Human-Computer Interaction Series

Editors-in-chief

John Karat
IBM Thomas J. Watson Research Center, Yorktown Heights, USA

Jean Vanderdonckt
Université catholique de Louvain, Louvain-la-Neuve, Belgium

Editorial Board

Gaëlle Calvary, LIG-University of Grenoble 1, Grenoble, France

John Carroll, School of Information Sciences & Technology, Penn State University, University Park, USA

Gilbert Cockton, Northumbria University, Newcastle, UK

Larry Constantine, University of Madeira, Funchal, Portugal, and Constantine & Lockwood Ltd, Rowley, MA, USA

Steven Feiner, Columbia University, New York, USA

Peter Forbrig, Universität Rostock, Rostock, Germany

Elizabeth Furtado, University of Fortaleza, Fortaleza, Brazil

Hans Gellersen, Lancaster University, Lancaster, UK

Robert Jacob, Tufts University, Medford, USA

Hilary Johnson, University of Bath, Bath, UK

Kumiyo Nakakoji, University of Tokyo, Tokyo, Japan

Philippe Palanque, Université Paul Sabatier, Toulouse, France

Oscar Pastor, University of Valencia, Valencia, Spain

Fabio Pianesi, Bruno Kessler Foundation (FBK), Trento, Italy

Costin Pribeanu, National Institute for Research & Development in Informatics, Bucharest, Romania

Gerd Szwillus, Universität Paderborn, Paderborn, Germany

Manfred Tscheligi, University of Salzberg, Salzburg, Austria

Gerrit van der Veer, University of Twente, Enschede, The Netherlands

Shumin Zhai, IBM Almaden Research Center, San Jose, USA

Thomas Ziegert, SAP Research CEC Darmstadt, Darmstadt, Germany

Human-computer interaction is a multidisciplinary field focused on human aspects of the development of computer technology. As computer-based technology becomes increasingly pervasive – not just in developed countries, but worldwide – the need to take a human-centered approach in the design and development of this technology becomes ever more important. For roughly 30 years now, researchers and practitioners in computational and behavioral sciences have worked to identify theory and practice that influences the direction of these technologies, and this diverse work makes up the field of human-computer interaction. Broadly speaking it includes the study of what technology might be able to do for people and how people might interact with the technology.

In this series we present work which advances the science and technology of developing systems which are both effective and satisfying for people in a wide variety of contexts. The Human-Computer Interaction series will focus on theoretical perspectives (such as formal approaches drawn from a variety of behavioral sciences), practical approaches (such as the techniques for effectively integrating user needs in system development), and social issues (such as the determinants of utility, usability and acceptability).

Stuart Reeves

Designing Interfaces in Public Settings

Understanding the Role of the Spectator in Human-Computer Interaction

Springer

Stuart Reeves
Horizon Digital Economy Research
University of Nottingham
Nottingham
UK
stuart@tropic.org.uk

ISSN 1571-5035
ISBN 978-1-4471-2622-5   ISBN 978-0-85729-265-0 (eBook)
DOI 10.1007/978-0-85729-265-0
Springer London Dordrecht Heidelberg New York

British Library Cataloguing in Publication Data
A catalogue record for this book is available from the British Library

© Springer-Verlag London Limited 2011
Softcover reprint of the hardcover 1st edition 2011
Apart from any fair dealing for the purposes of research or private study, or criticism or review, as permitted under the Copyright, Designs and Patents Act 1988, this publication may only be reproduced, stored or transmitted, in any form or by any means, with the prior permission in writing of the publishers, or in the case of reprographic reproduction in accordance with the terms of licenses issued by the Copyright Licensing Agency. Enquiries concerning reproduction outside those terms should be sent to the publishers.
The use of registered names, trademarks, etc., in this publication does not imply, even in the absence of a specific statement, that such names are exempt from the relevant laws and regulations and therefore free for general use.
The publisher makes no representation, express or implied, with regard to the accuracy of the information contained in this book and cannot accept any legal responsibility or liability for any errors or omissions that may be made.

Printed on acid-free paper

Springer is part of Springer Science+Business Media (www.springer.com)

For Rachel, and my parents

Preface

Over the last twenty years, perhaps best marked by the emergence of the ubiquitous computing programme, digital interactive technology has found itself in increasingly diverse contexts, and correspondingly applied in a growing number of creative ways. One key development is the increasing prevalence of computing power and significant digital infrastructures in everyday public places, such as museums and galleries, city streets and arts venues. This book addresses the challenges that such settings pose to the design of interactions that occur with, as well as around, computer interfaces. It comes at a time when there is an ever-growing body of work within the field of human-computer interaction that investigates technology in a wide range of public and performative settings. As such this book offers a timely empirical and conceptual contribution to this burgeoning body of work.

The purpose of this book is to provide both practical and theoretical use for a variety of audiences, particularly speaking to computer supported cooperative work and human-computer interaction communities; but it also proves a reference point for other fields, such as museum studies and performance literatures. This broad perspective means that this book can provide the resources for a shared or bridged perspective between computer scientists, artists, technologists, curators, and performers. Accordingly, Chaps. 4–7 present a series of broadly accessible empirical studies of interaction with technology 'in the wild', gradually building up a body of concepts, culminating in a design framework for public interactions with technology (Chap. 8). In the conclusion (Chap. 9), the book meets up with the introduction, suggesting a variety of ways in which elements of the book may be 'read' for these different audiences.

The bulk of this book was developed while working at the University of Nottingham's Mixed Reality Laboratory. My Ph.D. supervisors Steve Benford and Claire O'Malley (not forgetting my original supervisor, Mike Fraser, who escaped to Bristol) are owed the greatest debt. Much of the work in this book would not exist in its current form without their ideas, creativity, experience, encouragement, feedback and care. I also owe a debt of gratitude to my Ph.D. examiners, Paul Luff and Boriana Koleva, for their insights and contributions to the final stages of the process. Various others have helped me in some way along this journey, so I list them here (in no particular order, and no doubt omitting several): Andy Crabtree, Jennifer Sheridan, Alan Dix, Holger Schnädelbach, Martin Flintham, Tom Rodden, Barry Brown, Eric Laurier, Katie Fraser.

Being stationed at the Mixed Reality Lab itself was instrumental in developing the studies presented in this book. Many of the projects drawn on here are the result of years of hard work by various members of the lab, particularly for Equator projects.

Various artist groups, including Welfare State International, Blast Theory, as well as individuals such as Brendan Walker of Aerial, and Rachel Feneley of Lakeside Arts, Nottingham, are also to be acknowledged for making the studies present in this book possible.

Nottingham   Stuart Reeves

Contents

Chapter 1
Introduction

The growing interest in cultural, artistic and entertainment applications of interactive technologies in settings such as museums, galleries, theatres and even clubs, combined with the spread of mobile devices into the streets, means that interaction with computers is an increasingly ubiquitous and public affair. This book shows how crafting interaction for public settings raises a host of new challenges for human-computer interaction (HCI), widening the focus of design from concern about an individual's dialogue with their interface to also consider the ways in which interaction affects and is affected by third parties (e.g., spectators, bystanders, and so forth).

In examining such interactional settings, and the issue of how to design for the growing use of technology within them, this book considers what it means to 'perform' with an interface in public, raising and discussing questions such as:

- How might interfaces support users in performing their interactions within a wide range of expression, and fit well with such activities?
- What are the ways in which a third party might experience a user's interaction with an interface?
- How are participants made aware that a performance is occurring and understand the boundaries and limits of the performance, especially in public settings where performance may be interleaved with other activities?
- How does transition between users occur (for example when a current user hands an interface over to a new user in a setting such as a crowded public gallery), and how might we reflect this in design?
- How do orchestrators conduct their work and the ongoing shaping of a performance, typically from 'behind-the-scenes'?

In answering these questions, a broad, generic view of 'performance' is assumed, with the analytic work presented here addressing both traditional conceptions of performance—as found in theatres and concert halls—as well as more everyday 'performances'. This definition of 'performance', then, comes to encompass both explicitly-staged expressive interaction by musicians, actors, storytellers, dancers and other artists in front of an audience, and seemingly more 'mundane' and 'implicit' settings, where users present and perform their everyday social interactions with technology in a public setting. This covers, for instance, situations where people conduct mobile phone conversations on the streets, or use laptops on trains.

We shall see how this concept of 'performance' becomes a far more explicitly designed affair in a variety of settings; from more obvious and familiar sites of performance such as theatres, to exhibitions, galleries, amusement arcades, theme-parks and museums, where observing others' interaction is very much part of the experience, and has typically been carefully considered within the design. In exploring this more everyday conception of performance, many of the observations presented here share a common concern derived from classic computer-supported cooperative work (CSCW) workplace studies, particularly in showing how users often subtly conduct their interaction so as to be visible to others, promoting mutual awareness, such as in control room environments (see [4]).

As we explore answers to these questions, at its core this book presents a framework for understanding and designing interaction with technological interfaces in public settings. This is presented in full within Chap. 8, however a series of study Chaps. 4–7 will begin build up many of these framework concepts through empirical analysis of various instances of technology situated in public performative settings.

There are four key aims of this book and the framework presented within it (some of which are in common with related work [1, 2]). These aims for the book's contributions are individually detailed as follows.

- As the spread of interactive devices extends into varied public settings, it becomes more and more important to recognise and share the existing domain-based understandings within them or 'craft knowledge' that is involved in other disciplines such as performance or curation. These understandings are built up over time through practical experience, conceptual developments and fashions or trends within a particular domain's culture. As such the framework provides a set of *sensitising concepts* [3], drawing both from empirical studies of this craft knowledge in action in addition to this knowledge as it is contained within related literatures. These sensitising concepts help identify some salient points for interface designers concerned with developing interactive technologies for public settings to use as a resource in their work.
- The framework provides a way of articulating common concerns between several different communities (e.g., artists, technologists, designers, curators, computer scientists), and as such offers a 'boundary object' [6] for inter- and multi-disciplinary work. This is intended to help establish a *shared language* or common frame of reference. This shared language should also be respectful of individual domain competencies, particularly since the core ideas in this book are formed from a hybrid understanding of these fields. As a result it should enable such communities a means by which to communicate the issues raised by this book. This is particularly pressing with in the increased collaboration that occurs between such communities, such as in the growing penetration of technology in museums and galleries, the increasing use of sophisticated communications technology within performances of all kinds, and the general spread of devices into public.

- The framework establishes a number of boundaries and delineations of a design space, and at the same time generates a perspective for approaching that design space. In this way it also provides a collection of *constraints and strategies*, for both describing and navigating through the range of opportunities and challenges when creating new kinds of spectator interfaces. The development of this series of constraints and strategies is motivated by a lack of existing frameworks within the literature, as reviewed in Chap. 2.

- Finally, the framework—and this book as a whole—attempts to construct a *new perspective on interaction* in HCI, contributing to a broader understanding of the nature of human-computer interaction, in which traditional concerns for HCI are opened out to consider third parties, such as the bystander, the spectator, and audiences in general. Whilst the issues considered in this work certainly touch on some concerns already familiar to the HCI community, such as interaction with sensors, mutual awareness, privacy and more performative, theatrical views of interaction (e.g., [5]), there are also new issues that result from this concern for the third party, such as expression, magical effect, (un)wittingness and how interaction often comes to be a framed affair. In this way, this book collects together a growing, but as yet often unaddressed, concern within HCI, providing further studies of the impact of technology in public settings, but also offering a framework for designing within these spaces.

For a wide variety of researchers, practitioners, designers and artists who are interested in or currently working with technology in public settings, this book overall should appeal in terms of providing a palette or 'toolbox' of strategies for working with technology design in these challenging environments. Furthermore, for HCI researchers, the book contributes to an ongoing conceptual discussion over third parties to interaction and performance that has begun to emerge in recent years within HCI discourse. Finally, this book's particular use with artists and designers is in offering a framework that provides a common reference, shared language or 'boundary object' when collaborating with technologists.

In the concluding chapter we'll return to assess these core contributions that the reader may 'take away', and also reexamine the series of questions that this chapter opened with. These questions will also be revisited in a brief review of the literature surrounding the topics this book addresses, in Chap. 2.

The core arguments of this book are made in four empirical study chapters and a subsequent framework chapter (Chaps. 4–7 and Chap. 8, respectively). The study chapters introduce various basic components of the framework, which are then drawn upon, amongst other literatures, for the extended discussions of the framework chapter. The next sections provide an overview of the main features of the framework, and, in doing so, maps out the content of subsequent chapters. Although the main focus of this book is the framework, and the related various concepts that are introduced as part of the four studies, it should be noted that the study chapters alone also provide relatively independent in-depth examinations of a range of semi-public, public, implicit and explicit performance scenarios.

1.1 Core Framework Concepts

The first of the framework's concepts and observations is that of identifying different roles within interaction with an interface, contrasting the *participant*[1]—who is directly engaged with an interactive system—with the *audience*—a third party who experiences the manipulations involved in, and the effects that are a result of, the participant's conduct. Moments in which audience members *transition* to being participants are also introduced, exploring how the features of the environment and the interactive system make this possible to perform smoothly.

The roles of participant and audience are then expanded to consider the work of 'professional' members of a public performance setting: *actors*—who guide participants' conduct with the interface as well as sometimes physically guiding within a space—and *orchestrators*—who ensure the smooth running of the technology in support of actors, participants and audience. In order to ensure this smooth running, orchestrators at times must perform interventions, which may involve *transitioning* to an actor.

The introduction of orchestrators also creates a logical distinction between the settings in which orchestrators operate—i.e., a hidden area *behind-the-scenes*—and the settings participants, actors and audience conduct themselves—i.e., a visible area *centre-stage*. A further expansion to these settings is *front-of-house*, an area in which participants or audience are inducted into the centre-stage.

These observations on both roles and settings are then expanded by the introduction of the *frame*, a notion that circumscribes all the action that takes place within the public setting as a whole. Roles are then related as members of the frame in two main ways: firstly in terms of how they are involved either in the frame's construction—orchestrators and actors—or involved in its interpretation—participants and audience; and secondly in terms of which setting each role typically occupies—behind-the-scenes, centre-stage or front-of-house. These settings now form logical subdivisions of the frame through the way in which it is constructed.

Finally the introduction of a frame that 'surrounds' elements of the public setting in some way also creates the possibility of being 'outside' that frame. This possibility introduces a further role—the *bystander*—which is used to describe someone who is not a member of the frame, nor aware of it, and yet is unwittingly implicated in conduct taking place within the frame.

1.2 An Overview of Study Chapters

In presenting the framework, the studies are employed as exhibitors of—albeit with different individual relationships to—key framework concepts. Whilst these relationships are in reality quite complex, for the purposes of simplicity they are presented here as beginning 'narrowly', looking at the individual components of public

---

[1]Note that this, and other terms in a heavier type, have specific meanings in the context of this book, and will be explained in greater depth over its course.

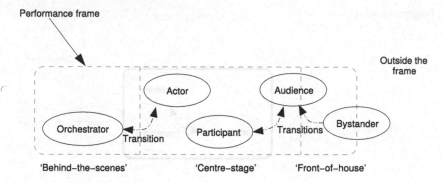

Fig. 1.1 Simplified summary of the framework's component parts, fully addressed within Chap. 8

settings, then being broadened out, developing these concepts to consider the entirety of a given setting, as well as concepts which then circumscribe such settings (i.e., the frame). The following list outlines which topics each chapter addresses, and in doing so, forms a very brief introduction to the framework by diagrammatically highlighting which components of the summary diagram in Fig. 1.1 they speak to.

- Chapter 4 focusses upon an augmented reality interactive exhibit sited within a public art installation (One Rock). It examines and dissects how visitors to this exhibition interacted with one another and the augmented reality device. In doing so, the chapter examines how a simple division of visitors performing actions with the device—*participants*—and those spectating on those actions—*audience*—forms (see Fig. 1.2[2]). As part of this the chapter details participant manipulations of an interface, which include direct input and gestures around that input. The output of those manipulations, including peripheral effects, such as the impact of the effects upon participants are also explored. Picking apart manipulations and effects of the device helps to describe how conduct with that device is experienced by audience to it. The chapter also discusses how *audience-participant transitions* occur; how visitors moved from being audience to a participant's manipulation of the device, to becoming a participant actively engaged with it themselves.
- The second study, Chap. 5, explores a storytelling event (The Journey into Space) in which participants used interactive torches in order to trigger sounds that were integrated into the ongoing story. Building upon the previous chapter's audience and participant roles, it develops a distinction between non-professional and professional members of the storytelling. As part of this, it explores the work of the *actor* running the storytelling, and how she came to guide participants' interactions, through guiding participant engagement with the torches themselves, as well as physically guiding them to avoid

---

[2]Elements of relevance for each study are indicated in black; other elements of the framework are left grey.

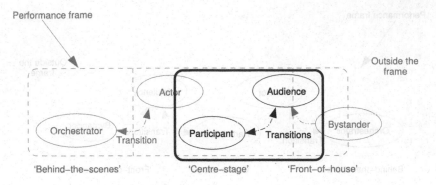

Fig. 1.2 Framework components covered by Chap. 4

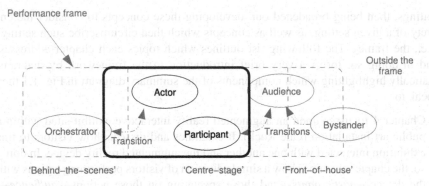

Fig. 1.3 Framework components covered by Chap. 5

or mitigate the effects of interference within a complex sensor space (see Fig. 1.3).

- Chapter 6, presents the third study, a scientific and artistic performance event (Fairground: Thrill Laboratory) in which members of the public attached to telemetry equipment, embarked on a fairground ride and had physiological data (heart rate and acceleration), as well as video and audio streamed live to a watching audience. The chapter expands upon audience, participant and actor roles to consider the work of *orchestrators* ensuring the smooth-running of the technology. It also presents a basic division of work between orchestrators who operate *behind-the-scenes*, hidden from the audience, and actors, who operate in a revealed *centre-stage* area (see Fig. 1.4).
- The final study, Chap. 7, looks at a performance art game (Uncle Roy All Around You) where members of the public, equipped with hand-held mobile devices were sent out into the streets of a city in order to find a special character within the game. Participants were given ambiguous clues that tended to implicate passers-by, and they were also required to enter offices, hotel rooms, retrieve postcards from car park kiosks and so on. In exploring the ambiguity of the participant's experience, this chapter introduces the concept of the *frame* in which the vari-

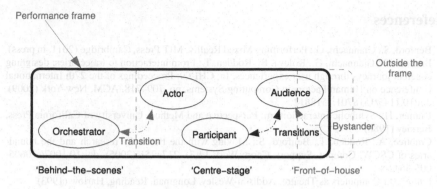

Fig. 1.4 Framework components covered by Chap. 6

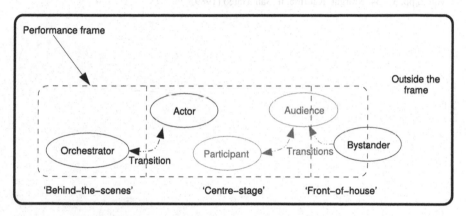

Fig. 1.5 Framework components covered by Chap. 7

ous roles presented operate. The constructed and interpreted boundaries of the frame determine what conduct is part of the game, which objects are 'props' and which places are 'sets'. From this develops the role of the *bystander*, someone who is implicated in the frame but is unaware of its existence. Subdivisions of the frame—behind-the-scenes and centre-stage settings—are expanded to include *front-of-house* areas in which participants are inducted. The chapter also explores interventions in the form of *orchestrator-actor transitions* (see Fig. 1.5).

In setting the scene for these studies and the framework they contribute to, we must first take a step back in order to cover the increasingly wide range of literature that is concerned with innovating and evaluating technology deployed in public settings. This corpus of work must also be placed in the context of the fields of HCI and CSCW, and in terms of their conceptual shifts in focus, particularly in the ways in which interests in human-machine dyadic interactions have expanded to cover wider forms of social interaction around interfaces.

References

1. Benford, S., Giannachi, G.: Performing Mixed Reality. MIT Press, Cambridge (2011, in press)
2. Benford, S., Giannachi, G., Koleva, B., Rodden, T.: From interaction to trajectories: designing coherent journeys through user experiences. In: CHI'09: Proceedings of the 27th International Conference on Human Factors in Computing Systems, pp. 709–718. ACM, New York (2009). doi:10.1145/1518701.1518812
3. Blumer, H.: Symbolic Interactionism: Perspective and Method. University of California Press, Berkley (1986)
4. Crabtree, A., Rodden, T., Benford, S.: Moving with the times: IT research and the boundaries of CSCW. Comput. Support. Coop. Work 14(3), 217–251 (2005). doi:10.1007/s10606-005-3642-x
5. Laurel, B.: Computers as Theatre. Addison-Wesley, Longman, Reading, Harlow (1993)
6. Star, S.L.: The structure of ill-structured solutions: boundary objects and heterogeneous distributed problem solving. In: Gasser, L., Huhns, M.N. (eds.) Distributed Artificial Intelligence, vol. 2, pp. 37–54. Morgan Kaufmann, San Mateo (1989)

Chapter 2
From Individuals to Third Parties, from Private to Public

With the spread of mobile devices into public settings and the increasing use of technology in cultural, artistic and entertainment venues, a corresponding need to understand the ways in which we might design successfully for such settings has developed. This chapter explores the steadily diversifying spread of technology, showing how the need for a general synthesis of existing conceptual and techno-logical developments is becoming increasingly important. Central to this endeavour is the claim that we need new perspective on interaction with technology in public settings.

The first section explores a brief history of HCI and computer-supported cooper-ative work (CSCW) studies, examining how concern has shifted from the individual interacting with the machine to social 'constellations' in which groups collaborate via and around technology. After this we shall see how, more recently within this and other work, researchers' focus has begun to shift towards these new kinds of settings, drawing not just from HCI, but also museum studies, performance art and games studies. Finally, we will return to the questions posed in the introduction, exploring them in light of this exploration of literature, in order to see how the ques-tions might be answered, and in what ways those answers leave us asking further questions.

It is of course difficult to provide a completely comprehensive review of the developments in this area over the last fifteen or twenty years within (and outside of) HCI research. However, the purpose for this chapter is to provide a general overview and, particularly, to 'set the scene' for subsequent studies in this book. Furthermore, we shall revisit and expand upon this core body of literature in each chapter, particularly within Chap. 8's framework.

2.1 Individuals to Third Parties

Paul Dourish notes HCI's "origin myth", being HCI's initial emergence from the convergence between computer science and psychological, cognitive and social psy-chological models of interaction [35, p. 61]. In order to justify the claim that this book forms part of a growing conceptual perspectival shift within HCI, it is worth spending some time here with this "myth" in order to understand the HCI context in which the concepts presented in here fit, and how examining third parties to interaction is increasingly pertinent to recent developments.

2.1.1 Understanding Individuals

Over the course of the computer's relatively brief history, it has rapidly migrated in role from computation to communications device [105]. Driving this change in role is the increasing ubiquity of the computer, which historically began "reaching out" to those with less specialised expertise and knowledge about computational technology or lesser inclination to accommodate it. This is perhaps most evident in the way the computer has become a general workplace staple (such as in business communications, scientific computational uses, and so on) [53]. The computer has also been actively adopted by groups and individuals beyond its original use as a tool for work, in no small part thanks to its growing prevalence in the home, the unexpected importance and rise of the internet [81], and—of particular relevance for this book—its increasing ubiquity in the form of mobile devices like phones, laptops, music players and a host of other embedded devices. This ubiquity, coupled with the remarkable flexibility of the computer and technological developments in areas such as networking, has led to the repeated push of computation into new and diverse settings beyond the workplace and home, such as the public spaces of museums, galleries, performance and the streets.

These developments have often resulted in shifts in the focus of computer science research as well as the growth of new application areas. Research into human-computer interaction evolved in part as it became clear to developers of software with interface components that "the interface *is* the system, at least from the viewpoint of the users" [5]. Early work within HCI concerned itself with the various metrics and models that could be employed in order to assist a user's task performance (amongst other concerns), the intellectual base of which grew from a background of experimental psychology and ergonomics. Quantitative and predictive low-level measures such as work rate and fatigue metrics, keystroke-level models, Fitts' Law, and models such as GOMS [24] initially dominated HCI. These models typically attempted to provide tools for analysing a single user's interaction with two-dimensional interfaces involving mouse and keyboard work. Such low-level perceptual, motor and cognitive models and metrics only dealt with very fractional slices of time, however, and different cognitive models gained increasing currency as researchers began to consider the interface as entering into a "dialogue" with the user—a dyadic relationship—and therefore stepping beyond viewing the interface as terminal [53]. Instead, Norman, developing concepts from Gibson [48], presented a formulation of the interface that is concerned with perceptual affordances (actionable properties that are perceived by a user). In the interactional dialogue, a user and designer's "conceptual models" of the functionality the interface provides access to are often found conflicting, resulting in "gulfs" of execution and evaluation where the user struggles to successfully predict the outcome of an action [82].

2.1.2 From Dialogues to Constellations

But the lower-level perceptual and dialogic views of interaction also began to be pushed wider as researchers started to broaden HCI in various ways.

The limitations of the lower-level experimental techniques typically used to evaluate interfaces became increasingly apparent, as such methods often did not reflect the settings in which human-machine dialogues would come to be played out. HCI was for a while "confined to rather small controlled experiments, with the presumption that the findings could be generalised to other settings" [4]. Those "other" settings—primarily workplaces—in reality consisted of multiple intertwined dialogues between workers themselves via or around the interface, as well as those of the human-machine dyads. Generally it had become increasingly clear that "[t]he interface [was] no longer a private affair between a single user and a single piece of technology as [was] classically studied in HCI" [21]. The scope of the observations of older HCI work also typically lacked in understanding a user's continued engagement with interfaces. As Buxton argues, HCI has had a tendency to focus on the 'first ten minutes' of interaction as opposed to the 'next ten years' [2].

There were also more fundamental philosophical issues tied to this shift in perspective. It was suggested, for instance, that these settings could be addressed through avoiding a logical separation of 'the users' and 'the interface', with less direct focus upon the interface engineering issues (as found in Office Automation [55]) and more upon understanding the surrounding milieu of social action within which the interface comes to be embedded [30, 54]. Other philosophical shifts recommended viewing users' conduct at the interface more as an ongoingly produced moment-by-moment form of 'conversation' in which circumstances are continually adapted to rather than being explicitly planned affairs [99]. Social psychology studies also began to reveal how cognition could be seen as more of a distributed phenomenon [72], providing some consonance with the view of interaction as being more than just a single user and an interface and that interaction as being ongoing and dynamic.

Perhaps prompted by the increasing importance of networking and the internet [81], especially in the role network communications within the workplace, research began to examine collaborative work rather than relying on a focus upon the individual and machine in order to solve the problems of human-computer interaction. CSCW in particular sought to address the "design of computer-based technologies with explicit concern for the socially organized practices of their intended users" [98]. In this stream of work, HCI came to be broadened by accounts of collaborative work provided both by studies of groupware and face-to-face interaction (e.g., [96, 97]) and various influential ethnographic, ethnomethodologically-informed, studies of technology in use at the workplace

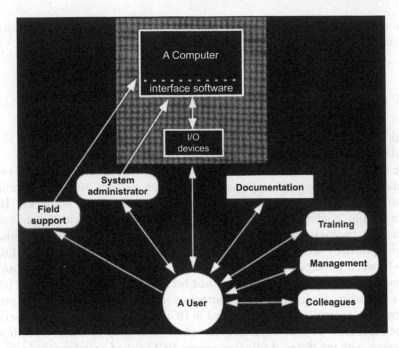

Fig. 2.1 A new vision of the interface, reproduced from [54]. [Image used with permission; ©Jonathan Grudin]

(e.g., [21, 58, 61, 65, 68, 99]). Many of the various parties conducting such studies were 'outside' the traditional field of HCI, such as ethnographers and anthropologists, social psychologists, and so on, but had as their topic of interest how social organisation is played out with and around technology.

This was a significant 'turn to the social', and represented the growing importance of ethnography as a rich technique for uncovering previously unaccounted-for social features of interaction with and around computer technology. More generally, the impact of these studies within HCI demonstrated the increasingly common concern for a more holistic view of interaction, exploding the typical HCI definitions of the interface as a purely technological artefact to encompass social constellations *as* the interface (see Fig. 2.1) [54].

In its focus upon collaboration around and through this exploded vision of the interface, Bannon suggests that CSCW became "an answer to certain problems within extant fields of research, such as mainstream HCI, and CMC (computer mediated communication) studies, and their relation (or lack thereof) to the understanding and design of computer systems that truly support the needs of people working together" [4]. Or, as Heath et al. describe of working environments, reforming understanding of these needs involves seeing how "collaboration, as a delimited form of cooperative work, is simply a gloss to capture a complex configuration of momentary arrangements through which two or more individuals, sequentially or simultaneously participate in particular tasks or activities" [60].

2.1.3 From Constellations to Third Parties

However, within earlier, now seminal CSCW research, which examined private settings like the office [21, 37, 99], air traffic control at an airport [69], or rail network
control rooms [65] (also see [58] for a companion study of the rail drivers' perspective), there has also been a notable concern for issues relating to a third party
experience of interaction through observations on aspects such as peripheral awareness and tacit coordination.

For example, in [65], operators in the London Underground control room under
study rendered otherwise 'invisible' activities visible for others, through methods
such as talking out loud, and ensuring the sensitivity and relevancy of such actions
with respect to co-workers through continual (mutual) monitoring. Such peripheral
awareness was also shown to be maintained through objects as well as conduct.
Hughes et al. [69], for example, discusse how an air traffic controller's 'flight strip'
(a literal strip of paper used to coordinate airspace) is employed not only as an
artefact with which a given controller may work, but crucially as a publicly available
common resource for fellow controllers. Some of these issues were also reflected
upon within virtual environments, such as in the MASSIVE system [8], in which
a spatialised model of interaction [9] governing what members of the environment
could at times see and hear, came to provide a peripheral awareness structure as an
important feature in everyday virtual interactions.

Although these studies are for the most part examinations of collaborative activity amongst participants who are equally engaged in some task, key features of
the spectator experience are hinted at, and to some extent brought into relief above
the apparent 'flatness' of the equally-weighted participatory settings under examination. These features (noted above) will later come to play an important role in
how we build up an analysis of a more performative view on interaction.

2.2 Private to Public Settings

The previous section documented how the initial HCI view of an individual's interaction with a single machine gradually evolved into constellations of mutually
aware, often peripherally-interacting users engaging in practical, mundane, everyday work via and around the interface. Relatively recently, however, computation
has extended beyond the settings which gave birth to such perspectives, "reaching out" from private[1] workplaces into public museums, galleries, artistic performances, clubs and the streets. In common with [34], this book argues that concepts
drawn from workplace studies have relevance to settings in which the term 'work'
is more explicitly used as an analytic device (although see [89] for an alternate perspective). This ever increasing ubiquity of technologies in such settings not only

---

[1]CSCW has also begun to concern itself with other private spheres, such as the home.

provides challenging new applications of such concepts, but may further complexify the picture, such as through 'blurring' the very boundaries between private and public domains [80].

This section takes a tour through the literature documenting these new settings, indicating the need for a coherent framework that draws together the various observations presented within this disparate corpus. At first it examines how studies of museums and galleries have explored the interactions of visitor groups at the exhibit face, the role of third parties to those interactions, and the ways in which they are integral to understanding the social nature of the visit. Subsequently it looks at some of the literature documenting the growing reach of technology into more everyday public settings such as city streets, and how the arts—which have for a long time been concerned with the relationship between performer and spectator—have developed a growing interest in and use of novel technologies.

2.2.1 Studies of Museums and Galleries

Like the trajectory of HCI's programme, studies of museums and galleries began with an early relationship with psychology, such as work by Melton and Robinson in the 1920s and 1930s, to later application of behaviourism [93], cognitivism [1], environmental psychology [15], and, more rarely, ethnography [78]. Measures such as 'dwell time,' number of objects viewed and routes traced during visits were (and still are) routinely derived from survey data in order to determine the quality of a visitor's experience [75]. There are some problems with this approach, however, not only in that interactions take place between a "lively triadic interplay" of visitor, exhibit and environment [102], but also since visiting typically occurs with others. Blud notes that studies "have tended to ignore the nature of the visitor, or visitor group, and have focused instead on the nature of the exhibit, and how effective different types of exhibit are in stimulating learning" [17]. Indeed, the role of the spectator has been problematised by 20th century art within galleries for some time [70].

Recently, however, particularly with the introduction of interactives in museums and galleries, new interest has been generated in moving beyond quantitative metrics in order to understand the exhibit face as a site of collaboration and coordination between friends, family and even strangers. Many of these developments in understanding the sociality of museum and gallery visits, particularly those on the importance of third parties to interaction, have occurred outside the traditional museum studies literature.[2] Of particular centrality in this body of work is the Work, Interaction and Technology group, which also undertook the influential studies of the London Underground rail network mentioned earlier [65]. Using video recordings captured at many major museums and galleries, WIT group work (such as [62]) has

---

[2]Interesting, however, artists have attempted to draw the spectator into the artefact (such as a painting) for a long time [91].

examined the ways in which visitors collaboratively conduct themselves, through gesture and talk, at the exhibit face. Like the group's previous work, much is made of the tacit coordination between visitors in museums and galleries. Sometimes this collaborative action proves problematic for the way existing exhibits have been designed. In [63], for example, observations on the deployment of "conventional input and display technologies" used in exhibits in this particular study were found to "undermine the collaboration of others by restricting the ability of people gathered at the exhibit to see the screen". Elsewhere, the ways in which co-visiting groups subtly "configure" one another's engagement with the exhibit is detailed, as well the notion that such engagement has a distinct interactional 'trajectory' in which action at previous exhibits may configure the approach to the next [77] (this concept of interactional trajectories has found broader application within HCI; see [10, 11], which we will return to later in the book).

Crucially here, observations are also made on the behaviour of third parties and general awareness of others in configuring conduct of visitors, such as in aiding and encouraging participation or perhaps in hindering others [76]. One particularly notable study (discussed in depth in subsequent chapters) examines the humorous interactions by visitors engaging with an exhibit, and how this activity drew the attention of bystanders, who, being oriented by their spectating of others, subsequently engaged with the object themselves [64]. In a further study, documenting an interactive video-based exhibit called the Ghost Ship [66], visitors were observed designing their actions to appear within the artwork, although interactions between strangers were limited. To remedy this Hindmarsh et al. recommend recognising and designing for "companions and strangers, whether they are in the same physical space or indeed remote spaces" through providing "opportunities for interaction" since, as their studies have suggested, the "actions and activities of individuals are often produced with intimate regard to the actions of others in perceptual range".

In light of some of these observations, a system designed to support a form of 'aural spectating' in museums is of interest here. The Sotto Voce system (which also will be revisited later on) permits co-visitors (rather than strangers) to eavesdrop upon their fellow visitor's PDAs (users were presented with selectable items for each room). Several themes of operation emerged, such as eavesdroppers "free riding" on the other's exhibit exploration, and visitors drawing on overheard content as a locational resource [3, 52].

Numerous other studies have further charted the growing presence of interactives within exhibition. The Augurscope device [90], for example, provided a mobile window onto a virtual recreation of a castle, which visitors could then move around the real site. Developing this, the Storytent [45, 51, 95] enabled visitors (particularly children) to take part in activities linking virtual visualisations of mediaeval buildings and stories with the corresponding real site through augmenting physical artefacts such as paper, or projecting onto the surface of a tent. Other exhibitions have attempted to embed interactives more seamlessly into the environment visitors would experience by 'hiding' the technology [43]. Alternate approaches to augmenting the experience have involved distributed systems designed to provide for sharing the experience of a museum's various objects between remote and local museum visitors [23], again involving implicit spectating. Finally, designing museum and gallery interactives has also opened up a seam of research that examines the use of ambiguity in a variety of aspects of design [46]. Ambiguity comes to play a role in provoking spectator curiosity in work such as the Tonetable [19], in which non-linear mappings between visitor interactions with the system and the effects of those interactions encourage further engagement and exploration. This will be particularly relevant later on in Chap. 8's framework.

Beyond museums, interactive technology has also reached public or semi-public settings outside of the confines of the exhibition, such as in educational and recreational uses. Some have begun to embed technology into relatively complex educational and creative indoor environments, such as the KidsRoom [18], which involved an interactive storytelling setting for groups of children. Others push out into the streets using mobile technology. For instance, technologies to support tourism on city streets have been developed to enable the sharing of photographs and physical presence (through positioning) with others [22]. Educational experiences such as the Periscope [103] within the Ambient Wood [57] involved the design and deployment of various technologies (displays, RFID readers, etc.) within a woodland setting. Another educational game, Savannah [13], saw players assuming the role of 'lions' hunting prey with PDAs whilst travelling around a virtual savannah, which in reality was a school playing field. Finally, studies of spectating at rally events have highlighted the importance of "spectating [as] a venue for conversation and sociability" [42].

The summing of this work indicates that, within an increasingly wide array of deployments of technology in public settings, issues of spectatorship and third parties arise frequently as concerns for design.

2.2.2 Technology on-the-Streets and in the Arts

As the spread of technologies such as public displays, wireless internet infrastructure, or personal mobile technology has become more prominent as everyday components within public and semi-public spaces, so corresponding interest in the impact of technology within mundane everyday settings, such as mobile phones on the streets (e.g., [47, 74]), has risen.

One of the more interesting results of this spread, however, is the way in which technology has also become an important part of many art installations, performance art pieces and musical performances. Such performances may be played out in semi-public settings, such as the Schizophrenic Cyborg system, in which a remote orchestrator controlled a display attached to a performer's chest whilst they were present at a party [92]. Performances are also conducted in more prominent public settings including city streets, such as the performance art game discussed in subsequent chapters, Can You See Me Now? [44]. (See the many systems documented in [104] or the theoretical concerns regarding interaction with interfaces expressed in [41], for example.) Whilst street performance has always been a staple within the performing arts, and also considering how interactivity similarly has been a long-standing concern for artists (see [70]), more recently it has become apparent how technology provides exciting new ways in order to augment performances in a variety of contexts (e.g., the installation piece Desert Rain [73] and Toshio Iwai's visually augmented pianos [104, p. 767], both discussed later in Chap. 8) as well as performers themselves (e.g., see [85, 86, 94] detailing various systems for instrumenting dancers or their environments). Technology has also begun to provide increased interaction between audience and performer, such as in Stelarc's Muscle Stimulation System piece where audience members could 'activate' parts of the performer's body [104, p. 159] (see Chap. 8).

More generally, performances inherently trade upon the conduct of third parties (the audience) and the dynamic ways in which the relationship between performer and spectator unfolds. Thus, such contexts in which technology is deployed, and the importance of audience to those activities that are played out, provide fertile grounds for studying public interaction.

The highlighting of performer skill for spectators is just one of the possibilities of augmentation. For many performers, making performances legible when using technology is important to their practices, as when control sensors may be purposefully attached to hands or arms (e.g., [40, 106], examples which shall be explored in more depth in Chap. 8) in order to provide the scope for what Bowers and Hellström term "expressive latitude" [20]. This aspect of interaction has also been explored in terms of interactives in museums and galleries, where 'expected' interactions that users naturally conduct their activities with may map with varying levels of directness to what is actually sensed by the interface [14]. This obviously has impacts for the experience of the spectator, however others note that non-linear mappings may also provide a design opportunity through provoking intrigue [19].

In one example, in the interactive martial arts games of [56], a performer's expertly skilled martial arts moves are conducted on stage in front of an audience, and also tracked and mapped to a corresponding projected avatar within a game environment. Technology might also push the physical boundaries of where audiences may be in order to engage in spectatorship. For example, in one system, a poet's bodily actions and spoken words were synchronously relayed to an audience located in a CVE as well as the real audience they were performing to. Poets were represented as avatars in the virtual world with the gestures of the performer driving those of their avatar [12]. The ways in which such systems are designed is made all the more pertinent by the advent of mainstream performances taking place simultaneously in the real world and popular internet-based virtual environments [6]. In other, more directly participatory events, designing for spectators may require explicit separation from performers. For example, the Tonetable, an installation that enabled up to four visitors to collaboratively interact with sound and visuals via a series of trackballs [19], initially suffered from spectator crowding, meaning that some essential aural 'sweet spots' were obscured. A redesign of its deployment had to take into account these crowding effects and the impact upon sound, resulting in separate areas being used for those 'performing' with the device and those spectating.

Studies of performance have also identified different performative roles or tasks that have often been inspired by studies of museums, galleries and workplaces. Ensuring the smooth running of a performance via control room and orchestration work has received recent attention, identifying routine activities such as monitoring work via technology as well as both subtle and deliberately highlighted intervention conducted by orchestrators to ensure the smooth running of the performance [31, 33, 39, 73]. Other studies have explored the role orchestrators play in collaboratively producing and maintaining narrative with players of an interactive mobile phone messaging-based game [32]. The design challenges presented when technology is used to manage relationships between performers and audience have also been covered, as in [12]. Observations on the nature of orchestrator roles and relationship between them, other performers and audience members within performance environments will be important for the studies presented in later chapters, the analysis they develop and the framework that is constructed.

Collected works or anthologies of artistic involvement with technology, such as [104], provide ample documentation of the increasingly central role interactive technology takes in supporting, or sometimes being the centre of, performance. Much of the presentation of the framework covered in Chap. 8 uses a wide range of examples from such literature, covering artists including Stelarc and Pamela Z.

Theoretically, however, academic artistic concern has often resided with increasing active engagement in the performance, characterised by transforming "viewers into participants" [41]. Frameworks dealing with the role of technology thus address how technology modulates a performer's relationship to the technology as a varyingly active participant (e.g., [29]) rather than exploring how spectators may be party to that very relationship. Some frameworks, however, have begun to examine the role that technology may play in performativity, particularly in "tripartite interactions" between collaborating performers and "observers" [92]. This book builds upon the observations of such frameworks through picking apart further details of the spectator experience, enriching them with a wider set of performative roles, and investigating more dynamic aspects of performance with interfaces in public settings, such as the ways in which members of a performance context transition between particular roles.

Techniques for mass spectator or audience participation have also generated interest within other contexts. Some large-scale interactives have been constructed in order to permit public use of musical instruments for visitors to an exhibition [84]. This and other demonstrations, such as the aggregation of audience behaviour to engage in large-scale gaming or mass participation events [25, 79] and even clubs [67], provide relevant examples of the need for new ways of understanding a variety of diverse public settings in which, through the impact of more prevalent and widespread sensor technology, bystanders and spectators may become drawn into some collaborative activity.

Finally, this section must address a number of recent examples of games. The game, as a form, is used in many of the settings presented above to serve the purposes of the designers, artists or educationalists. However, a number of more 'pure' demonstrations of gaming in public settings typically involving mobile technologies (usually classed as 'locative' or 'pervasive' gaming) have begun to emerge as well. One such game is Treasure [26], in which players take to the streets with PDAs, collecting coins from a game map derived from wifi network coverage. Another game called AR Quake [101] used augmented reality in order to transpose the gameplay of a popular first-person shooter into the real world by overlaying tracked virtual monsters on the local environment. Other games have taken place on various forms of mobile phones, such as Hitchers, in which virtual 'hitch hikers' are picked up and dropped by players as they physically move between phone cells [38].

Whilst there are further examples of game systems running on a variety of mobile technologies and played out in locations where strangers are present (e.g., [16, 28, 83, 88]), as well as early work on the social features of game-play (Huizinga in particular, discussed below), little documentation and even fewer frameworks exist on how player interaction with such systems either involve or are experienced by third parties (although there are design frameworks concerned with how individuals may interweave technology use into everyday life [27]). Some observations are forthcoming, however. One 'farming' type game called Yoshi [7] often involved "distinctive back and forth movements" by players; this conduct, given that it was typically played in the streets of urban or suburban areas, would tend to draw attention from passers-by. A player also reported being asked by one such stranger whether they were lost and reported receiving "strange looks" from other pedestrians. Finally, a recent study of the social gameplay practices surrounding Nintendo DS users considered issues such as how the small display impacted the experience of play for spectators in multiplay gaming, how the design of the device "actively work against" ad-hoc play formations involving strangers, and in referencing published work that contributes to the framework within this book [87], the ways in which such problems might be addressed by designing for the spectator [100].

2.3 Revisiting Opening Questions

So far we have threaded together one way to view the forms of literature and the settings they document that have been reviewed here. However, although this literature contains, say, observations on mutual awareness, configuration effects of bystanders and public interaction on-the-streets, there are few frameworks presented within it which seek to systematically address this wide range of public settings in which computational technology may increasingly be found. As such it becomes apparent that there is a need to synthesise this sometimes disparate work; in order to provide an overarching set of design understandings (in the form of sensitising concepts, a shared language, constraints and strategies and a new HCI perspective as mentioned in Chap. 1), we will seek to encompass the earlier observations highlighted in this chapter as well as develop and enrich them into a general framework.

It is also relevant here to note once again the relevance of Goffman's analysis of interaction in public, his dramaturgical perspective (e.g., [49]), and the ways in which this perspective will be drawn upon throughout the work presented in this book. In order to answer the key opening questions, several of Goffman's concepts are of use. Firstly, and primarily, Goffman's use of the performance metaphor as an analytic lens through which to examine social conduct, is present both within the analytic findings of study chapters (e.g., conceptualising interaction in terms of "performers" and "audience"), and fundamental to the framework. Another concept that we shall continually revisit in this book is the 'frame' [50], and the way that social situations are organised by the 'frameworks' of members and how conduct is interpreted within the context of the social frame. Goffman also developed notions of performative settings (or "regions") such as "front", "back" and "outside". These are used to differentiate the ways presentation of the self occurs in social action: for instance, front-stage reflects framings in which a 'performer' conducts themselves in front of an 'audience', whereas back-stage involves alternate settings that audiences do not have access to, where a performer may operate using an alternative framework. Later on we will use these ideas of 'setting-ed' interaction and performance frames in building up a design framework for interaction.

The opening questions hinted at both the form and breadth of the challenges that any framework addressing this space would need to consider. From this brief review of the ways in which investigations in HCI have moved from understanding an individual's interaction with a machine to beginning to consider the role of third parties to interactions, and from interest in private to public settings, it is apparent that these opening questions either remain unanswered or only partially answered. In closing this chapter we'll look once again at these questions.

- How can we design interfaces that support users in expressing their interactions, and that fit well with existing expressive activities such as music and dance?

Sections of the work we have seen in this chapter document the activities of performers and artists who have increasingly adopted technology in order to express themselves (see [104] in particular). What is not clear for the most part is how the craft knowledge of artists like Stelarc in their use of technology may be drawn upon in order to inform the design of interfaces. Understanding collections of such craft knowledge and how they may be repurposed can in turn guide the design of expressive interfaces within more mainstream HCI. This book will seek to collate some of this craft knowledge, and in response to these, will develop a set of strategies not only to address expressivity, but will also provide other strategies which engender, for instance, ambiguity in the interactional experience, or magical effect.

- How should a third party experience a user's interaction with an interface?

It has been made clear that, particularly within studies of museums and galleries, as well as workplace studies, understanding how to support users in expressing their interactions is intimately tied with how those interactions are experienced by others, however such observations are only just beginning to enter into the main stream of HCI. The framework directly addresses this issue, starting in Chap. 4 with a basic division of third parties and users. In this book we shall begin seeking to integrate existing observations—and contributing new ones—into a larger framework that presents an understanding of interaction with technology in public settings *in general*.

- How can participants be made aware that a performance is occurring and understand the boundaries and limits of the performance, especially in public settings where performance may be interleaved with other activities?

Some descriptions delineate the transient and negotiated rules of games, specifically Huizinga's [71], in which players are seen as coordinating around a set of rules—the "magic circle"—separate from the shared 'rules' of everyday life. Other descriptions, particularly Goffman's concept of framings [50], relate to the question of how, particularly in public settings, participants can be made aware that a performance is occurring, and, in commonly orienting to the socially organised boundaries of a given performance framing, may come to understand how to collaborate with others in the performance (in the case of Huizinga these boundaries form the heart of the organisation of a game). However, such work remains mostly unapplied to the design of technology situated in public environments. This book will integrate such perspectives into its observations on third parties and expressivity.

- How can interfaces be designed to accommodate transitions between roles, for example when a current user hands an interface over to a new user in a setting such as a crowded public gallery?

This survey has demonstrated how workplace and museum studies literature have for some time been examining in detail how colleagues or visitors may negotiate around an interface, and how objects, such as museum artefacts, may be 'handed over' between visitors as a typical part of the visit. There is room for building upon this work, understanding how it might fit within a larger context of performance and performative action by professionals expressing themselves with technology, handing that technology over to co-performers or non-professional participants. In this book we will investigate, in some depth, key moments of transition both in the analysis of such moments in each study chapter, but also more generally as a fundamental part of the framework.

- How can we design for orchestration; the ongoing shaping of a performance, typically from 'behind-the-scenes'?

Existing literature highlighted above seeks to understand how behind-the-scenes orchestration might fit in to a wider view of performance in which various professionals collaborate and coordinate in order to run the performance. This activity can be understood to fit within the context of less explicit performance situations such as the workplace or the museum, however it remains unaddressed within the literature. This book attempts to join these contexts up.

Before closing, it is perhaps useful to think about two main ways in which the literature presented here may be thought of more systematically. The first is through a division of private and public settings, ranging from private spaces like offices and homes, to semi-public spaces such as museums and galleries, to 'open air' public spaces like streets. The second division differentiates everyday, 'mundane' settings from deliberate performance settings, ranging from interactions occurring in offices or streets, to virtuosic conduct with technology taking place in front of paying audience members.

Later on we will build upon these simple divisions of this wide range of work in order to understand what the spread of computation into public settings means for design, and how understanding that meaning can form the basis for a framework. In particular, Chap. 4, examining social interaction around augmented reality exhibit, will begin to pick apart divisions between third parties and users actively engaged in some interaction, exploring the relationships between the two and how their conduct is intertwined with interaction with an interface.

Before these studies are presented, however, there are various methodological and analytic issues that we must attend to in order to understand the findings discussed within them. The following chapter situates this book within the tradition of ethnomethodologically-informed ethnography found commonly in CSCW, and explores how this, and Goffman's dramaturgy, influence the studies and framework. It also takes a lens to the practical matters involved in using these conceptual orientations, particularly as it relates to video-based interaction analysis [59]. In addition to exploring these two sides of analysing and producing findings from empirical data, the chapter reveals the relationship between two sometimes awkward bedfellows, connecting with recent concerns voiced within HCI regarding "implications for design" [36].

Readers familiar with this tradition and these debates may wish to skip the next chapter and head straight to the series of studies in Chaps. 4–7.

References

1. Alt, M.B.: Evaluating didactic exhibits: a critical look at Shettel's work. Curator **20**(3), 241–258 (1977)
2. Anderson, R.I.: Conversations with Clement Mok and Jakob Nielsen, and with Bill Buxton and Clifford Nass. Interactions **7**(1), 46–80 (2000)
3. Aoki, P.M., Grinter, R.E., Hurst, A., Szymanski, M.H., Thornton, J.D., Woodruff, A.: Sotto Voce: exploring the interplay of conversation and mobile audio spaces. In: Proceedings of the SIGCHI Conference on Human Factors in Computing Systems, pp. 431–438. ACM, New York (2002). doi:10.1145/503376.503454
4. Bannon, L.J.: Perspectives on CSCW: From HCI and CMC to CSCW. In: Proceedings of International Conference on Human-Computer Interaction (EW-HCI), pp. 148–158 (1992)
5. Bannon, L.J.: Situating workplace studies within the human-computer interaction field. In: Luff, P., Hindmarsh, J., Heath, C. (eds.) Workplace Studies: Recovering Work Practice and Informing System Design, August, pp. 230–241. Cambridge University Press, Cambridge (2000)
6. BBC News Online: BBC Starts to Rock Online World. http://news.bbc.co.uk/1/hi/technology/4766755.stm, verified 07/10/10 (2006)
7. Bell, M., Chalmers, M., Barkhuus, L., Hall, M., Sherwood, S., Tennent, P., Brown, B., Rowland, D., Benford, S.: Interweaving mobile games with everyday life. In: CHI'06: Proceedings of the SIGCHI Conference on Human Factors in Computing Systems, pp. 417–426. ACM, New York (2006). doi:10.1145/1124772.1124835
8. Benford, S., Bowers, J., Fahlén, L.E., Greenhalgh, C., Snowdon, D.: User embodiment in collaborative virtual environments. In: CHI'95: Proceedings of the SIGCHI Conference on Human Factors in Computing Systems, pp. 242–249. ACM/Addison-Wesley, New York/Reading (1995). doi:10.1145/223904.223935
9. Benford, S., Fahlén, L.: A spatial model of interaction in virtual environments. In: Proceedings of Third European Conference on Computer Supported Cooperative Work (ECSCW), pp. 109–124 (1993)

10. Benford, S., Giannachi, G.: Temporal trajectories in shared interactive narratives. In: CHI'08: Proceeding of the Twenty-Sixth Annual SIGCHI Conference on Human Factors in Computing Systems, pp. 73–82. ACM, New York (2008). doi:10.1145/1357054.1357067

11. Benford, S., Giannachi, G., Koleva, B., Rodden, T.: From interaction to trajectories: designing coherent journeys through user experiences. In: CHI'09: Proceedings of the 27th International Conference on Human Factors in Computing Systems, pp. 709–718. ACM, New York (2009). doi:10.1145/1518701.1518812

12. Benford, S., Reynard, G., Greenhalgh, C., Snowdon, D., Bullock, A.: A poetry performance in a collaborative virtual environment. IEEE Comput. Graph. Appl. **20**(3), 66–75 (2000)

13. Benford, S., Rowland, D., Flintham, M., Drozd, A., Hull, R., Reid, J., Morrison, J., Facer, K.: Life on the edge: supporting collaboration in location-based experiences. In: CHI'05: Proceedings of the SIGCHI Conference on Human Factors in Computing Systems, pp. 721–730. ACM, New York (2005). doi:10.1145/1054972.1055072

14. Benford, S., Schnädelbach, H., Koleva, B., Anastasi, R., Greenhalgh, C., Rodden, T., Green, J., Ghali, A., Pridmore, T., Gaver, B., Boucher, A., Walker, B., Pennington, S., Schmidt, A., Gellersen, H., Steed, A.: Expected, sensed, and desired: a framework for designing sensing-based interaction. ACM Trans. Comput.-Hum. Interact. **12**(1), 3–30 (2005). doi:10.1145/1057237.1057239

15. Bitgood, S.: Environmental psychology in museums, zoos, and other exhibition centers. In: Bechtel, R.B., Churchman, A. (eds.) Handbook of Environmental Psychology, pp. 461–480. Wiley, New York (2002)

16. Björk, S., Falk, J., Hansson, R., Ljungstrand, P.: Pirates!—Using the physical world as a game board. In: Proceedings of IFIP TC.13 Conference on Human-Computer Interaction (INTERACT), pp. 9–13 (2001)

17. Blud, L.M.: Social interaction and learning among family groups visiting a museum. Mus. Manag. Curator. **9**(1), 43–51 (1990)

18. Bobick, A., Intille, S., Davis, J., Baird, F., Pinhanez, C., Campbell, L., Ivanov, Y., Schütte, A., Wilson, A.: The KidsRoom: a perceptually-based interactive and immersive story environment. Presence: Teleoperators and Virtual Environments **8**(4), 367–391 (1999)

19. Bowers, J.: TONETABLE: a multi-user, mixed media, interactive installation. In: Proceedings of COST G-6 Conference on Digital Audio Effects (DAFX-01), (2001)

20. Bowers, J., Hellström, S.O.: Simple interfaces to complex sound in improvised music. In: Extended Abstracts on Human Factors in Computing Systems (CHI), pp. 125–126. ACM, New York (2000). doi:10.1145/633292.633364

21. Bowers, J., Rodden, T.: Exploding the interface: experiences of a CSCW network. In: Proceedings of the SIGCHI Conference on Human Factors in Computing Systems, pp. 255–262. ACM, New York (1993). doi:10.1145/169059.169205

22. Brown, B., Chalmers, M., Bell, M., MacColl, I., Hall, M., Rudman, P.: Sharing the square: collaborative leisure in the city streets. In: Proceedings of ECSCW, pp. 427–429. Springer, Berlin (2005)

23. Brown, B., MacColl, I., Chalmers, M., Galani, A., Randell, C., Steed, A.: Lessons from the lighthouse: collaboration in a shared mixed reality system. In: Proceedings of Conference on Human Factors in Computing Systems (CHI), pp. 577–584. ACM, New York (2003)

24. Card, S.K., Newell, A., Moran, T.P.: The Psychology of Human–Computer Interaction. Lawrence Erlbaum Associates, Inc., Mahwah (1983)

25. Carpenter, L.: Cinematrix, Video Imaging Method and Apparatus for Audience Participation. US Patent, Nos. 5210604 (1993), 5365266 (1994)

26. Chalmers, M., Barkhuus, L., Bell, M., Brown, B., Hall, M., Sherwood, S., Tennent, P.: Gaming on the edge: using seams in pervasive games. In: Proceedings of the Second International Workshop on Gaming Applications in Pervasive Computing Environments at Pervasive 2005. Springer, Berlin (2005)

27. Chalmers, M., Galani, A.: Seamful interweaving: heterogeneity in the theory and design of interactive systems. In: DIS'04: Proceedings of the 2004 Conference on Designing Interactive Systems, pp. 243–252. ACM, New York (2004). doi:10.1145/1013115.1013149

28. Cheok, A.D., Fong, S.W., Goh, K.H., Yang, X., Liu, W., Farzbiz, F.: Human Pacman: a sensing-based mobile entertainment system with ubiquitous computing and tangible interaction. In: NetGames'03: Proceedings of the 2nd Workshop on Network and System Support for Games, pp. 106–117. ACM, New York (2003). doi:10.1145/963900.963911
29. Cornock, S., Edmonds, E.A.: The creative process where the artist is amplified or superseded by the computer. Leonardo **6**(11) (1973)
30. Crabtree, A.: Designing Collaborative Systems: A Practical Guide to Ethnography. Springer, Berlin (2003)
31. Crabtree, A.: Informing the evaluation of *Can You See Me Now?* in Rotterdam: runners' and control room work. Technical Report Equator-03-004, School of Computer Science & IT, Nottingham University, May 2003
32. Crabtree, A., Benford, S., Capra, M., Flintham, M., Drozd, A., Tandavanitj, N., Adams, M., Row-Farr, J.: The cooperative work of gaming: orchestrating a mobile SMS game. Comput. Support. Coop. Work J. Collab. Comput. (JCSCW) (2007). Special Issue on Leisure Technologies
33. Crabtree, A., Benford, S., Rodden, T., Greenhalgh, C., Flintham, M., Anastasi, R., Drozd, A., Adams, M., Row-Farr, J., Tandavanitj, N., Steed, A.: Orchestrating a mixed reality game 'on the ground'. In: Proceedings of the SIGCHI Conference on Human Factors in Computing Systems, pp. 391–398. ACM, New York (2004). doi:10.1145/985692.985742
34. Crabtree, A., Rodden, T., Benford, S.: Moving with the times: IT research and the boundaries of CSCW. Comput. Support. Coop. Work **14**(3), 217–251 (2005). doi:10.1007/s10606 -005-3642-x
35. Dourish, P.: Where the Action Is: The Foundations of Embodied Interaction. MIT Press, Cambridge (2001)
36. Dourish, P.: Implications for design. In: Proceedings of ACM Conference on Human Factors in Computing Systems (CHI), pp. 541–550. ACM, New York (2006). doi:10.1145/1124772. 1124855. URL http://www.isr.uci.edu/~jpd/classes/readings/Dourish-Implications.pdf
37. Dourish, P., Adler, A., Bellotti, V., Henderson, A.: Your place or mine? Learning from long-term use of audio-video communication. Comput. Support. Coop. Work **5**(1), 33–62 (1996)
38. Drozd, A., Benford, S., Tandavanitj, N., Wright, M., Chamberlain, A.: Hitchers: designing for cellular positioning. In: Dourish, P., Friday, A. (eds.) Proceedings of Ubicomp. LNCS, vol. 4206, pp. 279–296. Springer, Berlin, Heidelberg (2006)
39. Drozd, A., Bowers, J., Benford, S., Greenhalgh, C., Fraser, M.: Collaboratively improvising magic: an approach to managing participation in an on-line drama. In: Proceedings of European Conference on Computer-Supported Cooperative Work (ECSCW), pp. 159–178. Kluwer Academic, Dordrecht (2001)
40. Dykstra-Erickson, E., Arnowitz, J.: Michel Waisvisz: the man and the hands. Interactions **12**(5), 63–67 (2005). doi:10.1145/1082369.1082416
41. Edmonds, E., Turner, G., Candy, L.: Approaches to interactive art systems. In: GRAPHITE'04: Proceedings of the 2nd International Conference on Computer Graphics and Interactive Techniques in Australasia and South East Asia, pp. 113–117. ACM, New York (2004). doi:10.1145/988834.988854
42. Esbjörnsson, M., Brown, B., Juhlin, O., Normark, D., Östergren, M., Laurier, E.: Watching the cars go round and round: designing for active spectating. In: Proceedings of the SIGCHI Conference on Human Factors in Computing Systems, pp. 1221–1224. ACM, New York (2006). doi:10.1145/1124772.1124955
43. Ferris, K., Bannon, L., Ciolfi, L., Gallagher, P., Hall, T., Lennon, M.: Shaping experiences in the Hunt Museum: a design case study. In: Proceedings of ACM Conference on Designing Interactive Systems, pp. 205–214. ACM, New York (2004). doi:10.1145/1013115.1013144
44. Flintham, M., Benford, S., Anastasi, R., Hemmings, T., Crabtree, A., Greenhalgh, C., Tandavanitj, N., Adams, M., Row-Farr, J.: Where on-line meets on the streets: experiences with mobile mixed reality games. In: Proceedings of SIGCHI Conference on Human Factors in Computing Systems (CHI), pp. 569–576. ACM, New York (2003). doi:10.1145/642611.642710

45. Fraser, M., Stanton, D., Ng, K.H., Benford, S., O'Malley, C., Bowers, J., Taxén, G., Ferris, K., Hindmarsh, J.: Assembling history: achieving coherent experiences with diverse technologies. In: Proceedings of European Conference on Computer Supported Cooperative Work (ECSCW), pp. 179–198. Oulu University Press, Oulu (2003)
46. Gaver, W., Beaver, J., Benford, S.: Ambiguity as a resource for design. In: Proceedings of Conference on Human Factors in Computing Systems (CHI), pp. 233–240. ACM, New York (2003). doi:10.1145/642611.642653
47. Geser, H.: 2001 Towards a sociological theory of the mobile phone. Unpublished report
48. Gibson, J.J.: The Ecological Approach to Visual Perception. Erlbaum, Hillsdale (1979)
49. Goffman, E.: The Presentation of the Self in Everyday Life. Doubleday, New York (1959)
50. Goffman, E.: Frame Analysis: An Essay on the Organization of Experience. Harper & Row, New York (1974)
51. Green, J., Schnädelbach, H., Koleva, B., Benford, S., Pridmore, T., Medina, K., Harris, E., Smith, H.: Camping in the digital wilderness: tents and flashlights as interfaces to virtual worlds. In: Extended Abstracts on Human Factors in Computing Systems (CHI), pp. 780–781. ACM, New York (2002). doi:10.1145/506443.506594
52. Grinter, R.E., Aoki, P.M., Szymanski, M.H., Thornton, J.D., Woodruff, A., Hurst, A.: Revisiting the visit: understanding how technology can shape the museum visit. In: Proceedings of ACM Conference on Computer Supported Cooperative Work (CSCW), pp. 146–155. ACM, New York (2002). doi:10.1145/587078.587100
53. Grudin, J.: The computer reaches out: the historical continuity of interface design. In: Proceedings of the SIGCHI Conference on Human Factors in Computing Systems, pp. 261–268. ACM, New York (1990). doi:10.1145/97243.97284
54. Grudin, J.: Interface. In: Proceedings of the 1990 ACM Conference on Computer Supported Cooperative Work (CSCW), pp. 269–278. ACM, New York (1990). doi:10.1145/99332.99360
55. Grudin, J.: Computer-supported cooperative work: Its history and participation. IEEE Comput. 27(5), 19–26 (1994)
56. Hämäläinen, P., Ilmonen, T., Höysniemi, J., Lindholm, M., Nykänen, A.: Martial arts in artificial reality. In: Proceedings of the SIGCHI Conference on Human Factors in Computing Systems, pp. 781–790. ACM, New York (2005). doi:10.1145/1054972.1055081
57. Harris, E., Price, S., Weal, M.: Data recording and reuse: supporting research and digitally augmented learning experiences. Position paper for EQUATOR Record and Reeuse workshop (2004)
58. Heath, C., Hindmarsh, J., Luff, P.: Interaction in isolation: the dislocated world of the London Underground train driver. Sociology 33(3), 555–575 (1999)
59. Heath, C., Hindmarsh, J., Luff, P.: Video in Qualitative Research. Sage, Thousand Oaks (2010)
60. Heath, C., Jirotka, M., Luff, P., Hindmarsh, J.: Unpacking collaboration: the interactional organisation of trading in a city dealing room. Comput. Support. Coop. Work 3, 147–165 (1995)
61. Heath, C., Knoblauch, H., Luff, P.: Technology and social interaction: the emergence of 'workplace studies'. Br. J. Sociol. 51(2), 229–320 (2000)
62. Heath, C., vom Lehn, D.: Configuring reception: looking at exhibits in museums and galleries. Technical report, Kings College, London (2003)
63. Heath, C., vom Lehn, D.: Misconstruing interactivity. In: Hinton, M. (ed.) Interactive Learning in Museums of Art and Design. Victoria and Albert Museum (2003)
64. Heath, C., Luff, P., vom Lehn, D., Cleverly, J.: Crafting participation: designing ecologies, configuring experience. Vis. Commun. 1, 9–34 (2002)
65. Heath, C., Luff, P.K.: Collaboration and control: crisis management and multimedia technology in London Underground line control rooms. J. Comput. Support. Coop. Work 1(1–2), 69–94 (1992)
66. Hindmarsh, J., Heath, C., vom Lehn, D., Cleverly, J.: Creating assemblies: Aboard the Ghost Ship. In: Proceedings of ACM Conference on Computer Supported Cooperative Work (CSCW), pp. 156–165. ACM, New York (2002)

67. Hromin, D., Chladil, M., Vanatta, N., Naumann, D., Wetzel, S., Anjum, F., Jain, R.: Code-BLUE: a Bluetooth interactive dance club system. In: IEEE Global Telecommunications Conference (GLOBECOM), vol. 5, pp. 2814–2818 (2003). doi:10.1109/GLOCOM.2003. 1258748
68. Hughes, J., King, V., Rodden, T., Andersen, H.: Moving out from the control room: ethnography in system design. In: CSCW'94: Proceedings of the 1994 ACM Conference on Computer Supported Cooperative Work, pp. 429–439. ACM, New York (1994). doi:10.1145/192844. 193065
69. Hughes, J.A., Randall, D., Shapiro, D.: Faltering from ethnography to design. In: Proceedings of the 1992 ACM Conference on Computer-Supported Cooperative Work (CSCW), pp. 115–122. ACM, New York (1992). doi:10.1145/143457.143469
70. Huhtamo, E.: On the origins of the virtual museum. In: Nobel Symposium (NS120) on Virtual Museums and Public Understanding of Science and Culture (2002)
71. Huizinga, J.: Homo Ludens: A Study of the Play-element in Culture. International Library of Sociology and Social Reconstruction. Routledge, Cambridge (1944)
72. Hutchins, E.: Cognition in the Wild. MIT Press, Cambridge (1996)
73. Koleva, B., Taylor, I., Benford, S., Fraser, M., Greenhalgh, C., Schnädelbach, H., vom Lehn, D., Heath, C., Row-Farr, J., Adams, M.: Orchestrating a mixed reality performance. In: Proceedings of SIGCHI Conference on Human Factors in Computing Systems (CHI), pp. 38–45. ACM, New York (2001). doi:10.1145/365024.365033
74. Lasen, A.: 2002 A Comparative Study of Mobile Phone Use in London, Madrid and Paris. Unpublished report. URL http://www.surrey.ac.uk/dwrc/papers/CompStudy.pdf
75. Lawrence, G.: Rats, street gangs and culture: evaluation in museums. In: Kavanagh, G. (ed.) Museum Languages: Objects and Texts, pp. 9–32. Leicester University Press, Leicester (1991)
76. vom Lehn, D., Heath, C., Hindmarsh, J.: Exhibiting interaction: conduct and collaboration in museums and galleries. Symb. Interact. **24**(2), 189–216 (2001)
77. vom Lehn, D., Heath, C., Knoblauch, H.: Configuring exhibits. In: Knoblauch, H., Kotthoff, H. (eds.) Verbal Art Across Cultures: The Aesthetics and Proto-aesthetics of Communication, pp. 281–297. Gunter Narr Verlag, Tubingen (2001)
78. MacDonald, S.: Behind the Scenes at the Science Museum. Berg (2002)
79. Maynes-Aminzade, D., Pausch, R., Seitz, S.: Techniques for interactive audience participation. In: Proceedings of IEEE International Conference on Multimodal Interfaces (ICMI) (2002)
80. Moss, M.L., Townsend, A.M.: How telecommunications systems are transforming urban spaces. In: Wheeler, J.O., Aoyama, Y. (eds.) Fractured Geographies: Cities in the Telecommunications Age. Routledge, London (1999)
81. Myers, B., Hollan, J., Isabel Cruz, T.U.: Strategic directions in human computer interaction. ACM Computing Surveys **28**(4) (1996)
82. Norman, D.A.: The Design of Everyday Things, 1st edn. Basic Books, New York (2002)
83. Pac-Manhatten website: http://pacmanhattan.com, Verified 07/10/10 (2004)
84. Paradiso, J.: The Brain Opera technology: new instruments and gestural sensors for musical interaction and performance. J. New Music Res. **28**(2), 130–149 (1999)
85. Paradiso, J., Hu, E., Hsiao, K.-y.: Instrumented footwear for interactive dance. In: Proceedings of the XII Colloquium on Musical Informatics (AIMI), pp. 89–92 (1998)
86. Park, C., Chou, P.H., Sun, Y.: A wearable wireless sensor platform for interactive art performance. In: Proceedings of Fourth Annual IEEE International Conference on Pervasive Computing and Communications (PerCom), pp. 52–59 (2006)
87. Reeves, S., Benford, S., O'Malley, C., Fraser, M.: Designing the spectator experience. In: Proceedings of SIGCHI Conference on Human Factors in Computing Systems (CHI), pp. 741–750 (2005). doi:10.1145/1054972.1055074
88. Sanneblad, J., Holmquist, L.E.: "Why is everyone inside me?!" Using shared displays in mobile computer games. In: Proceedings of International Conference on Entertainment Computing (ICEC) (2004)

89. Schmidt, K.: 'Keep up the good work!': The concept of 'work' in CSCW. In: International Conference Series on the Design of Cooperative Systems, pp. 265–286. Springer, Berlin (2010). doi:10.1007/978-1-84996-211-7_15

90. Schnädelbach, H., Koleva, B., Flintham, M., Fraser, M., Izadi, S., Chandler, P., Foster, M., Benford, S., Greenhalgh, C., Rodden, T.: The Augurscope: a mixed reality interface for outdoors. In: Proceedings of SIGCHI Conference on Human Factors in Computing Systems (CHI), pp. 9–16. ACM, New York (2002). doi:10.1145/503376.503379

91. Shearman, J.: Only Connect... : Art and the Spectator in the Italian Renaissance. Princeton University Press, Princeton (1994)

92. Sheridan, J., Dix, A., Lock, S., Bayliss, A.: Understanding interaction in ubiquitous guerrilla performances in playful arenas. In: Proceedings of British HCI Conference (2004)

93. Shettel, H.H.: Exhibits: art form or educational medium? Museum News 52(1), 32–41 (1973)

94. Sparacino, F., Wren, C., Davenport, G., Pentland, A.: Augmented performance in dance and theater. In: International Dance and Technology 99 (IDAT99) (1999)

95. Stanton, D., O'Malley, C., Ng, K.H., Fraser, M., Benford, S.: Situating historical events through mixed reality: adult-child interactions in the Storytent. In: Proceedings of 2nd International Conference on Computer Supported Collaborative Learning (2003)

96. Stewart, J.: Single display groupware. In: Adjunct Proceedings of the SIGCHI Conference on Human Factors in Computing Systems (CHI), pp. 71–72. ACM, New York (1997)

97. Stewart, J., Bederson, B.B., Druin, A.: Single display groupware: a model for co-present collaboration. In: CHI'99: Proceedings of the SIGCHI Conference on Human Factors in Computing Systems, pp. 286–293. ACM, New York (1999). doi:10.1145/302979.303064

98. Suchman, L.: Notes on Computer Support for Cooperative Work. Working paper WP-12 (1989)

99. Suchman, L.A.: Plans and Situated Actions: The Problem of Human-machine Communication. Cambridge University Press, Cambridge (1987)

100. Szentgyorgyi, C., Lank, E., Terry, M.: Renegade gaming: practices surrounding social use of the Nintendo DS handheld gaming system. In: Proceedings of the SIGCHI Conference on Human Factors in Computing Systems (CHI). ACM, New York (2008)

101. Thomas, B., Close, B., Donoghue, J., Squires, J., Bondi, P.D., Piekarski, W.: First person indoor/outdoor augmented reality application: ARQuake. Pers. Ubiquitous Comput. 6(1), 75–86 (2002). doi:10.1007/s007790200007

102. Umiker-Sebeok, J.: Behavior in a museum: a semio-cognitive approach to museum consumption experiences. Signif. Behav. J. Res. Semiotics Commun. Theory Cogn. Sci. 1(1), 52–100 (1994)

103. Wilde, D., Harris, E., Rogers, Y., Randell, C.: The Periscope: supporting a computer enhanced field trip for children. Pers. Ubiquitous Comput. 7, 227–233 (2003)

104. Wilson, S.: Information Arts: Intersections of Art, Science and Technology. MIT Press, Cambridge (2002)

105. Winograd, T.: From computing machinery to interaction design. In: Denning, P., Metcalfe, R. (eds.) Beyond Calculation: The Next Fifty Years of Computing, pp. 149–162. Springer, Berlin (1997)

106. Z, P.: Audible image/visible sound: Donald Swearingen's Living Off The List. 21st Century Music 8(1) (2000)

Chapter 3
Studying Technology in Public Settings

This chapter addresses the problem of studying technology in use in uncontrolled and complex settings found in public and semi-public places. As well as covering the conceptual approach taken in the empirical studies presented in the book and the framework, this chapter seeks to provide background to some of the more practical concerns that were involved in producing what are a heavily interrelated set of studies and a design framework. In describing the mesh of the conceptual and practical, it is hoped that this will provide adequate context for the reader's understanding of what is presented in this book.

The first sections of this chapter broadly cover the more conceptual side of the methodological approaches and analytic perspectives that have been employed in addressing and overcoming the significant problems that are posed by studying technology in-action within public settings. Firstly it is the insights of ethnomethodology [6] and conversation analysis that are introduced to the reader and the ways in which they relate to the studies presented in later chapters. As Rawls summarises, "[e]thnomethodology [...] is the study of the methods people use for producing recognizable social orders [...] to discover the things that persons in particular situations *do*, the methods *they* use, to create the patterned orderliness of social life" [7]. Other interactionist traditions, particularly Goffman's dramaturgical concepts for understanding social interaction [8, 9], have also informed data collection and analysis, and strongly directed the construction of the framework in this book. As such a central aim of this chapter is in exploring the philosophical rationales that were formative in engaging in this work.

After covering some of this more conceptual ground, this chapter explores the practical aspects of data collection and analysis, and the distinct material challenges it presents in terms of studying interaction 'in the wild'. Part of this challenge is the more general issue facing researchers studying all manner of public settings in which technology is deployed, namely the difficulty in piecing together what are typically very fragmented, distributed and mobile data resources. This chapter examines the use of a variety of tools that have been employed in order to assist with managing diverse and fragmentary data sets in order to provide context and background to the empirical studies.

S. Reeves, *Designing Interfaces in Public Settings*, Human-Computer Interaction Series,   29
DOI 10.1007/978-0-85729-265-0_3, © Springer-Verlag London Limited 2011

The final topic this chapter addresses is a discussion of the conceptual relationship between the framework and the components of this framework as they are developed in the studies. This discussion becomes vital when seeking to connect two 'layers' of work: the findings that are developed in naturalistic video-based data analysis, and the conceptual generalisations of a framework. In doing this, we shall expand and elaborate the opening chapter's diagrammatic summary of framework components.

3.1 Concepts for Understanding Public Settings

This book takes an interactionist and naturalistic perspective on interaction with technology, drawing upon a tradition of ethnomethodology and to some extent conversation analysis (see [6, 7, 17] for various founding works) for the ways in which it approaches observational work and analysis of (typically video-based) data.

Ethnomethodology takes as its topic the methods people employ in managing the problem of intersubjectivity—that is, the techniques and strategies members of society use in making sense of one-another's subjective perspective on everyday experience, and through these methods, achieving a significant measure of shared understanding. This shared understanding is seen as a mundane and routine accomplishment that is achieved in everyday interaction, creating an observable and accountable social order that participants in interaction orient towards.

As we saw in the previous chapter, historically within HCI this perspective has gained increasing currency in the shift from understanding HCI as a dialogue between a single user located at a machine, to seeing such interactions as consisting of constellations of potentially distributed users performing their activities with *and around* multiple machines. Various influential accounts have advanced varieties of the interactionist perspective and the ethnographic technique in particular in order to illuminate this view on HCI. Ethnomethodology's concerns have in turn influenced these accounts, particularly evident in certain CSCW literature such as Lucy Suchman's well-known book Plans and Situated Actions [21], along with several other seminal workplace studies (e.g., [2, 12–14]).

Ethnomethodology is concerned with the accountable ways in which social interaction is conducted by members of society. Everyday activities are seen as being organised and crafted, moment-by-moment, in a way that makes them relevant to the ongoing situation, context and setting in which action is produced. Garfinkel suggests that these crafted, "account-able" activities are made so by virtue of them being "observable-and-reportable, i.e. available to members as situated practices of looking-and-telling" [6, p. 1]. This action is inherently reflexive, in that the very procedures for making actions accountable to the shared sense of social organisation are the selfsame procedures members used in order to "produce and manage settings of organized everyday affairs" [6, p. 1]. For instance, turn-taking, a focus point for much conversation analytic research, is a major feature of talk. Research conducted on turn-taking in conversation has found that participants engage in a number of methods for managing the distribution of turns in talk and rights-to-talk, such as constructing sentences in such a way so as to be recognisable as the end of a turn, deferring the end of a turn in order to maintain the opportunity to continue speaking, participants collaboratively 'repairing' conversational breakdowns in turn-taking, and so on (see [18, 19]). These studies show how utterances are made in a way that is accountable to speakers' shared orientation towards turn-taking and its role in everyday conversation. They also demonstrate the indexicality of these utterances; that is, the fact that talk is 'indexed' to the context in which it is produced. Just as these things can be said about verbal conduct, so they can be relevant to bodily conduct as well. Indeed, we will see turn-taking—verbal and bodily—in action within later study chapters, particularly in how it is employed within handing over technology and managing its use.

In contrast with mainstream sociology, ethnomethodology is not concerned with the construction or application of theories to explain social phenomena. It is not interested in how objective 'social structures' influence social interaction. It is not concerned with applying a formal method to the analysis of data in order to generate 'findings' and situate those findings within a theoretical framework in order to explain them. Instead, it discards notions of applying sociological method, offering a 'philosophical commitment' towards understanding and making sense of empirical data.

Within the data collected for the studies presented here, these age-old problems of intersubjectivity remain at the heart of the analytic endeavour. In producing their findings, the studies examine the accountable, indexical and reflexive nature of social interaction, and seek to understand social order as a shared, collaborative achievement by members of the settings under study. Understanding *how* shared understanding and collaborative action is accomplished around what is often quite sophisticated technology is the main thrust of the analysis, and, as suggested earlier, follows on in tradition and form from a relatively well-established stream of HCI and CSCW concerned with naturalistic and interactionist understandings of human-computer interaction. The analysis attempts to understand just how coordination is managed around an augmented reality device (Chap. 4), an interactive storytelling system (Chap. 5), a digitally augmented fairground ride (Chap. 6) or a performance art mobile experience (Chap. 7). Through this, we can better understand in detail the material ways in which technology is used, and, as a result, be better informed when coming to decision-making in design (and inspirations for design).

Following from this point, the relationship of this perspective on interaction with the presentation of analysis must be clarified. This book is not a purely sociological work. Whilst in some sense all attempts at understanding interaction in a range of contexts is 'doing sociology' in one fashion or another, the analyses presented here are, broadly-speaking, two-layered affairs in which an upper layer of 'structured design reasoning', as found in Chap. 8's framework mostly but also addressed in each study chapter's discussion, is informed by a lower layer of analytic observations about interaction with interfaces in public settings as directed by concerns of how interaction is worked out moment-by-moment, with and around technology. It is important to acknowledge that there is the potential for unease in the relationship between (more broadly) ethnographies and work that seeks to develop implications from naturalistic studies of social interaction. However, whilst paying attention to many of the pitfalls encountered in this relationship, particularly with regard to recent debates on ethnomethodologically-informed ethnography and its use in design [4, 5], it is clear that overall the relationship is beneficial.

Now we can turn, for a moment, to the major informant for the 'structured design reasoning' in this book, particularly through examining the interactionist-oriented work of Goffman.

Goffman's dramaturgy and frame analysis have both informed the framework, and the way that the analyses presented in study chapters have been developed in order to exhibit different components of this framework. As discussed in Chap. 2, the dramaturgical perspective begins by considering all social interaction as 'performance', i.e., using a theatrical performance metaphor as a self-awaredly 'ironic' lens with which to view and interpret how social interaction is done. In Goffman's analysis, an individual's performance "front" is stably and fixedly maintained for an audience by that individual as a performer, in order to help "define the situation for those who observe the performance" [8, p. 22]. This enables an audience to orient appropriately to the conduct of the individual, and therefore negotiate the subjective experiences of each member. This basic distinction between performer and audience serves as a starting point from which to begin to unpack members' interactions with and around technology. We will see how, in the first study chapter, this simple demarcation of roles can provide a basis for building up a rich framework for interaction with technology in public settings. Further to this, we will see later on how Goffman's settings of front-stage and back-stage may be applied to interaction in technology-filled environments and inform our analysis and understandings of them for the purposes of design.

Goffman's dramaturgical perspective involved the mutual construction of situational "definitions". Goffman's analysis of members' "frameworks" within which social interaction is interpreted and constructed provides another important insight in the analysis of these studies and the construction of the framework. In the final study and in the framework chapter, we will expand upon how these framings come to feature in technology-mediated interactions between members of a performance, and the way that technology may be designed with framings in mind, as well as considerations for situations where members may be 'outside' frame boundaries.

In the ways outlined above, then, Goffman's dramaturgy and notion of framings has been used both in conducting analysis and building up concepts of the framework. It has thus been used in order to bridge and structure the 'gap' between the findings of an ethnomethodologically-informed analysis of interaction and the design structures presented particularly in the framework chapter.

3.2 Practical Approaches to Studying Public Settings

One of the key features of working with the conceptual orientations outlined above has been developing rich descriptions of interaction with technology in the wild. Such detailed descriptions work as a sensitising tool, highlighting forcefully to the analyst the haecceities and contingencies ('just-thisness') of everyday actions. Collecting data is important to building these thick descriptions of social order and how it is constructed, methodically, by members of society. Using data we can understand what members' methods are, how social order in settings as diverse as theatrical performances, city streets or funfairs, is accomplished and achieved, daily, by the work of their participants. This has meant gathering data from a wide range of sources, often in challenging environments. As such, diverse forms of data were collected as part of the studies that contribute to this book, including audiovisual data, log data (system and sensor logs), observational notes, technical and non-technical documents, photographs, interviews and other audio recordings.

For the studies in this book, video data features as the main analytic resource, and considerable time was spent conducting analytic work around a corpus of video recordings and other associated data. Reflecting the conceptual orientation presented in the previous section, the primacy of video is due to the way in which it provides a powerful resource to study the "orderliness and patterns in people's routine interactions, [whilst] operat[ing] at a finer level of detail than conventional ethnographic observation" [16]. The simple faculty to repeatedly see everyday activity, and to draw together multiple instances of common fragments of social interaction, helps the analyst access the 'backgrounded' and routinely performed-but-ignored ways in which social action is organised. This taken-for-granted aspect of social organisation was something famously Garfinkel highlighted in "breaching experiments" which exposed mundane social order through disruption of it [6]. Heath, Hindmarsh and Luff suggest, quoting Agar, that this repeatability of video supports "a critical way of seeing" which "comes out of numerous cycles through a little bit of data, [and] massive amounts of thinking about that data" [1], in [11, p. 59]. Thus, video forms a key role in enabling the analyst to begin to see how these mundane and routine activities are achieved as an orderly and ongoing accomplishment of interaction between people in a given setting.

The beguiling richness of video and its repeatability should not be so overwhelming, however, that neglecting its obvious problems be permitted. Whilst the opportunities and pitfalls of video-based interaction analysis have been covered elsewhere (e.g., [10, 11, 16]), some issues will be touched on below that are of particular relevance for the settings under study.

The term 'video-based' is used here to mean a particular hybridised form of video analysis in which a large range of other data sources were integrated what was primarily video-driven analytic work. So, whilst other resources—such as interviews, questionnaires, informal discussions, log file data, and simulations or reconstructions of events—are important, by and large these other resources were drawn on in order to develop a deeper appreciation for what is sometimes quite opaque to the observer on the video record. Indeed, these other resources also provided a capacity to initiate lines of enquiry which would not have been apparent from video or observational records alone. For instance, Chap. 4's study employed a simulator in order to recreate the interactions with a device, and in Chap. 6 a more general replay system was used to visualise log data alongside multiple video recordings. More generally, similar approaches are providing greater purchase on the study of increasingly disparate and distributed interfaces (see [3]). Greater detail on these particular systems is provided in their corresponding chapters.

A variety of video perspectives have been captured in each study. Some were recorded through a largely unattended 'ambient' style of camera-work using a tripod (as found in Chaps. 4 and 5), whereas others involved roaming situationally-embedded camera-work as part of observation, shadowing and enquiring of participants (in Chap. 7), and yet others still used a mixture of these two (in Chap. 6). Obviously, the 'camera effects' upon those being filmed is quite different when generally unobtrusive fixed cameras are employed, compared to filming in a rather more pointed (literally) and mobile way without fixed positions. Further to this, it is clear that, especially given the often distributed nature of the environments under inspection, only a series of disjoint 'slices' of the action may ever be captured for review at any time, and as a result, much work must be done in order to perform a 'recovery' of what is typically a fragmented timeline of conduct. This last problem was particularly so for Chap. 6's study, in which a significant part of the experience for the participant takes place on a fairground ride. A further issue to take note of is that the limited duration of the settings under study (being 'events') meant that there was no way in which extensive recordings over a large amount of time could be made, and no way in which any analyst could, say, 'drop in' over a long period in order to get acquainted with the setting. By their very nature these settings were not fixed and stable environments, but rather transient ones which occurred 'one time only', a fact that to some extent shapes the findings derived from them. A more sustained engagement in particular settings, however, would have meant a smaller selection of settings could be covered within the research period. As such, a trade-off between engagement and diversity was unavoidable. Nevertheless, three of the four studies presented later involved professional performers, so in another sense the studies examine the competence of such professionals, mitigating the issue of sustained engagement.

How the video collected for the various study chapters has been examined is worth discussing here, as well as how selections from that set were made. Once again, more specific details are covered in individual chapters, however, some broad comments can be made here. For the most part there was a large bulk of video recordings for any given event, and in order to develop a full understanding and appreciation for the setting in which interaction occurs, whether it was an exhibition or performance, this bulk must be systematically inspected. Heath, Hindmarsh and Luff discuss three general phases typically involved in the study of a video-based corpus [11, p. 62]; the studies in this book follow a similar approach. They highlight three phases of work which typically correspond to increasing levels of transcription detail: a preliminary review, involving basic cataloging of a data corpus and its approximate contents (similar to video editor's 'logging' of raw footage); a substantive review, in which the corpus is catalogued and annotated in greater detail (e.g., when conversations occur and approximately what their contents were, brief descriptions of physical conduct in terms of gross movements or positions); and finally an analytic review where portions of the corpus are studied in detail, typically using transcription systems and rich description of bodily interaction. This third phase—the analytic review—is strongly informed by any observation in person and familiarity with the setting in general, perhaps through interviews, informal discussions, personal engagement in development work, exploration of log files, and so on.

Once the corpus has been subject to analytic review, it becomes useful to select segments that provide exemplars or exhibits to drive the analysis presented in each chapter. In the context of this book, the significance of these 'vignettes' of action may have emerged from a wider appraisal of the corpus or be more directed by the concerns of the framework. Specifically, the first two study Chaps. 4, 5 are more 'foundational' in the sense that the topics of particular interest, such as the play of roles such as 'participants' and 'actors', emerged chronologically earlier and thus did more in forming some of the basis of the framework than in being resources with which to investigate particular framework topics. In later studies (Chaps. 6 and 7) there has been a tendency for a reversal in this relationship. In other words, topics of interest derived from emergent themes in the earlier studies came to be sources of enquiry for the data corpus of later studies.

Referring to 'emergent themes' in this way might at first be considered to be strongly related to the quantification of interactions, where bodily and verbal conduct is coded and significance is attached to frequency, so as to give force for a particular argument that may be advanced. However, this book does not take that particular approach, and instead concerns itself with the concrete particulars of complex social interaction around technology. As Schegloff explains regarding the study of naturally occurring events rather than "experimental or otherwise elicited data":

> [...] no number of *other* episodes that developed differently will undo the fact that in these cases [the event] went the way it did, with that exhibited understanding, and with an object of study made available to inquiry, demanding an account along those lines [20].

Finally, a further influence in selecting data is to some extent presentational. For some studies, providing a general overview of the settings in which the studies took place is quite essential for communicating how the experience appeared from different members' perspectives. In Chap. 6's study, for instance, the vignettes provide a way of looking at the action from a variety of perspectives, both physically (i.e., within different spaces), and within the different capacities of members of the event (e.g., behind-the-scenes staff, audience). On the other hand, some vignettes have also been chosen as a kind of 'breaching experiment' [6]. Technological breakdown is a continual feature, especially of the first two studies, and is represented in many the vignettes due to the kinds of features breakdown exposes, such as in making more visible the backgrounded contingencies of the settings under examination.

3.2.1 Challenges in Collecting and Analysing Data

There are various challenges posed by collecting and analysing data that is drawn from interaction 'in the wild'. When compared to controlled, lab-based environments, there are a host of initial access and consent issues, as well as practicalities such as setting up video cameras, following participants in distributed settings, making sense of conduct, and so on.

In each of the settings studied, piecing together fragmented interaction is a key problem. Whilst large amounts of data, including video, log files, notes and so on, may be collected, there is typically never enough information to fully and comprehensively capture the true scope of the event. This poses methodological problems when coming to perform analysis; the analyst must first piece together these constituent but incomplete parts, and attempt to make sense of them within the context of a broader knowledge of the event, typically derived from observation and first-hand experience of being present. This fragmented record often excludes what might be critical moments or critical data, further encumbering the process of analysis outlined previously.

There are also considerable methodological challenges in the varied role of the author in these studies. Achieving a full understanding of the setting under study often became a time-consuming and potentially uncertain process when not present for the event itself. This was particularly the case for Chap. 6's Fairground: Thrill Laboratory and Chap. 7's Uncle Roy All Around You, which both involved distributed teams and complex arrangements of technology. The fragmented record thus requires even more care in these situations since first-hand experience cannot be relied on. Instead, interviews, informal conversations and general attention to the mundane specifics of the event become vital in order to fill out this knowledge gap.

Developing this further, mobile interaction such as that found in Uncle Roy All Around You also poses special problems, particularly in that it becomes highly desirable in combining the fragments of the experience, to be able to recreate or 'see' what the player in the experience saw. Within these mobile settings, fully capturing interaction with a device is typically precluded by the necessity of not interfering with the experience for players. This was very much so for Uncle Roy All Around You, given that a significant element of the experience was that of 'alone-ness'. This further underlines the partial and fragmented view that comes to challenge the analyst when investigating interaction in the wild.

In real terms, these problems were tackled ways appropriate to each setting under scrutiny, and so a variety of video perspectives has been captured in each study. Some were recorded through a largely unattended 'ambient' style of camera-work using a tripod (as found in Chaps. 4 and 5), whereas others involved roaming situationally-embedded camera-work as part of observation, shadowing and enquiring of participants (in Chap. 7), and yet others still used a mixture of these two (in Chap. 6). Obviously, the effects of the camera upon those being filmed is quite different when generally unobtrusive fixed cameras are employed, compared to filming in a rather more pointed (literally) and mobile way without fixed positions. In both cases, however, it is easy to sometimes overestimate the impact cameras have on participants [11, p. 47–49].

Given the often distributed nature of the environments under inspection, only a series of disjoint 'slices' of the action may ever be captured for review at any time, and as a result, much work must be done in order to perform a 'recovery' of what is typically a fragmented timeline of conduct. This problem was particularly true for Chap. 6's study, in which a significant part of the experience for the participant takes place on a fairground ride.

A further issue to take note of is that the limited duration of the settings under study (being 'events') meant that there was no way in which extensive recordings over a large amount of time could be made, and no way in which it was possible to 'drop in' over a lengthy period in order to get acquainted with the setting. By their very nature these settings were not fixed and stable environments, but rather transient ones which occurred 'one time only', a fact that to some extent shapes the findings derived from them. A trade-off between engagement and diversity is often unavoidable. Nevertheless, three of the four studies presented later involved professional performers, so in another sense the studies examine the competence of such professionals, mitigating the issue of sustained engagement.

3.2.2 The Author's Role

The role of the author in each of the studies potentially affects how data collection and analysis has been performed. I, as the author of this book, had a varying level of involvement in each of the systems and events under study that are presented in subsequent chapters. This involvement ranged from collaboration in designing, implementing, capturing and analysing data to an involvement in a secondary round of analysis only.

In Chap. 4, I was involved in the design (in collaboration with Welfare State International, the group coordinating the design and construction of the exhibition), as well as the implementation, data collection and analysis of the Telescope device within the exhibition. Data collection in this case involved setting up video recordings, doing observational work whilst being present at many runs of the performance. The author also constructed a simulator used in order to assist analysis by re-running logged data.

In contrast, I was not involved in the design or development of the system in Chap. 5's study of the Journey into Space event, but rather in an analysis-only role, although informal conversations further informed my understanding of the system and analysis of breakdown, repair and so on.

Differing from these previous two studies, Chap. 6's study did not involve me in either its design and development, or the capture of video or telemetry data. However, in addition to the video, log data and interview records being consulted collectively in a series of data-sessions, once again, extensive informal conversations were had between myself and various members of the event (mostly staff at the Mixed Reality Lab, at the University of Nottingham). This was done in order to successfully understand each element of the technology supporting the event across what were at times complex interactions over physically distributed sites.

Finally, similar to the study of Fairground: Thrill Laboratory in Chap. 6, I was not involved in the design, development or data capture of Uncle Roy All Around You (Chap. 7), and neither was I part of research team working on the earlier analyses of the game. Instead, the performance was examined quite some time after these previously-published analyses on the game were written when it became clear that aspects of the design of the game were highly relevant to developing concepts within the framework, and as such would be useful in helping to shape it.

3.3 Relating Studies and Framework

Finally in this chapter we turn to the details of the relationship between the studies and the framework. Firstly this is addressed in terms of the sense of their ordering, making explicit their chronology and the rationale for their presentation at the places they are found. Secondly the tangle between the findings of the studies informing the framework, and the framework informing the focus of the studies (as mentioned earlier in this chapter), is explicated in more detail on a chapter-by-chapter basis.

3.3.1 How the Chapters are Organised

This sequence of chapters in which the studies are documented is a logical ordering that differs from their actual chronology. The series of performance events on which Chap. 7's study is based were designed and implemented in the months running up to its premiere in June 2003. After the premiere in 2003, Uncle Roy All Around You toured twice during 2004, the collected data from which forms the basis of the study in Chap. 7. The first event, One Rock (Chap. 4), on the other hand, occurred around December 2003. The second study's event, the Journey into Space (Chap. 5), was run in May 2004. Finally, the Fairground: Thrill Laboratory events on which the third study is based (Chap. 6) took place during autumn 2006.

There are two main reasons why the chapters have been ordered in this logical—rather than chronological—fashion. Firstly, in order to assist simplicity, the smaller-scale events (One Rock, the Journey into Space) are tackled initially, with spatially larger, more complex settings (Fairground: Thrill Laboratory, Uncle Roy All Around You) being explored in later chapters. Secondly, building up from simpler components in smaller-scale settings enables the framework to be presented in a piecemeal way that is hopefully more comprehensible than systematically presenting each concept in turn. Thus the study chapters may present initial concepts, create 'problems' for later chapters to solve, refine previously-covered topics and finally exploit unusual situations in order to demonstrate the robustness of the concepts developed in previous chapters. More specifically, Chap. 4 introduces a basic distinction between participants and audience, however in doing so exposes some of the simplifications that result, glossing over non-professional and professional distinctions in participation that are further refined in Chap. 5. Chapter 6 expands the number of componential roles as well as increasingly refining descriptions of existing ones; Chap. 7, in testing the limits of how these concepts have been defined further develops and strengthens them.

3.3.2 Influence Between Studies and Framework

The way in which the framework itself has been developed is also of importance. Whilst the studies presented in this book are used to exhibit particular framework concepts, such as 'orchestration', or 'transition', the thoughts and ideas motivating the framework itself also stem from an ongoing analysis of a variety of literatures (such as analyses of interaction in museums and galleries, the growing body of HCI literature concerned with mass-participation and/or spectatorship, workplace studies within CSCW, performance art literature). Whilst the data has been approached in a way that seeks to discover emergent themes, there is an inevitable measure of cross-pollination between the ongoing understandings of the framework and the orientation to the recorded data regarding where focus is channelled. For example, when developing notions of orchestration and transition, this meant specifically spending more time inspecting orchestration activities behind-the-scenes (Chap. 6), or deeper examination of the point when intervention causes orchestrators to transition to actors (Chap. 7).

Also relevant at this point is the way in which the selection of each study has been made. Although each study attempts to reflect different features of the framework in comprehensive ways, there was also an element of opportunism in the selection of the studies as they individually arose as possible sources of investigation. Reinforcing this opportunism in choice and selection were the possibilities of working with professional artists.

The details of these relationships can now be addressed individually for each study chapter in order to inform the reader's understanding of how selections from the data were made.

For One Rock, given that this study was, chronologically, the first piece of analysis undertaken, concepts like participant and audience roles generally emerged from the data. Thus the study sets up and raises a number of issues which later studies will build upon and revise, in order to develop the framework. For example, although the role of 'participant' is used quite broadly, we will see in later chapters that there are more subtle professional and non-professional divisions such roles. Similarly, we shall also see subsequently how audience may be witting or unwitting of their role in participant interaction. A final point to note is that this study is presented using terminology that is harmonious with the framework, although one publication which this chapter is based upon used different language (e.g., the word 'bystander' was used for 'audience' [15]).

For the Journey into Space, chronologically the analysis was undertaken early on within the research period, a short time after examining One Rock and during a time when the framework was less well-formed. As in the One Rock study, the concepts generally emerged from the data to inform the framework rather as opposed to framework issues determining how selections from the corpus were performed. Once again, however, there is a measure of reflection onto the way in which this study is presented in this book from the framework itself, and terminology has been brought in line with framework.

The study of Fairground: Thrill Laboratory marks something of a shift in the relationship between the framework and studies as outlined above. In comparison to One Rock and the Journey into Space, Chap. 6's study builds upon concepts of roles such as audience, participants and actors, audience-participant transitions and spatialised manipulations and effects. Many of these notions are visible in the chapter's analysis, however, given that the study occurred chronologically later than these two previous studies, the relationship to the framework differed from them. The point here is that studying Fairground: Thrill Laboratory involved less of a 'blank slate' approach to the data than earlier chapters, in which emergent concepts developed the groundwork of the framework. Instead, topics of interest derived from the framework's development, informed how the data set was analysed and exactly which vignettes came to be presented in this chapter. This then motivated a desire to both build upon previous observations (such as participant and actor roles), and to provide concrete examples of new framework topics (e.g., orchestration and 'behind-the-scenes' work).

Finally, the study of Uncle Roy All Around You was also directed significantly by the concerns being developed within the framework, particularly the issue of how to account for the role of uninvolved or 'unwitting' members of a performance environment.

References

1. Agar, M.: The right brain strikes back. In: Fielding, N.G., Lee, R.M. (eds.) Using Computers in Qualitative Research. Sage, Thousand Oaks (1991)
2. Bowers, J., Rodden, T.: Exploding the interface: experiences of a CSCW network. In: Proceedings of the SIGCHI Conference on Human Factors in Computing Systems, pp. 255–262. ACM, New York (1993). doi:10.1145/169059.169205
3. Crabtree, A., Benford, S., Greenhalgh, C., Tennent, P., Chalmers, M., Brown, B.: Supporting ethnographic studies of ubiquitous computing in the wild. In: Proceedings of Conference on Designing Interactive Systems (DIS) (2006)
4. Crabtree, A., Rodden, T., Tolmie, P., Button, G.: Ethnography considered harmful. In: CHI'09: Proceedings of the 27th International Conference on Human Factors in Computing Systems, pp. 879–888. ACM, New York (2009). doi:10.1145/1518701.1518835
5. Dourish, P.: Implications for design. In: Proceedings of ACM Conference on Human Factors in Computing Systems (CHI), pp. 541–550. ACM, New York (2006). doi:10.1145/1124772.1124855. http://www.isr.uci.edu/jpd/classes/readings/Dourish-Implications.pdf
6. Garfinkel, H.: Studies in Ethnomethodology. Prentice-Hall, New York (1967)
7. Garfinkel, H.: Ethnomethodology's Program: Working Out Durkheim's Aphorism. Legacies of Social Thought. Rowman & Littlefield, Totowa (2002)
8. Goffman, E.: The Presentation of the Self in Everyday Life. Doubleday, New York (1959)
9. Goffman, E.: Frame Analysis: An Essay on the Organization of Experience. Harper & Row, New York (1974)
10. Heath, C., Hindmarsh, J.: Analysing interaction: video, ethnography and situated conduct. In: May, T. (ed.) Qualitative Research in Practice, pp. 99–121. Sage, Thousand Oaks (2002)
11. Heath, C., Hindmarsh, J., Luff, P.: Video in Qualitative Research. Sage, Thousand Oaks (2010)
12. Heath, C., Knoblauch, H., Luff, P.: Technology and social interaction: the emergence of 'workplace studies'. Br. J. Sociol. 51(2), 229–320 (2000)

13. Heath, C., Luff, P.K.: Collaboration and control: crisis management and multimedia technology in London Underground line control rooms. J. Comput. Support. Coop. Work **1**(1–2), 69–94 (1992)
14. Hughes, J., King, V., Rodden, T., Andersen, H.: Moving out from the control room: ethnography in system design. In: CSCW'94: Proceedings of the 1994 ACM Conference on Computer Supported Cooperative Work, pp. 429–439. ACM, New York (1994). doi:10.1145/192844.193065
15. Reeves, S., Fraser, M., Schnädelbach, H., O'Malley, C., Benford, S.: Engaging augmented reality in public places. In: Adjunct Proceedings of SIGCHI Conference on Human Factors in Computing Systems (CHI) (2005)
16. Ruhleder, K., Jordan, B.: Capturing complex, distributed activities: Video-based interaction analysis as a component of workplace ethnography. In: Lee, A.S., Liebenau, J., DeGross, J.I. (eds.) Information Systems and Qualitative Research, pp. 246–275. Chapman and Hall, London (1997)
17. Sacks, H.: Lectures on Conversation. Blackwell, Oxford (1995)
18. Sacks, H., Schegloff, E., Jefferson, G.: A simplest systematics for the organisation of turn-taking for conversation. Language **50**, 696–735 (1974)
19. Schegloff, E., Sacks, H.: Opening up closings. Semiotica **8**, 289–327 (1973)
20. Schegloff, E.A.: Reflections on quantification in the study of conversation. Res. Lang. Soc. Interact. **26**(1), 99–128 (1993)
21. Suchman, L.A.: Plans and Situated Actions: The Problem of Human–Machine Communication. Cambridge University Press, Cambridge (1987)

Chapter 4
Audience and Participants: One Rock

One Rock was a two-month public installation developed by Welfare State International, an arts company located in Ulverston, Cumbria. The focus of the exhibition was a large rock in Morecambe Bay, on the north-west coast of England. The aim was to use the various geological, microbiological, historical and social aspects of the rock to engender and renew fascination with the surrounding locality and its features. The installation was created inside an exhibition space approximately a mile away from the physical rock.

The exhibition attracted varying numbers of people,[1] both in terms of group sizes and daily throughput (from individuals through to groups of forty). Automated progression between stages of the installation precluded any latecomers (who would be asked to wait until the next run), so once a performance had started, the group inside stayed until the end without any additional visitors entering the space. A single performance lasted for twenty minutes in total. A docent was usually on hand during the performance, providing different levels of intervention for the visitors. When visitors entered the space, for example, some docents described briefly the experience, where others said nothing.

The exhibition itself was structured specifically around three ways of viewing the rock: 'macro'—reflecting the macro-level detail of the rock, 'micro'—reflecting microscopic details of the rock, and 'mythic'—reflecting mythic elements associated with the rock. The space was physically divided up into three parts to reflect these three aspects, with all sections involving dramatic changes in lighting and a loud accompanying soundtrack. (See Fig. 4.1 for an overview.)

The 'macro' section was deliberately passive and meditative with coordinated visuals and sound showing the rock and its surroundings (Fig. 4.2, left). The entrance area contained a model of the rock which matched the dimensions of the real rock, which is approximately the size of a small car. The macro section provided a physical representation of the rock to give visitors a sense of its place within the local ecology of the Bay.

---

[1]Unfortunately, no full visitor numbers are available.

S. Reeves, *Designing Interfaces in Public Settings*, Human-Computer Interaction Series,   43
DOI 10.1007/978-0-85729-265-0_4, © Springer-Verlag London Limited 2011

Fig. 4.1 Exhibition space floor plan

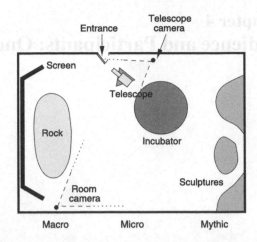

Fig. 4.2 The physical model of the rock; the Telescope and the Incubator; and the 'mythic' section

Once the initial sequence on the large screen ended visitors moved towards the second, more interactive micro section (Fig. 4.2, centre). This area of the exhibition contained a bespoke augmented reality (AR) device called the Telescope, which was placed approximately two metres from a display feature of the exhibition called the Incubator. The Incubator was a metal structure lit from below that supported hundreds of bottles containing microbes, sea life and other residue collected from around the rock. It also held concealed speakers for associated sounds. During this part of the exhibition when visitors were exploring the Incubator and using the Telescope, views of microscopic sea-life were projected onto the opposing wall. The micro section allowed visitors to experience the 'unseen' world of the rock, studying its microscopic life and substance.

The final mythic section adjacent to the area where the Telescope and Incubator were located was primarily sculptural, using traditional materials including those collected from the Bay. These forms illustrated various social and historical local legends that 'the rock might tell of' if it could speak (Fig. 4.2, right).

Fig. 4.3 The Telescope

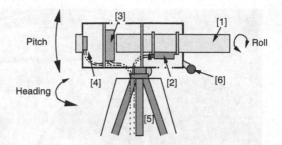

After spending some time in this section, visitors were attracted back to the main screen for a final audiovisual sequence, after which the lights were raised and visitors left the room.

The exhibition was in some sense a carefully designed and planned 'performance' presented for the stimulation and enjoyment of the visitors as well as providing interactive elements to explore. Overall, the reaction to the exhibition was positive. Comments recorded in the visitors' book continually made reference to the beauty and audiovisual impact of the "shifting light images" and sound effects.

The following subsections describe the Telescope's software and hardware construction, as well as the design rationale for its particular form and workings.

4.1 Telescope Hardware and Software

The Telescope construction is shown in Fig. 4.3. Looking into the viewing tube or eyepiece (1) reveals the contents of the screen (3), which displays a processed video feed from a webcam located at the front of the body (4). The Telescope can be moved using the handles (6) which rotate the entire body section about the pivot of the tripod (5). The light switch on the right handle triggers a halogen lamp attached next to the webcam. A digital compass (2) is attached to the underside of the viewing tube, and detects changes in the heading and pitch of the Telescope's upper section. Rotation of the tube is calculated from the roll of the compass as it is rotated by the viewing tube.

The software that was developed combined code for the electronic compass and provided a video handling and display service in order to present the augmented content overlaid on the webcam video feed.

4.2 Telescope Design, Constraints and Aesthetics

The Telescope (see Figs. 4.4 and 4.5) could be rotated to examine the bottles in detail (see Fig. 4.6). The device provided visitors with a way of conjuring video sequences out of the bottles on the Incubator. The artistic intent behind the Telescope was to be able to create the illusion that prefabricated microscopic images and videos from

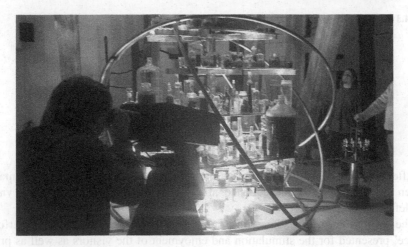

Fig. 4.4 The Telescope in use, pointing towards the Incubator

Fig. 4.5 A plan view of the spatial organisation of the local environment around the Telescope

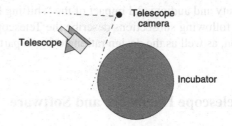

the rock could emerge from the glass bottles by 'zooming' into them. Bottles that the Telescope was pointing at to were registered in such a way that connections could be created between them and the digital content. Figure 4.6 illustrates the view that visitors would see when using the Telescope. In the centre, video content is 'emerging' in front of a bottle. The bottle is indicated by a green polygon which signifies to the user that this view has associated video content. Just to the edge of the display, another green polygon indicates a video associated with another bottle.

As an element of the overall installation, the Telescope needed to fit within the artistic thematic of the piece. Indeed, the 'telescope' metaphor emerged through discussions on the various ways in which the public could currently view the physical Bay at a distance. Real pay-per-view telescopes are available in waterfront towns around the Bay, and provide ways of inspecting it in more detail. In addition, the Telescope metaphor was relevant to conveying some sense of the dangers of viewing the Bay too closely.[2] The display inside the Telescope was also informed by this metaphor, and was intended to emulate the sense of distance experienced when using a real telescope. An AR approach was also particularly interesting for this

---

[2]A short time after the exhibition, for instance, around 20 people died in Morecambe Bay after rapidly rising tides trapped and then drowned them [1].

Fig. 4.6 View experienced looking through the Telescope. (*1*) is the augmented content overlaid on the video pass-through, (*2*) and (*3*) are bottles of interest as presented to the viewer, marked as being of interest with a green polygon

exhibition, as the juxtaposition of the physical specimens and their 'invisible world' fitted well with the overlay of physical specimens with digital content.

Challenging some of these aesthetics, however, were more practical considerations. For example, the Telescope needed to be robust enough to last through the two-month exhibition, yet not supersede the impact of the digital content (the microscopic images) and physical target (the Incubator). The sturdy casing of the Telescope was therefore covered in black paint and cloth so as to reduce its physical impact and to some extent 'background' the device within the exhibition.

A further issue was that of registration. AR devices often rely on a registration scheme embedded in the environment. The significant and constant changes in lighting would have seriously challenged an image processing algorithm. More importantly, however, the aesthetics of the Incubator, and indeed the surrounding space, meant that concessions over the inclusion of fiducial markers (for example, placed on the bottles to be examined) could not be made. Therefore, only sensor data obtained from a digital compass, measuring pitch, roll and heading could be depended upon.

The device also had to be calibrated for the exhibition space in ways that impacted both physical and digital components. For example, increasing the Telescope's distance from the Incubator obtained a more realistic telescope effect but led to a poorer display resolution.

Finally, the lighting changes that featured in the exhibition meant that the Incubator was not illuminated at all times. Therefore, visitors using the Telescope outside of the 'micro' section were unable to see the Incubator well. For this reason a halogen lamp was placed inside the Telescope in order to provide temporary illumination of the jars. The light switch was intended for users studying the Incubator when the lights were low. The background light level was accounted for when drawing both the regions and video file overlay; in low light, neither regions nor media were visible, whereas when the Incubator's internal lights were on, the regions and media appeared (as seen in Fig. 4.6).

4.3 The Telescope in Use

Over the course of the two-month exhibition, data was collected at various intervals, during a series of several weekends throughout the length of the exhibition. To study the Telescope in use, however, this capture also extended to a general data collection of the exhibition as a whole with interaction at the Telescope featuring as part of this. The analytic data corpus consisted of approximately five hours of video data shot from two positions in the exhibition space (marked in Figs. 4.1 and 4.5), as well as log files of the electronic compass sensor readings taken at corresponding times. The two video cameras were placed to give an overview of the exhibition space and a close-up of the Telescope. The camera recording the Telescope obtained audio from a plate microphone attached to the front of the device, allowing conversations to be heard above the ambient music and sounds of the exhibition. As with each of the studies in this book, visitors were made aware of the recordings taking place and their subsequent use in research, and encouraged to voice any concerns to a member of the curation team.

These camera views were played alongside the analysis tool that was developed as part of the study of this data, depicted in Fig. 4.7. The bottom window of the figure shows one camera view, although recordings from both cameras were usually watched concurrently. The tool was developed in order to reconstruct the Telescope's movement from the sensor logs and provide a view of what visitors would have seen. In the figure, the simulated view window (top left) shows a video of a micro-organism that is zoomed to full, obscuring the webcam feed. The reconstruction of this view was a necessary feature of the analysis, as there were a significant number of cases in which visitors reacted to or commented on what could be seen on the display inside the Telescope. Another window (top right) shows a real-time 3D graphical reconstruction of the Telescope, the movement of which was derived from recorded logs of compass data. This simple graphic enables the analyst during an examination of the data to manually synchronise between the simulated view and the camera views by visually comparing the video of the Telescope with the motions of the 3D model. Video segments needed to be repeatedly viewed in tandem with the simulated view in order to better understand often subtle interactions. Thus repeated viewings were made possible by skipping to certain points in the log data using the controls shown in the centre of Fig. 4.7.

Samples from this data have been worked into a series of vignettes that attempt to provide representative examples of cases that have been studied throughout the collected data. The resulting vignettes describe various facets of the Telescope's use by visitors, being selected in order to examine firstly how visitors might engage as participants, perhaps with others, at the Telescope itself. Secondly, the selections

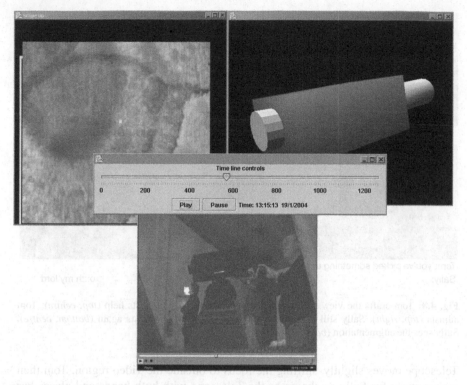

Fig. 4.7   The One Rock analysis tool

attempt to demonstrate how other visitors might be audience to a participant's interactions, and thirdly how participants using the Telescope and audience to Telescope
interactions might exchange roles (transition).

4.3.1 Participation with the Telescope (Vignettes 1 & 2)

This first two vignettes in this chapter deal with the nature of participation and
participant roles within the Telescope's use by visitors. As part of this, the vignettes
explore collaborative ways in which participants rapidly handed over the device
between them, particularly in the crafting of views for one another.

The first vignette takes place when the Incubator lights are on. Tom, who is an
exhibition docent, is talking to two female visitors, Sally and Fay, about the Telescope. He approaches the device with them, and begins to adjust the viewpoint. Tom
lines up the view through the Telescope at the edge of a video, and provides a brief
description of its operation (Fig. 4.8,[3] top, left). Just as he disengages, however, the

---

[3]Note that several of the photos in this chapter have been artificially lightened.

what am I looking at?   **can't see what I'm looking at**

Tom: you've picked something up   **oh it's gone now**
Sally: **o:::h my lord**

Fig. 4.8 Tom crafts the view for two visitors (*top, left*). Sally requests help (*top, centre*), Tom adjusts (*top, right*), Sally still has problems (*bottom, left*), Tom adjusts again (*bottom, centre*), Sally sees the augmentation (*bottom, right*)

Telescope moves slightly, shifting the focus to outside the video region. Tom then makes space for Sally as she grabs the Telescope with both hands and places her left eye to the viewing tube. As she grabs the device, the view through the Telescope jumps again, moving the focus to between two regions. After approximately three seconds, Sally looks over the Telescope, still holding the handlebars, and says (Fig. 4.8, top, centre):[4]

Sally: what am I looking at? (4.0) can't see what I'm looking at

Just before Sally looks up (on her first "what"), the Telescope focus moves inside a region and a video starts to play. Sally hands over Telescope to Tom who then very briefly checks the view (Fig. 4.8, top, right). When Tom checks the view, he sees that there is a video on-screen, the same video Sally unwittingly lined up just as she asked her question.

Tom: right (.) oh there you go you've got something yo-y-you've err (.) on screen ((points at eyepiece)) now you've act- you've picked something up you've picked er a beastie up there you've picked a blob (.) a live microbe

Tom disengages from the Telescope at "got something" and Sally then reengages (Fig. 4.8, bottom, left). Unfortunately, an anomalous movement (possibly due to magnetic field jitter) shifts the focus of the Telescope again to the other side of the

---

[4]The transcriptions in this book have been constructed using a simplified "Jeffersonian" system, see [7]. "(...)" in these transcriptions indicates that part of the data has been skipped for purposes of clarity.

region such that the focus is now too far to the left of the region and again no video is playing.

Sally: have I?=
Tom: =yes can you see what it is?
(0.2)
Sally: no o::h↑

Tom laughs and moves in on Sally's "o::h" as Sally backs away from the Telescope. He grasps the eyepiece and places his right eye on it (Fig. 4.8, bottom, centre). The view he sees is the same as Sally's when she says "have I?".

Tom: oh it's gone now um=
Sally: =what that blue there was a blue=
((Tom pushes the Telescope's view to the right in order to get the focus inside the region))
Tom: =try and line it up with the green squares (.) ah there you go (0.2) yeah yeah (0.8) those are living ((Tom hands over the Telescope to Sally)) (0.4) living microbes in the inside the jars
(0.8)
Sally: o:::h my lord

Finally, then, Sally sees what Tom has been intending her to see all along (Fig. 4.8, bottom, right).

When Sally first uses the Telescope, Tom frames her use of with a description of its operation. Sally's grab of the Telescope's handlebars, however, disrupts the viewpoint that Tom has configured. Due to the 'single-user' properties of the Telescope (i.e. a private view), Tom is unable to monitor the display during the handover. Thereafter follows a further problem—albeit one not caused by accidental movement of the Telescope's body, but an anomalous jump in viewpoint—which also follows a similar pattern: Sally says "have I?" and "no o::h" after which Tom moves in to perform another correction. Tom, building on his previous description, now provides a more detailed account of how to locate the content, "try and line it up with the green squares".

There are therefore three attempts at configuring the viewpoint for a handover between visitors before any success. The interface does not allow a shared perspective on the content and so the docent is unable to reconstruct or correlate a fellow participant's difficulties in using the interface without drawing from second hand information, namely accounts of the problems occurring, or by taking over himself. For this reason, the two causes of breakdown in this sequence—the accidental bumping of the Telescope and the anomalous jump of viewpoint—indicate that attempts at repairing the problem may be required repeatedly until the set up view just happens to survive during the handover. As a result, the docent is unable to craft the experience for the visitor.

The second vignette begins with Pauline briefly peering through the eyepiece of the Telescope, whilst Tom explains the contents of the glass bottles to the group she is in. She spends some time examining the view (about eight seconds), and then pulls away from the Telescope, making a distasteful expression and saying "wriggling" (Fig. 4.9, left). She moves away to examine the Incubator. Pauline's view prior to pulling away can be seen in Fig. 4.9 (right).

wriggling

Fig. 4.9 The moment of Pauline's reaction (*left*) to what she sees (*right*)

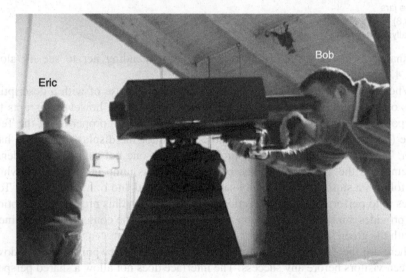

Fig. 4.10 Bob uses the Telescope with Eric, Pauline and David (not visible in images) standing nearby

Later on, at the end of the same show, Pauline, David and Eric are standing nearby. The house lights have come on and they appear to be discussing the structure of the room. Bob begins using the Telescope by placing his left eye to the viewing tube and moving it around (Fig. 4.10). He then turns the Telescope light on using the button on the handlebars. As with the first example, Eric and Pauline turn their gaze and subsequently bodies directly towards the Telescope (Fig. 4.11, left). After a few seconds Eric moves towards the Telescope, followed by Pauline. Bob pulls up from the Telescope eyepiece, his right hand releasing the light switch (Fig. 4.11, right) and then the handlebar, looking in the approaching visitors' direction. He then creates space as Eric and Pauline move in.

there's the ((mumbles)) thing there

Fig. 4.11 Bob presses the light and Eric orients towards the Telescope via the Incubator (*left*). Bob disengages from the Telescope as David (again, not visible), Eric and Pauline approach (*right*)

how weird (0.2) .h huh

Fig. 4.12 Eric looks through the Telescope whilst Pauline stands next to him, with David on the left (*left*). Eric disengages momentarily, comparing augmented and disaugmented views (*right*)

Eric and Pauline take over, with Eric grabbing the handlebars (Fig. 4.12, left). Pauline here uses the same word she had used earlier, "wriggling", to describe the function of the Telescope to her co-visitor. Bob overhears, shown in the following dialogue:

Pauline: there's the ((mumbles)) thing there ((Pauline points to the Telescope))
(1.8)
Eric: mmm (0.2) does that help?
Pauline: hhh if you wanna see something wriggling down there ((Bob laughs))
((Pauline laughs and looks up at Bob, Eric glances over the top of the Telescope))
Eric: ((moving head back to the Telescope eyepiece)) how weird (0.2) .h huh

During this short exchange, Eric rapidly glances over the top of the Telescope at the Incubator, with his gaze aligned in the general direction of the Telescope's orientation. During this he maintains physical contact with the handle bars (see Fig. 4.12, right), and afterwards returns his eye to the eyepiece whilst uttering "how weird". Thus Eric manages to rapidly move from an augmented view of the Incubator to a 'disaugmented' (i.e., normal) view, but retain a hold upon the device, later returning to the view he momentarily left.

4.3.1.1 Participants

From these vignettes, we can start to piece together some of the features of participation with and around the Telescope device. Whilst participation often involved
rapid engagement and disengagement with the Telescope, participation has also
been shown frequently to be a collaborative affair, with participants often grouping
around the device in formations. From here it becomes important to address some
key aspects of this, such as the ways in which participants *hand over* the device
between them via the possibilities physically afforded by the Telescope for rapid
engagement and disengagement, and the attempts of participants to *frame one an-
others' participation* through talk and the crafting of views. Further to this, we can
start to consider the ways in which *manipulations* of the device are readily available
and indeed visible for participants, and yet the *effects* of those manipulations are not.
The visibility of these manipulations permits participants to engage in coordinative
work around the Telescope, particularly via maintaining mutual awareness.

The key issue raised the first vignette is how visitors, as participants using the
Telescope, identify and repair disparities in content during handovers by rapidly
switching places. The problematic handovers between Tom and Sally show how
the Telescope's design limits other participants' ability to see what those using the
Telescope are seeing. That the Telescope is a 'private' device means repair of these
discrepancies is problematic. Nevertheless, the amount of time taken to perform
several iterations of the configure-handover-view cycle is a matter of seconds. Repair is eventually possible, enabled by the rapidity with which participants using the
Telescope can move between looking through the eyepiece, holding the handlebars
but talking to surrounding participants, and handing over to become a surrounding
participant themselves.

The second vignette also highlighted how participants hand over the device, however provided an example of participants sharing experiences of content, and the
ways in which previous participation (in this instance, Pauline) can inform how
others' participation is framed (Eric's). Another aspect highlighted in the second vignette is that participation even without discrepancies, as seen in the first vignette,
involves participants exploiting an alternately 'augmented' or 'disaugmented' view.
It is notable that participants may maintain their physical engagement with the device (as Eric does) but not the display (i.e., not looking through the eyepiece, but
holding the handles and being in an observable position of use). Such characteristic
'alignment' actions occurred relatively frequently as was seen in the vignette with
Eric's rapid switching between being engaged with the augmentation, and disaugmented as he maintained engagement with the device, in order to check the alignment between his view and the real world. We shall see such activities once again
in the fourth vignette.

In order to understand handover, which is core a feature of participation in both
vignettes, we also must appreciate the physical features of the Telescope that participants had access to as resources in their negotiation. Indeed, participant manipulations of the physical attributes of the Telescope fundamentally shape the way in
which social interaction plays out around it and many of its physical features support the resources required by participants. We have seen in the second vignette

how access to the augmentation was simply afforded by the eyepiece, and, when successfully configured by a docent or previous visitor, provides a relatively stable experience that is less sensitive to 'handover' instabilities, namely, jumps of alignment between users.[5] Due to the Telescope's handles and mounting being separate to the eyepiece, it is also easy for participants to make room around the device while still holding on to it, as a way of sharing, handing over and inviting others to use it. In addition, it facilitates rapid handover to others and rapid disengagement or reengagement by an individual, which is useful for negotiating social interactions such as repairing breakdowns in communication when instability or interference does occur (as seen in the first vignette when Sally and Tom are trying to 'see' the same thing).

This last point leads us to consider that, when such instabilities do occur in handing over the device, a participant may go to considerable lengths to set up an experience for another participant, both in terms of verbally framing their experience but also in carefully manipulating the Telescope to provide them with an appropriate view when they engage. This need to position the display for others is clearly important, but is also potentially difficult, and handovers between participants can be at times dangerous moments for social interaction. We have seen that a combination of physical instability, sensor instability and an inability to see the effects of manipulation when disengaged from the display can cause problems here, as in the case of the first vignette. Fortunately, in the case of the Telescope the problematic aspects of the design can often be resolved. Due to the physical form of the viewing tube, the Telescope permits swift handovers between participants since the action involved in engaging and disengaging with the augmented view is simple and takes little time. The design therefore does at times result in quick and seamless negotiations, as well as even providing for humorous interactions between participants, or participants and audience members as addressed shortly in the fourth vignette.

More generally, this raises the issue of beginning to think of participants' use of and engagement with the Telescope in terms of manipulations and effects, which is explored in more detail in the next section. Participants may be engaged with manipulating the Telescope (moving it left, right, up or down) as well as being engaged with the effects of those manipulations (i.e., looking through the eyepiece) in order to direct their view on the augmentation. However, the effects of those manipulations are not available to other participants. This became problematic particularly in the first vignette where Sally and Tom spend time resolving the effects of progressive manipulations of the Telescope that are unavailable to the other participant who is not manipulating the device. It is also problematic when considering what resources are available for audience spectating upon the Telescope's use as we shall see in the next two vignettes.

---

[5]It is useful to consider the case with head-mounted displays (HMDs) in which shared alignments are extremely difficult to obtain.

4.3.2 Audience and Transition (Vignettes 3 & 4)

Classifying visitors as participants does not tell the whole story. For example, in the second vignette Pauline and Eric are drawn to the Telescope via its light being activated by Bob. Here the physical features of the Telescope and its relationship to the environment played a part in the swift transition of visitors spectating upon some use within the local milieu to becoming engaged users of the device. These next two vignettes will explore this, beginning to divide up visitors into participants and audience, and how they might make the transition between one role and the other.

In this vignette, the exhibition docent, Tom, is using the Telescope. The exhibition space is dark at this point in the performance, and the Incubator is not illuminated. Tom presses the button to turn the Telescope light on. This is noticed by visitors local to the Incubator, and after a short time, some orient themselves towards the structure, and others actually step closer to it (Fig. 4.13, centre and right). In the course of these relocations, some visitors bend over to examine the bottles in detail, whereas others stand back, maintaining their orientation. Still others move around the circumference of the Incubator itself. Some of the motions of visitors is illustrated in Fig. 4.14.

The Telescope's light in this example not only affects the attention of both the current user and other visitors, but also causes a visitor (Jenny) to move towards the Telescope. As with others of the group, Jenny's gaze is intermittently cast on the Incubator, but her movement is directed towards the Telescope (she is also marked in Fig. 4.13). She stops a short distance away from the device. Tom finishes using the Telescope, lets go of the light switch and, at this very instant, Jenny turns her head from the Incubator towards Tom. Tom disengages from the Telescope, and arcs around Jenny, creating space so she can use it.

The light cast upon the Incubator brings about Jenny's initial movement towards the Telescope. However, when she adopts a position of proximity, it is the light turning off which brings her gaze away from the Incubator and towards the device. Tom's use of the light may at first appear to have a 'moth effect' on the gathering visitors, but Jenny's movements highlight that using the Telescope can cause further visitors to engage with or even use the device.

Shortly after this, Tom has set up the Telescope's orientation for Jenny to see a video of diatoms in the centre of the view (Fig. 4.15).

In this fourth vignette, Freddy approaches the Telescope for the first time. The Incubator lights are on. After getting into a comfortable position with the handlebars, he begins to move the Telescope around. He zooms in to watch a video emerging from a bottle. A few seconds later, Pauline walks directly between the Telescope and the Incubator. Freddy stops and briefly glances up and over the Telescope at Pauline (Fig. 4.16, left). Freddy's movement is noticed by Pauline who looks to her left, and then crouches down (Fig. 4.16, right). In response to this ducking movement, Freddy jerks his head back to the Telescope slightly. He then moves back up again and grins at Pauline while she laughs. Finally, Freddy moves his head back down to look through the Telescope.

Fig. 4.13 The Telescope's light illuminates the Incubator and many visitors move or look towards it (movement indicated where visible with *arrows*). Jenny (*circled*) moves towards the Telescope. The Telescope itself is mostly not visible on these images, however is positioned to the *left side*

The Telescope's view here is also subject to a spatial interference, caused by Pauline's movement within the field of view of the camera. The camera has some 'sensor-like' properties (we can think of it as a 'visual sensor'), in that the image experienced by the Telescope user can be disrupted in a way that is different to disruption of a normal camera image. This is because the image also contains the augmentation (i.e., microbe imagery) that is overlaid on the video feed of the target of the augmentation, namely, the Incubator. This combined image can be 'interfered

Fig. 4.14 Perspective view
of the approximate movement
of visitors around the
Incubator just after the light
on the Telescope is switched
on

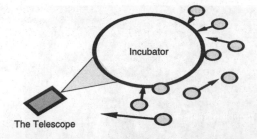

Fig. 4.15 Tom crafts a view for Jenny (*left*) and then hands over the device to her (*right*)

Fig. 4.16 Freddy looks up (*left*) from his view through the Telescope and Pauline ducks (*right*, *circled*)

with' by moving within part of the camera's field of view, causing the background (the target of the augmentation) to be obscured, but not the foreground (the augmentation itself). In terms of sensors, the Telescope's relationship to the local environment is unbalanced, in that the onboard sensor (the electronic compass) has no reference to the local surroundings. These surroundings may easily produce sources of interference from by passers-by that affect the camera but not the internal compass. The presence of Pauline here 'breaks' the combined image forming the augmentation by disrupting the visual sensor, i.e., occluding the Incubator and its bottles. This disruption is then repaired by Freddy through the process outlined above.

4.3.2.1 Audience and Participant

The impact of participant bodily conduct, talk and Telescope use, including the changes in lighting it creates, informs and affects visitors' engagement with the device and the Incubator. In these vignettes (as well as the second vignette to some extent) we can see such cases in which the conduct of those engaged with the Telescope—participants—impacts and is impacted by the conduct of those visitors in the vicinity, but not engaged with the device. This section examines such visitors, exploring a simple division between visitors as *audience* as well as participants.

Firstly we must consider the aesthetics of the device and space, returning to the notion of manipulations and effects raised at the end of the first two vignettes, how the configuration of manipulations an effects might appear to visitors spectating upon this scene, and both aspects impact upon the movement and engagement of those visitors.

The sheer physical size and visibility of the Telescope to the audience (i.e., those visitors not engaged directly with the Telescope or its current user, such as those in the third vignette surrounding the Incubator) is notable, and the fact that, despite the use of black paint and fabric, attracts much attention. Unexpected benefits were derived from this attention (in a similar way to the Ambient Wood project's Periscope device [10]), most prominently in the way in which the Telescope requires gestural manipulation, and due to the size of the Telescope, this manipulation is often large and highly visible to the audience. Furthermore, as seen in the third vignette, the Telescope light amplifies this visibility to the audience, as well as amplifying the visibility of any manipulations, and through both of these, increases the visibility of the Incubator, constructing a connection between the Telescope and it (a central feature in transition, as noted below). In the third vignette this resulted in the 'moth effect' when participant manipulations of the Telescope's light drew audience members to the Incubator.

In turn, the augmented content which is viewed by a participant is not, however, accessible to that audience. This combination of very revealed manipulations and hidden effects of those manipulations (i.e., via a concealed display) potentially creates immediate surprise and ongoing fascination, something that we may characterise as an 'intriguing' device for the audience (this is discussed systematically in Chap. 8). As part of these revealed manipulations, it is also very clear when someone is looking through an eyepiece at some form of display. This enables audience to infer both what that participant is doing with the display and in what directions they might be doing it. However, there are also disadvantages to this 'intriguing' approach as demonstrated by the problems in the first vignette with participants sharing views. The lack of shared perspective on the augmentation, which is lost by hiding the effects, is a source of these troubles.

Both the Telescope and Incubator in One Rock are legitimate objects of interest for participants and audience. The Telescope is some way from the Incubator and has to be pointed at it in order to view the augmentation. While it can be expected that participants use the device, it should also be anticipated that audience will attend directly to the objects the device implicates, such as a painting, sculpture or a part of a building, and so on. This results in spatial interference, as experienced by Freddy due to Pauline's movement. The fourth vignette thus illustrates how a participant using the Telescope (Freddy) coordinates with an audience member (Pauline) to resolve a problem. Freddy initially engages with the Telescope. He notices a disruption of his view, and pulls up from the Telescope in order to work out what is happening. He maintains physical engagement with the device by holding on to the handlebars, and checks the real world view against what he has just experienced in the augmented view. (We have seen a similar 'alignment checking' operation by Eric in the second vignette.) Pauline indicates an understanding of his movement by belatedly making an attempt to avoid blocking his augmented view, and Freddy is able to both recognise this fact, and share a moment with Pauline that shows his recognition. There are a series of resources that are drawn upon to retain a view of the Incubator: the ability to 'disaugment' yet maintain engagement on Freddy's part; the ability to recognise and orient to such an activity on Pauline's part; and their ability to acknowledge and complete such a process quickly (in this case, approximately two seconds between Freddy moving his view away from the Telescope and returning to it). In this example, the Telescope's physical form allowed Freddy to assess a discrepancy and subsequently resolve it. Freddy and Pauline resolved the interference in this instance, however this point raises the issue of how audience and participant might interact in order to resolve the disruption. Here, resolving this interference was achieved not only with reference to the Telescope's physical features, but also to the environment itself and the way in which the Telescope implicated the Incubator and as part of this, audience members. Pauline ducking when in front of the Telescope exhibits one of the ways in which audience and participants might demonstrate awareness of one another.

4.3.2.2 Transition

As mentioned before spatial interferences occur due to elements of the local environment (the Incubator) being interesting artefacts in their own right, without using the Telescope to view them. Thus we encounter frequent obstructions of the Telescope view by visitors passing between it and the Incubator. This apparent relationship between the Incubator and Telescope is key when considering how audience members might become participants, and how, in addition to physical configuration, participant conduct may come into play when audience members *transition* to become participants.

Attending to and being attracted by the Telescope is one of the primary mechanisms behind transitioning from audience to participant. The third vignette demonstrated how a participant's (Tom) activities may impact those who are audience to that conduct, illustrated through the movement of the crowd of visitors as well as Jenny's gradual movement towards the Telescope. Whilst audience and participants are separate roles, there remains a relationship between the two. This is shown through the way in which audience were at times implicated in the conduct of participants at the Telescope, particularly when grouped around (or in the way of) the Incubator. As noted previously, the highly visible structure of the Telescope, the large gestures required to manipulate it, and the link to the Incubator created by its light and the further reinforcement of this link via manipulations of the lit Telescope, are some of the features which initially draw audience attention. We have seen that when some of this audience attention is drawn to the Incubator as a result of Telescope manipulations as in the third vignette, the actions of the participant not only impact audience behaviour with regard to their interaction with the Incubator, but also help draw audience in Telescope's general direction, so the audience member begins the transition to participant. Once the audience member is drawn in, the participant, Tom, makes space for the new participant to manipulate the Telescope, framing and crafting that participation, as seen in the first vignette.

4.4 Discussion

Within the vignettes there has been a subtle interplay between various movements and interactions made by participants and audience at One Rock, both with and around the Telescope. This section provides a summary discussion of some of the themes drawn out over the course of the analysis, and related design challenges that result. These themes have been the roles of *audience* and *participant*, and *audience-participant transitions*. In addition, the ways in which the simple division of participant and audience is present within some existing literature is explored, as well as the concepts of manipulations and effects, and the 'intriguing' nature of the experience.

4.4.1 Audience and Participants Within Other Literature

In the analysis, there are two main roles that visitors have been subdivided into: participants and audience. Before summarising these notions of audience and participant, however, it is worth reviewing observations that have been made within existing literature, particularly those derived from the examination of public settings.

Studies of museums and galleries have shown repeatedly that both companions and passers-by or strangers can shape each others' experiences and conduct [8], and have also described how different 'divisions of labour' are adopted at the exhibit face, such as members of social groups reading labels for others [4]. Furthermore, and of more importance to the observations here, visitors often spectate and draw on the activities of others to learn how to use and appreciate interactive exhibits [6], which is an observation replicated to some extent by the tacit coordination seen in the control room studies mentioned in Chap. 2 (e.g., [3, 5]).

Some systems have been designed explicitly with the support for visitors in the periphery, such as forms of 'eavesdropping' enabled between visitors with audioguide-like technology, as demonstrated in Grinter et al. [2]. The system supported visitors assuming a less active role, such as those who, like the previous example of label-readers and label-listeners, wished to eavesdrop on their fellow visitor's experience rather than interact directly themselves.

So, rather than identify behavioural characterisations of visitor types such as 'busy', 'greedy' or 'selective' models (e.g., [9]), in general, then, this literature instead identifies two main roles: the participants who interact and collaborate at the exhibit face, and the audience who observe their activities directly or in the periphery. There is also a degree of interaction between the two roles as they configure one another's conduct. The roles of audience and participant visitors may assume are thus primarily based upon the way in which visitors present themselves and their conduct to others within the collaborative setting. The use of different roles as categories of visitor activity are used as an attempt to provide pointers towards certain patterns or regularities of this presentation of conduct observable within a public setting.

4.4.2 Participants in One Rock

The role *participant* has been introduced in this chapter as a label for visitors who are either directly engaged in manipulating the Telescope, or part of some grouping local to the device. In the vignettes participants collaborated with one another to craft views, resolve discrepancies in those views and framed one another's participation with the Telescope using talk and gesture.

Participant access to the Telescope's display raises an important consequence for design in that we typically need to consider a shared environment in which some participants have an augmented view while other participants have a 'plain', or unaugmented view. This will be especially true in public environments such as exhibitions, where there are many visitors flowing through the experience and it is unfeasible to ensure they are all equipped with a display to participate with. Interactions between participants who are on an 'uneven footing' are therefore an important design consideration.

The notion of participant, however, has glossed the activities of the docent, Tom, and the members of the public. The docent was not strictly a 'visitor' participant, but rather participated in interactions, crafting and designing perspectives for others as part of his professional work.

4.4.3 Audience in One Rock

The role *audience* has been introduced as a label for visitors for whom a participant's interaction with the device is visible or perceptible in some way; either they are spectating upon a participant or are situated locally in the surrounding environment.

A key feature of the role of audience has been how the audience experiences, is aware of, and becomes implicated in participant conduct. Here the audience experience of the Telescope is strongly determined by visibility of the manipulations required by participants to use it, and the visibility of effects of those manipulations. This combination provides a potentially 'intriguing' aspect in that it plays a part in drawing audience members to the Telescope. Such a strategy has particular relevance for experiences in museums, galleries and exploratoria in general. These kinds of environments often trade on successfully engendering curiosity or intrigue in visitors in order to create engagement with exhibits. We can now see how this strategy (and later as part of a wider range of strategies) may play a role in constructing such a design.

In discussing the role of audience in interaction around the Telescope and Incubator, the analysis has also examined interference and the resolution of that interference between participant and audience. Interference is a result of the way in which the Telescope's design approached registration of the device, and different approaches to this problem have implications for the aesthetics of the environment. Generally there are two forms of sensor support that can be envisaged for the Telescope: environmentally-registered techniques such as fiducial markers (where the target has a marker attached) or device-registered techniques such as the Telescope's compass (where the target is determined by dead reckoning). For device-registered systems such as the Telescope, we saw how interactions between audience and participant resulted in only certain discrepancies occurring (i.e., the video but not the augmentation was obstructed by passing audience). Environment-registered, on the other hand, could provide cues for the system to integrate such obstructions together (e.g., if one obstructs a fiducial, the system registers that obstruction). It is worth noting that in both cases, however, the perspective of the participant and audience differs, due to the 'intriguing' design of the Telescope.

Finally, following on from this, it is useful to consider how a design strategy for the Telescope could, alternatively, have explicitly guided audience around such spaces of interference. For example, this could have meant physically restricting audience movement between the Incubator and the Telescope (e.g., using a barrier), or perhaps instead relying on the apparent link created by the light on the front to inform audience conduct (clearly this occasionally failed as exhibited in this study). The next chapter will explore this notion of guiding work and how it plays out within a performance setting.

4.4.4 Audience-Participant Transitions

Audience and participants do not maintain one particular role throughout their experience. Instead, audience become participants and participants become audience during their time in the space. We have observed how Jenny, in the third vignette, moved from being audience to participant Tom's conduct with the device, to becoming a fellow participant of Tom's, and then finally engaging with the Telescope herself.

These transitions had various stages and features: firstly being drawn to the Incubator; the impact of the implicit link between the Telescope and the Incubator; and participants inviting, making room and handing over the device to others. At this point we can address some of these features, considering how, once again, the manipulations required to use the Telescope, and the effects of those manipulations may play in supporting or hindering transition.

It has been noted that the effects of manipulating the Telescope are only visible for a single participant via the 'peephole' style display. The way in which the effects are hidden to the audience has interesting trade-offs with respect to transition. On the one hand, as has been noted previously, hiding effects and revealing manipulations can create something of an 'intriguing' design that assists transition by drawing in audience. On the other, however, the hidden nature of these effects can cause problems for interactions between participants, especially when it comes to lining up and maintaining views for others during handover and when sharing and discussing content within a group. Thus, the interests of audience-participant transitions and participant collaboration potentially conflict.

4.5 Summary

This first study has examined an augmented reality device, the Telescope, in the context of a public artistic exhibition, One Rock. Through examining this setting, this chapter has introduced two key roles: the role of the *participant* and the role of the *audience*. Participants engaged directly by manipulating the Telescope as well as collaborating beside other participants who might instead be manipulating it. Participant work involved framing one another's experience of the augmentation, negotiating handover between participants via this framing as well as physical manoeuvres such as making space and using the physical features of the Telescope to smooth this process. Participant work also involved resolving problems and discrepancies of views, not only with other participants but at times with audience members. Being an audience member, in turn, involved experiencing participants' activities with and around the Telescope in a number of ways, either through observing the direct manipulations required to move it, or indirectly through its impact on the environment (via its light, for example) and through this possibly becoming implicated in that observed participant conduct.

Fundamental to both participant and audience roles is the way in which transitions between them play out. We saw, for instance, that the visibility of participant manipulations of the Telescope not only impacted audience focus upon objects in the environment and their movement around it (particularly through lighting the Incubator), but also drew some audience in towards the Telescope, and in so doing making the transition from audience observing participant Telescope use to being participants themselves.

Finally, there were a number of associated concepts introduced alongside the main notions of participants, audience and audience-participant transitions. Both participant use of the Telescope and audience experience of that use was considered in terms of manipulations and effects. For the participant, manipulations of the physical structure of the device are undertaken as part of engaging interactively with its digital interface. These manipulations modify the effects that are experienced. However, it was noted that whilst the manipulations are revealed to all, and, furthermore, are relatively obvious in their scale, the effects of those manipulations—the augmented content—is hidden from all but the participant at the eyepiece of the device. So, although the audience experiences these very obvious manipulations, their effects are not apparent. It was suggested that such a combination might be thought of as a strategy for generating a level of 'intrigue', drawing audience into the Telescope and thus transitioning to participants.

In some sense the division offered here between participant and audience is too simplistic. For example, it was noted how the docent was a different kind of participant than members of the general public due to his professional status and the work he performed in crafting and guiding visitors as they encountered the Telescope and the exhibition in general. Further to this, the design issue of how spatial interference might be resolved between participants, or between participant and audience, has been touched on. The next chapter builds upon the basic division in roles introduced here and begins to fracture the notion of the participant to consider professional and non-professional specialisms of that role. It will enrich the observations in this chapter through exploring a more explicitly managed interactional environment in which guiding work by a professional actor (a storyteller) is employed to guide participants through spaces of manipulations and effects.

References

1. BBC News Online: Tide kills 18 cockle pickers (2004). Http://news.bbc.co.uk/1/hi/england/lancashire/3464203.stm, verified 07/10/10
2. Grinter, R.E., Aoki, P.M., Szymanski, M.H., Thornton, J.D., Woodruff, A., Hurst, A.: Revisiting the visit: understanding how technology can shape the museum visit. In: Proceedings of ACM Conference on Computer Supported Cooperative Work (CSCW), pp. 146–155. ACM, New York (2002). doi:10.1145/587078.587100
3. Heath, C., Jirotka, M., Luff, P., Hindmarsh, J.: Unpacking collaboration: the interactional organisation of trading in a city dealing room. Comput. Support. Coop. Work **3**, 147–65 (1995)
4. Heath, C., vom Lehn, D.: Misconstruing interactivity. In: Hinton, M. (ed.) Interactive Learning in Museums of Art and Design. Victoria and Albert Museum (2003)
5. Heath, C., Luff, P.K.: Collaboration and control: crisis management and multimedia technology in London Underground line control rooms. Comput. Support. Coop. Work **1**(1–2), 69–94 (1992)
6. Hindmarsh, J., Heath, C., vom Lehn, D., Cleverly, J.: Creating assemblies: Aboard the Ghost Ship. In: Proceedings of ACM Conference on Computer Supported Cooperative Work (CSCW), pp. 156–165. ACM, New York (2002)
7. Jefferson, G.: Glossary of transcript symbols with an introduction. In: Lerner, G. (ed.) Conversation Analysis: Studies from the First Generation, pp. 13–31. Benjamins, Elmsford (2004)
8. vom Lehn, D., Heath, C., Knoblauch, H.: Configuring exhibits. In: Knoblauch, H., Kotthoff, H. (eds.) Verbal Art Across Cultures: The Aesthetics and Proto-Aesthetics of Communication, pp. 281–297. Gunter Narr Verlag, Tubingen (2001)

9. Sparacino, F.: The museum wearable: real-time sensor-driven understanding of visitors' interests for personalized visually-augmented museum experiences. In: Proceedings of Museums and the Web (MW2002), pp. 17–20 (2002)
10. Wilde, D., Harris, E., Rogers, Y., Randell, C.: The Periscope: supporting a computer enhanced field trip for children. Personal Ubiquitous. Computing 7, 227–233 (2003)

Chapter 5
Professionals and Non-professionals:
The Journey into Space

Building on the observations of the previous chapter, this study develops a distinction between non-professionals and professionals, moving beyond participants to consider the role of the *actor*. In using this term for users of interactive systems, this study demonstrates how the actor crafts the performance via a variety of methods, such as managing handovers and delivering instruction, in order to manage both desirable and undesirable interactions with the technology. A key emerging skill for the actor is the ability to guide the participants around a complex space of manipulations, effects and potential interference resulting from the space in which the torch technology is deployed. The event in question was the "Journey into Space", a storytelling event that took place at the Newark and Nottinghamshire county show over two days in May 2004. During this event, small groups (2–10) of young children aged approximately between 5 and 11 years were led by professional storyteller, Rachel Feneley, on an imaginary trip into outer space. The event employed an interactive torch (flashlight) system to augment this storytelling activity. By pointing the torch at various targets located on surrounding walls, sounds are triggered. The story itself unfolds in a series of stages, some of which involved the storyteller instructing and directing participant use of the torch in order to play the sounds at appropriate moments in the story's trajectory.

The event took place in a large, hexagonal, metal-framed marquee. The walls were covered with dark cloth to set the scene, with various images of planets, spaceships, and aliens that had been printed onto paper (and thus moveable). During each storytelling session (lasting approximately twenty minutes), the torch interface was used to trigger sounds that had either been recorded by the children or were pre-existing in the system. These sounds would then play when the beam was pointed at the particular target on the wall they had been assigned to (the images of planets and so forth are shown in Fig. 5.1). Figure 5.2 shows a floor-plan, and the bottom is a photo of the space (the red arrow indicates the orientation of the video camera performing torch recognition in the space, which was mounted on a horizontal section of the marquee frame just above head height). The area of the space was approximately nine by four meters.

S. Reeves, *Designing Interfaces in Public Settings*, Human-Computer Interaction Series,   67
DOI 10.1007/978-0-85729-265-0_5, © Springer-Verlag London Limited 2011

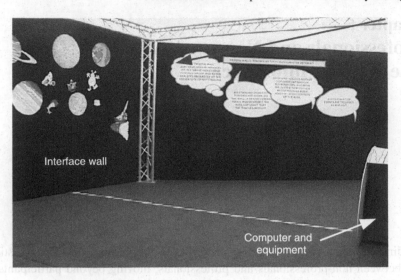

Fig. 5.1 The storytelling space, with an *arrow* indicating the direction of the torch interface camera

Fig. 5.2 Plan layout of the area in which the storytelling took place. [Image reproduced from [18]]

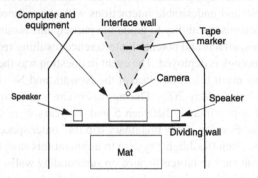

To provide some background to the vignettes, the story that Rachel told began with the children training to be astronauts, and then embarking on a trip into outer space in a spaceship. With this ship, they landed on and explored a planet in search of treasure, and then returned home as heroes to adoring crowds.

5.1 Other System Deployments

The torch technology had been used previously for interacting with graphical objects projected onto an immersive Storytent interface for young children [12]. It had also been used for an interactive exhibit in the caves underneath Nottingham Castle, in which visitors could shine their torches at points on the walls of a cave in order to retrieve information about the many inscriptions and marks on

Fig. 5.3 The arrangement of
participants at the
Nottingham caves exhibit.
[Image reproduced from [18]]

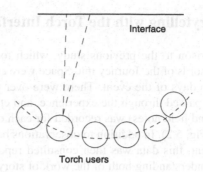

the walls [11]. A further use of this interface was its deployment as a digging tool
for a virtual "sandpit" [10], in which users could uncover artefacts by 'digging'
with their torch beams pointed at a projected display. Finally, a further study of
a more recent deployment of the technology (chronologically after this study was
conducted) has explored the potential for using the torch system to support learning [7].

A key feature that differentiates the study presented here, however, is that movement of the storyteller and the children around the space was highly varied, ranging from seated circles to 'free' formations exploring the space individually and in
teams. Further complicating matters was the fact that the marquee environment, with
its translucent ceiling and fabric walls, stretched a number of the assumptions relied
upon in previous experiences. At the time, this deployment 'in the wild' stretched
the interface beyond its use previously. In contrast, previous scenarios, such as the
Nottingham caves museum exhibit [11], were more spatially limited, typically re-
stricted to semicircular audience-like arrangements of the visitors to the exhibit, in
which a set of targets were attached to a smooth surface with users operating the
torches directly in front of the wall and some distance away from its surface (see
Fig. 5.3).

It was primarily the flexible use of space through the movement of the children
and storyteller within it, as well as the varied modes of torch use that helped to
initiate new forms of breakdown or failure of the interface which had previously
not been observed in earlier deployments. There are, however, a set of well-known,
'standard' failures that computer vision systems can succumb to, such as occlusion,
noise and spurious data in the image [13]. The intention here, however, is not to
simply exhibit these problems, but to illustrate how they are bound up in the social
circumstances of the work of the storyteller and the children in using the sensor
technology. Furthermore, as the analysis will highlight, the system's operation and
standard failures may be thought of in spatial terms. This is especially relevant for
public settings where users are moving through and navigating such a space during their manipulation of an interface and their experience of the effects of those
manipulations.

5.2 Storytelling with the Torch Interface

In comparison to the previous study, which took place sporadically over several weeks, records of the Journey into Space were collected intensively over the course of the two days of the event. There were over twelve separate groups of children in all that passed through the experience, and ethnographic data (video recordings, log files and field notes) was recorded for each of these groups (camera placements noted on Fig. 5.2). In addition to observations being conducted during the two days of the event, this data was then consulted repeatedly in order to develop a more detailed understanding both of the work of storytelling, and how this work meshed with the constraints and use of the technology. As a side note, constructing a simulator to replay interface events as in the previous chapter was not necessary since both manipulations of the interface and their effects were readily available to the analyst in the video record. However, discussions were had with the developers in order to provide technical insight into the root causes of breakdown in given situations.

Again, sequences from this data have been worked into a series of vignettes which are selections from a number of cases that were studied throughout the entirety of the collected data. The analysis uses these vignettes as well as observations from the larger set in order to draw out the analytic points.

One of the main motivations in studying the torch interface was understanding the more professional side of interactions in public settings. This developed from the previous study of One Rock in which, as noted, it became apparent that it was important to address both professional and non-professional divisions of participant roles. In order to do this, focus shifted to examining the nature of professional performer's work, how the performer ran a performance (in this case, storytelling) and in doing so how they appropriated and adapted the interactive technology. The following vignettes have been selected in order to present this performer's storytelling, mostly through describing instances of technological breakdown, detailing how that breakdown was managed, repaired where possible and adapted to over time forming a growing experience of technological contingencies.

In attempting to explicate the work of the actor, the first two vignettes provide some small initial exhibits of how breakdown was addressed by the storyteller. In doing so they introduce notions of interference and interaction spaces which are then explored in detail after each vignette. The second two vignettes, whilst also presenting elements of breakdown and repair, present longer instances of interaction, with particular focus on how the torches came to be woven into the story. The analysis of these vignettes then develops into a discussion of how the storyteller came to understand, manage and adapt to interference and interaction spaces.

5.2.1 Interaction Spaces (Vignette 1)

A group of (three) children and Rachel are sitting in a circle towards the left side of the space, and are about to blastoff earth by using the torch to perform this stage

too close (.) bit further back   ((Jenny glances back))

Fig. 5.4 Rachel gestures to Jenny to move away from the wall (*left*), Jenny gets the sound working (*right*). [Images reproduced from [18]]

of the story. The torch has been passed to a girl, Jenny, whom Rachel instructs. A recorded countdown sound has been associated with a spacecraft target on the wall. Rachel begins by guiding Jenny towards the location of the spaceship and positioning her so that the sound is more likely to be triggered.

> R: ((points towards interface wall)) you see the (.) craft over there? (0.4) get up close and
> point (.) point the (0.4) point the magic torch at the craft over there
> ((Jenny points the beam at the wall, but she has not pointed it at the right target))
> R: yeah (.) that one there (0.4) can you see?
> ((Jenny directs torch beam to the spaceship, there is no sound))
> R: that one there (0.6) you need to get a bit closer
> ((Jenny walks towards wall))
> R: keep going (0.2) keep going ((the countdown sound is triggered for a fraction of a second
> and then halts))
> (3.0)
> ((Jenny moves closer and closer to wall, arriving within centimetres of it))
> R: too close (.) ((gestures)) bit further back (0.8) bit further back
> ((Jenny slowly steps back from the wall, keeping the beam trained on the spaceship target;
> the countdown triggers, Jenny glances back towards Rachel and the group))

Rachel physically guides Jenny around the space in order to repair the technological breakdown they have suffered—i.e., the sound not triggering or triggering for too short a time. She does this by firstly instructing Jenny to move physically closer to the wall's surface (Fig. 5.4, left), and, when this strategy of moving around the space appears to partially solve the problem (i.e., the slight triggering of sound), Rachel instructs Jenny to move away (Fig. 5.4, right), whereupon the sound is triggered.

5.2.1.1 Defining Interaction Space

From this short vignette we can begin considering how and where successful manipulations of the torch interface occur. This first vignette exposes some basic interaction with the interface, but also reveals how the calibrated shape of the space

Fig. 5.5 Manipulation space.
[Image reproduced from [18]]

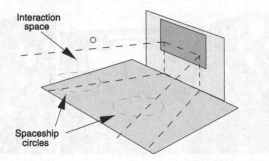

impacts this. Even though the torches were initially calibrated with the vision system, the nature of the fluctuating light within the space was at times a source of problems. The initial lack of sound triggering in this vignette as Jenny shines the beam at the wall was due to a combination of light levels, obliqueness of the beam as it was projected onto the wall and the group being situated generally outside of the area in which the torches were calibrated for the system. If the beam becomes too oblique or too weak here, the expectations of the vision system configured by this previous calibration will be compromised. When Jenny moved towards the wall the sound still failed to trigger. Rachel's management of these troubles via her instruction to Jenny to move closer to meant that the target then became obscured from the camera when Jenny got "too close", resulting in further positions away from the wall being successively tested until the sound triggered. The trouble was resolved only after this kind of experimentation by Rachel.

Thus we can begin to map out an approximate volume in which those manipulating the torch may safely move around and interact with the interface with success, as suggested in Fig. 5.5. This space itself is largely defined by the initial calibration of the torch, thus it is derived as an approximation from the positions and orientations of the torch captured during this calibration. The constraints of obliqueness modify this space, as do the ambient light levels, albeit in a less predictable way. Each of these aspects came into play as Rachel directed Jenny's use of the torch. The combination of each of these factors generates the shape of the space of successful manipulation that is experienced by the group. Training data and obliqueness ensure that this is a relatively static space, however this character is then less predictably altered by levels of light as they fluctuate during the day. Furthermore, it follows that within this manipulation space there may be particular 'sweet spots' in which torch manipulations and effects of those manipulations are most smoothly conducted and experienced (i.e., an optimal position to stand). For the Journey into Space, this spot was usually the main area in front of the wall (where the torch was calibrated) that provided consistently less problematic interaction. We shall see later how this information featured in adaptation.

Fig. 5.6 The group are hearing the sound (*left*), Paul gets in the way and Alice gestures (*right*). [Images reproduced from [18]]

5.2.2 Interference Spaces (Vignette 2)

In this second vignette, another group of four children and a helper—Alice—are also about to blastoff from the Earth (Fig. 5.6). They are sitting in a circle in between the left side and the centre of the space. After asking who would like to trigger the blastoff, Rachel passes a torch to Helen, seated to Rachel's right. A boy, Paul, is sitting to Rachel's left.

> R: who wants to have the magic torch first? ((torch is passed to H)) ok so when you're brave enough point it at earth and we're ready to take off

Helen points the torch at the Earth target, and the countdown sound begins to play, "Ten, nine, eight, seven, si...", at which point it breaks off and no "five" and so forth is heard. At the time when the break in sound was heard, Paul had leaned forward. This is then noticed by Alice who gestures for Paul to move his body back (Fig. 5.6, right). The sound then re-triggers and begins from ten again, this time completing. This situation of Paul obscuring the beam, Alice rapidly noticing this, gesturing to Paul, and Paul subsequently moving from the path of the beam took at most a second to compete.

It is also notable in this vignette that use of the torch by members of the circle is regulated by Rachel through assigning 'turns' with it to members of the group, thus managing how handover between children is done ("who wants to have the magic torch first?"). This provides an interesting comparison with the way in which handovers with the Telescope in Chap. 4 were managed. Whilst Rachel here instructs the children in a different manner, and negotiates handover between them in a more explicit fashion, the docent in the previous chapter also provided instruction to visitors and did much to smooth the handover via crafting the view of the Telescope.

Later on in this group's storytelling, and directly after the blastoff, Rachel provides the opportunity for some children to use the torch to 'look out the window' of their spacecraft, exploring this view by pointing the torch at different targets and listening for what sounds are assigned to the targets. During this period, Rachel uses the circle's orderliness to manage handover with the torch in order to let each child have their turn.

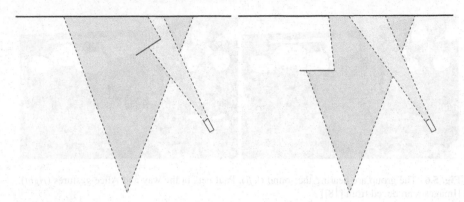

Fig. 5.7 Two forms of occlusion with the torch (*left*) and camera (*right*). [Images reproduced from [18]]

5.2.2.1 Defining Interference Space

At first it might seem that a space in which manipulations are unsuccessful would merely correspond to the inverse of the space in which manipulations *are* successful (i.e., the opposite of Fig. 5.5). This is not the case, however.

From this second vignette as well as the first, we can see that there are two main forms of interference that are possible: occlusion of the field of view of the camera (Fig. 5.7, right), and occlusion of the torch (illustrated in Fig. 5.7, left). The first form was exhibited in the first vignette when Jenny got too close to the interface wall, obscuring the target that was to be triggered. In order to resolve this, Jenny moved away from the wall successively with Rachel's instructions ("bit further back, bit further back") experimentally until the interference space was vacated. The second form is demonstrated here in this vignette, where Paul obscures the torch beam. Paul's obstruction of the torch was quickly noticed and then rapidly managed by Alice, Rachel's assistant in the storytelling at that time.

In a similar way to the space of successful manipulations, a spatial map of possible interference with those manipulations can be created, i.e., in the space which obstruction to the camera or the beam may in any way occur. The largest space of interference is created by the camera that is trained at the wall; its position and field of view define a (relatively) static interference space (Fig. 5.8, left). The torch itself, on the other hand, also defines an interference space, although it is smaller and mobile (Fig. 5.8, right).

There is a fundamental asymmetricity between the beam and the camera, rather simplistically since obscuring the torch beam is an 'observable', legible event for both the camera and the actor and participants as the beam may observably and inspectably be partial on the wall or absent altogether, whereas obscuring the camera is not (it is only available to the system). So, whilst the torch can be thought of as producing a controllable interference space, thanks to its beam and the social cues involved in its use (i.e., a kind of pointing), disruption of the camera image is internal to the system and provides no resources for Rachel to draw on in resolving any breakdowns.

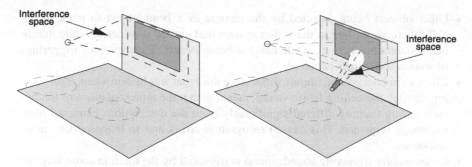

Fig. 5.8 Interference spaces. [Images reproduced from [18]]

We can begin to discuss these breakdowns and repairs as seen in the vignettes so far in terms of the basic legibility of these interference spaces. The torch provides greater and more legible resources to the users in order to repair breakdown. In contrast, the nature of the camera can cause problems simply because occluding the camera view is somewhat illegible.

There were, of course, other reasons for and effects of breakdown that have not been shown in these vignettes. The aural results of breakdown were various: sounds sometimes stuttered if they had been triggered already, halted halfway through playing or even failed to play at all; sounds started anomalously even though a torch was not trained on the wall; a sound successfully played might be a different sound altogether to the sound that was recorded and attached to the target. Sounds may also be triggered accidentally.

We can summarise the causes of the majority of breakdown into a short list, covering those already seen in the vignettes as well as others that were observed in the data but due to space limitations are not shown in this chapter. Breakdowns varied in terms of the speed with which resolution was possible; typically those involving the camera were more prevalent and more difficult to resolve than those with the torch.

- Obscuring a target: someone standing in front of a target on the wall being pointed at by a torch such that the target is no longer visible from the camera's perspective (as in the first vignette). Any sound playing will halt.
- A person or a thing in front of the torch: the beam is partially or fully obscured by someone standing between the torch and the wall (as in the second vignette).
- Making the torch beam too oblique or using the torch outside the area within which the torch was trained: the beam of the torch, when projected from an angle onto the wall, will be less and less detectable as a beam for the vision system (as in the first vignette). There are also recognition issues. If the system has been calibrated to recognise a torch being shone on the wall from a particular area of the space the range of angles it is expected to present will be coded into the recognition system. If it is shone onto the wall from an angle outside that set it might not be recognised or might be misclassified.

- Other objects being detected by the camera as a beam/object to track: originally there was a bug in the vision system that caused it to detect white, torch-beam-sized objects (e.g., white hats) as being beams. Thus spurious triggerings of sounds sometimes occurred.
- Changes in background illumination: since the event was held in a tent, light coming through the ceiling fabric varied, meaning that the representations of torches built during training differed significantly from the descriptions extracted from the image sequence. This caused recognition errors and so inappropriate audio responses.
- Unknowingly triggering sound: sound is triggered by the torch in some way but either without the intention or knowledge of the user (this will be explored in the fourth vignette).
- Inexplicable: breakdowns that were difficult to tie causally to other events.

5.2.2.2 Putting the Spaces Together

Developing on from interference and interaction spaces, we can begin to consider how the resulting superposition of these different spaces creates a complex spatial identity (which will now be referred to as 'spatial character'), circumscribed by the varied tolerances of the vision system, environment and the torch. We can see an approximation in the left of Fig. 5.9, and a plan view on the right, which perhaps go some way to visualising the interaction between these spaces. Obviously these diagrams cannot easily convey the sophisticated reality of the space's character, and at this point we should consider the rather non-trivial job faced by the actor not only in understanding this space, but also guiding others around it, as particularly exemplified by Jenny's difficulties with the torch in the first vignette. The camera space shown on the left of Fig. 5.8 alone would be a challenge for the actor to navigate and guide and succeed in instructing interaction successfully with the interface without cues, however the reality is that the exact boundaries of the space shift with the factors that have been examined thus far. So, the actor must manage this shifting

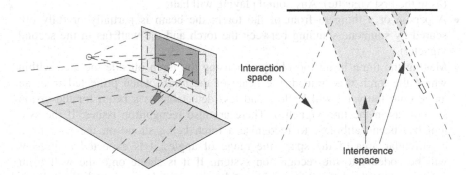

Fig. 5.9 Mapping the spaces (*left*); plan view (*right*). [Images reproduced from [18]]

character and the contingencies it produces in order for manipulations to be successful ones: e.g., ensuring children use the torch approximately 'here', that no-one is
obstructing the torch over 'here' in front of them, and that no-one is obscuring the
camera 'here', and so forth. As such, the design of the space places these concerns
in the hands of the actor (namely, Rachel) to manage, the details of which will be
addressed in the next subsection. (We will consider a design of space that places
these concerns in the environment later on in this chapter.)

5.2.3 Understanding, Managing and Adapting to Space (Vignettes 3 & 4)

In this third vignette, the storyteller, Rachel, has brought the children to the main
area near the wall. They 'board' the spacecraft by seating themselves in a circle,
however this time the circle is located directly in front of the wall rather than off
to one side of the space. They then go through a number of procedures to ready
the ship for blastoff (Fig. 5.10, top). The following vignette features Rachel, her
assistant Alice, and two of the children in the circle, Eric and Joe.

> R: okay (0.4) so (0.2) what we need to do before we set off is put on our spacesuits so put
> on your big boots ((Rachel mimes putting on boots))
> ((The children copy Rachel's mime))

Rachel then, in a similar manner, instructs the children to put on their 'space
suits', 'helmets' and so on.

> R: okay (0.2) seatbelts on
> ((All the children follow Rachel's miming lowering seatbelts))

Initially Rachel quickly instructs the group to form a circle on the floor. This
circle is created at a particular place in the space (directed by Rachel's pointing
and her own position in the space), and implicitly establishes an orderliness for the
rest of this segment of the story. The introduction of the bodily actions (i.e., repeated
miming of putting on boots, seatbelts, etc.) and how they are performed (i.e., through
each child taking their turn to mimic Rachel's instruction) builds upon the order
created by seating in the circle formation; Rachel instructs through demonstrating
some action which is then carried out by the rest of the group. At this point the torch
is introduced by Rachel as the next stage in the trajectory of the story.

> R: okay good (.) we're all ready to go (0.4) okay (.) so what I need to do (.) with the magic
> torch ((picks up one of the torches next to her)) (1.0) joe if I pass you the magic torch
> ((Joe takes the torch))
> R: if you press the button
> ((Joe presses the button to switch the torch on))
> R: and if you shine it o:::n ((points at wall))
> ((Children start looking at the wall))
> (0.4)
> R: the blue one there (.) the: earth on that one
> (1.0)
> ((Joe shines the torch on the Earth target but it makes no sound))

Rachel closely structures and instructs Joe's use of the torch in order to deliver the next stage, i.e., the blastoff. She does this by describing what action with the interface is next (e.g., "press the button", saying "shine it on" whilst pointing) which Joe then performs (see Fig. 5.10, bottom left and right). In doing so, Rachel shifts the focus of attention away from the circle to the wall. The newly-introduced torch and its use comes to be embedded within the unfolding of the story through such structuring and instruction. The torch here is treated as another component of the general activities of getting ready for blastoff (i.e., putting on boots, helmets, fastening seatbelts, checking buttons, and so on). Unfortunately, the beam fails to register any response from the system and does not trigger the sound associated with the Earth target (which would have been a recording of the children counting down from ten to one). Rachel attempts to remedy this as follows.

> R: okay (1.0) a:nd (0.2) we'll try (0.2) this time eric if you also (0.4) take the (.) the magic torch ((passes different torch to Eric)) (0.4) and if you shine it on the blue one (.) see what happens
> (3.0)
> ((Eric shines his torch on the Earth target but there is still no sound))
> R: ((looks around and laughs)) okay (0.2) so I want you to get in our takeoff positions (.) what you need to do is old hands with everybody
> ((The children hold each others hands))
> R: that's it (0.4) are you ready? (0.2) an we're gonna go from five to zero so we go FIVE
> All: FOUR THREE TWO ONE BLASTOFF ((mime blastoff))
> R: ah (0.2) we're flying

At first Rachel attempted here to remedy this by offering another child a different torch and instructs Eric to point the torch at the same target as had been suggested to Joe. When this repair fails to work, Rachel tries no further attempts at repair and instead abandons the torches entirely and performs the blastoff with the children herself.

Instruction in torch use and surrounding this, managed handovers of the torch—both in this vignette and the last—have become increasingly important parts of managing how the torches are deployed. Using the torches comes to be embedded within the organisation and logic of the circle. Rachel creates a set of procedures for the children to follow (such as donning helmets) which are then extended to include a further procedure (i.e., the blastoff) that involved the torch. Later still, as noted in the previous vignette, torch use is further extended into the 'looking out the window' procedure.

In this fourth and final vignette, a group of three children we have seen previously in the first vignette are beginning to 'explore a planet' in order to fulfil their 'mission' (to find treasure on the planet). Exploration occurs after blastoff, and once the period of travelling through space has ended. The object of missions may vary from attempting an encounter with aliens to locating and bringing back some object. The vignette begins with Rachel and three children, Tom, Jenny and Peter seated in a circle. Tom has one of the torches in his hands.

> R: okay (0.4) what we need to do is (.) get out of the (.) aircraft (.) jenny you gotta go first through the little chute over there ((points Jenny towards the location of the 'chute' in the direction of the wall)) (0.2) go through the little chute

put on your big boots

if you shine it o:::n

Fig. 5.10 Boarding the spaceship (*top*), blasting off using the torches (*bottom left* and *right*)

((Jenny bends down a little and walks forwards, see Fig. 5.11))
(0.8)
R: followed by Tom

Rachel then repeats the instruction until the other children—Tom and Peter—have also 'disembarked'; finally Rachel exits and arranges the group to face the wall.

The spacecraft circle provides the physical arrangement and structure with which to get to the next stage of the story (i.e., exploring the planet). This is accomplished by Rachel instructing the children through an imaginary 'chute' on one side of the circle in order to bring them to the wall in order to use the torches to perform the exploration. The children perform each instructed activity in their turn. The group is then arranged by Rachel at the wall.

followed by Tom

Fig. 5.11 Leaving the via the chute to explore the planet

R: let's see (1.0) ((points at a moon target)) point it at that one
((Tom points torch beam at interface wall and triggers alien sound))
(2.0)
R: NO (0.2) what does that mean?
((Tom triggers alien sound again))
(1.0)
R: OH NO what does that mean? (0.4) what's that noise? oh no what does that mean? (1.0)
th- eh there's an alien (0.6) okay (0.2) we need to split up in teams (0.2) jenny ((points at
Jenny)) (.) you're with me (0.2) tom you go with peter ((points at Peter)) (0.4) okay we're
gonna search the planet (0.2) you ((points to Tom and Peter)) go that side (0.2) we'll go this
side (0.4) okay we're looking for gold people ((walks away from the wall followed by Jenny))

Rachel instructs Tom on 'how to explore' by telling him to point the torch
at a particular target. The sound that is triggered (a sound of 'aliens' previously
recorded by the children) is then folded into the story ("oh no" and "there's an
alien") and leads to the group splitting up to search the planet for 'gold'. Rachel
guides the children to particular locations in the space through pointing. A short
time later Tom rushes towards the 'gold' target on the wall, quickly followed by
Peter.

R: now if you see an alien (0.2) what you got to do you got to communicate with the alien (.)
okay?
T: ((points the torch beam towards the 'gold' target, Fig. 5.11, left)) quick ((the torch bean
triggers the alien sound)) (5.0) get back ((moves the torch beam, a pre-defined sound (some
music) attached to the gold target starts to play))
J: ((runs towards the wall))
R: AH ((puts her hands on her head)) (0.4) you found th- you found the gold

Through some exploration of the wall with the torch and a measure of experimentation similar to that seen in this group's earlier vignette (when Jenny was guided

.hh WO:W   back to the ship

Fig. 5.12 Finding the gold (*left*), running back to the ship (*right*). [Images reproduced from [18]]

closer and further away from the target they were to trigger), Tom triggers the sound associated with the gold target. Rachel confirms this finding with her exclamation, and the story proceeds to the next stage.

> R: okay what we need to do (1.0) is (0.6) if we speak (.) really nicely ((walks over to the wall))
> (0.4) and we wish it off (0.6) okay? (1.0) come close
> ((The children move up close to Rachel))
> (1.0)
> R: okay (1.2) what we need to do (0.4) is we need to wish (0.2) the gold (0.2) off=
> T: =I wish I wish the gold was here
> R: okay let's do that (.) that sounds good ready? (0.2) do we have to close our eyes tom how do we do it?
> T: eyes closed
> R: okay (.) ready one two three all close our eyes (0.2) I wish I wish the gold was here ((Rachel takes the gold target from the wall)) (1.0) .hh WO:W (0.2) okay jenny (0.2) I'm going to keep you in control of the gold
> ((Tom triggers the alien sound))
> R: what we need to do (0.4) ((points at alien)) before the aliens come we need to get back into the ship ((points towards the place where the 'ship' is)) (.) everybody back to the ship ((The children run back to the 'ship' and form a circle again, Fig. 5.12, right))

In this final segment, Rachel here instructs the children to reform back into a group, clustering near the wall, in order to retrieve the object of their mission. During this Tom (possibly accidentally) triggers the alien target with the torch that is still in his hands. Rather than treat this as a disruption, Rachel quickly accounts for the alien sound and weaves it into the story, employing it as a means by which to return "to the ship" now that their mission is complete. She guides the children again through pointing back to the location of their spacecraft circle.

Finally it is worth summing up the overall structure and arrangement of activities that Rachel deploys within this vignette in order to progress the story. Here it involves getting the children off the spacecraft, engaging them in a search for and discovery of treasure, and getting them back on board again.

5.2.3.1 Adapting to Spatial Character

It is apparent in the vignettes and in the larger collection of data that Rachel comes to understand something of space's character (i.e., spaces of interference and successful manipulation) as evidenced by the adaptation of her conduct within them. A set of strategies developed as a result of both repeated experience and through Rachel's knowledge about the system.

Primarily this understanding and adaptation with various strategies develops from experiences during breakdown, which were either managed in situ (i.e., repaired) or avoided through adaptation. Some forms of breakdown were relatively simple to link to a cause (e.g., being clearly outside the space of successful manipulation) and therefore avoidable, whereas others of a less obviously causal nature were harder to avoid. In addition to troubles in discerning the causal link of breakdown, it was very difficult to predict when breakdown might occur. This was usually due to both the difficulties in controlling all children in the space and the anomalous nature of some breakdowns.

Rachel was sometimes able to weave the glitches into the story, as seen with her reaction to Tom's accidental triggering of the alien sound in the final vignette. Anomalously triggered sounds were repurposed and transformed, folded back into the ongoing story, and sometimes provided a sense of spontaneity and excitement. Such misplaced sounds became resources for further actions, and were recontextualised with respect to the orientation of the group. Rachel also sought to verbally complete those sounds that were interrupted halfway or stuttered to a halt. On the other hand, there were breakdowns that were too disruptive or 'unweavable' to fold back into the story. As a result these breakdowns caused the story itself to come to a halt, or at least slow down. In other instances further attempts to correct the problem might be made with the torch, as exhibited by Rachel's instructing of Jenny in the first vignette to move progressively away from the wall. At other times still, the breakdown was directly followed by some very rapid consultation between Rachel and the team in order to decide whether the failure was terminal, or whether another attempt should be made with the torch. Another strategy employed here in the case of seemingly unmanageable breakdown, was to simply ignore the breakdown and continue with the next part of the story as seen in the third vignette where Joe's attempts with the torch fail.

Other strategies were employed in order to pre-emptively avoid or manage breakdown altogether. For example, breakdown could be repaired by completely avoiding interference space, or avoiding certain forms of interaction with the interface. When standing, children frequently entered into a space of interference. Typically this would occur when children moved close to the wall, obscuring the targets or perhaps flagging themselves up as a false beam. This was overcome to some extent by the team informing Rachel about the issue of obscuring the camera's view, and so children could be directed to maintain a reasonable distance from the wall. A piece of tape was also placed on the floor in front of the wall (see Fig. 5.2, left, labelled 'tape marker') as a kind of guide to the boundaries of interference; its placement was based on the closest distance a child of average height could stand from the wall without obscuring any targets. This mark provided further resources beyond directions such as "don't stand too close to the wall", and instructions to move back. As such the action could be planned around these markers pre-emptively rather than reflexively dealing with interference. Other pieces of knowledge about avoidance strategies and ideal 'sweet spots' also came through information reported to Rachel about the interface's workings from the research team at the event. During times when children were sitting down, positioning was equally as important. Initially Rachel seated groups in circles on the edge of the space (as in the first, second and this final vignette), meaning that the beam of the torch became oblique and distanced, thus affecting the vision system by both the distortion of the beam and the potential problems with high light levels. Through discussion with the research team, it became clear that Rachel needed to conduct the spaceship circle in a more central location in order to overcome at least the obliqueness problem and so the groupings migrated towards a particular spot in the centre of the space, as seen in the third vignette (admittedly not a particularly successful example, however). It is notable that the location of the circle formation ends up situating the major-ity of interaction in a place that—when working properly—best facilitates story-telling through the technology. Finally of note is that torch use during exploration sequences declined as Rachel adapted to the technical problems associated with its use in such an unrestrictive way that heightened the chance of entering interference space.

There were, of course, other ways in which adaptations took place over the course of the two days. These adaptations developed over time with experience, constructed into an effective working body of knowledge about the torch technology in situ. These adaptations to the actor's work developed the telling of the story around the contingencies of the technology and the experiences of repair, just as the technology in use was shaped to fit the contingencies of the storytelling.

5.3 Discussion

This chapter has built upon the observations of the previous study chapter, implicitly addressing the role of the *participant*, for example. Primarily, however, has intro-duced a new role, that of the *actor*, who in this case was the storyteller. This section summarises the analysis, and subsequently draws comparisons with other systems, considering how the spatialised manipulations of a system may be thought of in terms of being hidden or revealed to varying extents.

5.3.1 The Actor's Work

Drawing on the analysis developed in the vignettes, this chapter has characterised the work of running a storytelling performance with the participants as consisting of instructing (e.g., via pointing, verbal instruction), spatially structuring activities (e.g., a seating in a circle, splitting into groups), organising handovers of the torch and managing the trajectory of the story (e.g., ensuring the next stage of the story is reached).

This *guiding work* is conducted by the actor, the nature of which shapes and is shaped by the technology. As introduced in the previous chapter's discussion, interaction with an interface can be thought of in terms of manipulations of the interface and the resultant effects those manipulations produce. Examining the actor's work and understanding the impact of technology on that work, the analysis has then explored how manipulations of the torch technology are spatialised. Such spatialised manipulations influence how and why breakdown occurs, how repair may be performed, and how adaptation to the spatiality of manipulations may be achieved by the actor. Thus, in order to understand the job of the actor in her work of instructing, structuring, organising torch handovers and managing trajectory of storytelling, the analysis has developed a sense of the ways in which the actor must also navigate the complex spatial character of the interactive environment, manage its contingencies, and adapt it to best fit the flow of the story as it progresses.

At this point a further concept can be integrated into our understanding of the nature of the actor's work. Picking apart 'guiding work' leads to a consideration of the way in which various forms of 'trajectory' come into play in the performative experience. Benford et al.'s conceptual framework on interactional trajectories has particular relevance here [2] (also see [1]). Two key trajectories of relevance here are "canonical trajectories", which represent an intended path through an experience, and "participant trajectories", which form separate path that is created by a participant through the same experience, and may diverge from the canonical trajectory. Benford et al. discuss management of divergent participant trajectories, and their reconvergence with canonical trajectories through orchestrator activities behind-the-scenes, as well as intervention in participant activity (which we will discuss in the next chapter). In a sense, then, the actor's guiding work may be conceptualised as managing this convergence between the trajectory of the story as it is intended and unfocussed participant interactions with the interface. Of interest from the point of view of work on trajectories is that this canonical trajectory was frequently improvised and adapted to the contingencies of the technology.

We can define the *actor* as being a professional and skilled member of the setting, who conducts the running of the performance in front of audience, and with participants. The adapting nature of the actor's guiding work, and has following essential elements:

- *Managing interaction on boundaries*: avoiding situating the spaceship circle near the edges of the space; making sure torch users were not standing too far away, too close or at too oblique an angle.
- *Constraining movement in the space according to context*: in the spaceship circle, torch use meant that children were instructed to sit down if they had stood up; during exploration of the planet, closeness to the wall was avoided.
- *Using the torches only at particular times and in particular ways*: Rachel began to abandon more 'free' torch use during the exploration phases because of increased

experience of breakdown. Torch use and handovers in the spaceship also circle became regulated and managed by instruction.

Generally, troubles with manipulations of the interface, as well as their resolutions, were for the most part essentially spatial in character, and autochthonous in that they were exhibited and generated by the arrangement of technology and participants in the space coupled with the forms of conduct occurring within that space. An appreciation of the complexities of this space had to be developed and managed by the actor. Some of the adaptations to this spatiality were due to explicit information or rules about the technology provided through instruction from the research team, whereas other adaptations were through Rachel's ongoing and developing appreciation for the interactions between the spaces of interference and spaces of successful manipulation, effectively building up her working body of knowledge of the system's spatial character. Finally it is important to note the way in which the simple positioning decisions and physical design of the space in general fundamentally generates interference spaces as well as 'sweet spots' and spaces where manipulation is preferable. This in turn therefore gives character to work that the actor must do in guiding participants, instructing them, and so forth.

5.3.2 Hiding and Revealing Spaces of Manipulations and Effects

Like the Telescope's camera, we can think of the camera in the Journey into Space as a simple visual sensor. Other systems with greater numbers of sensor units and more diverse hybrid sensor solutions can provide more sophisticated and subtle spaces of interference and manipulation. This section compares and contrasts the observations on actor's guiding work within the Journey into Space to consider such other systems also in terms of manipulation and interference spaces. Of particular interest here is how guiding work is only one strategy; here we consider how *hiding* or *revealing* spaces of manipulation and interference may be used in different contexts as different strategies.

The first example to examine is Treasure, put forth in [5]. This was a simple game in which players, equipped with Wifi-enabled PDAs, collected resources ("coins") distributed within their vicinity (in a city) and uploaded them when in wifi network coverage. Wifi coverage can be somewhat patchy and unreliable, meaning that locating a space in which manipulations will be successful can be difficult. Players' PDAs built up a map of this coverage as they played the game, so that players developed an understanding of locations to upload coins (i.e., wifi hotspots). Thus the spatial character of the network as experienced by players was exploited and repurposed as part of the game (the terminology "seamful design" is used to describe this technique [6]). For a game without such revealing of spatial character or one that does not in some way manage these spaces of manipulation, and movement about them for the player, patchy coverage could create serious breakdown. This problem was sidestepped by using breakdown as an unpredictable element in the game. The spatial character of this game arena was thus experienced as very much part of the game's dynamic as players 'discovered' network coverage and so the flow of players was self-managed rather than being shaped by some external, guiding influence.

A second example, which is revisited in later chapters, is Can You See Me Now? (CYSMN), a mixed reality game played between online players (drawn from members of the public) faced with a map of a city, and professional 'runners' on the ground in the city itself. Online players navigated the virtual map as the runners, equipped with GPS units and PDAs with which to see the online players' locations, attempted to catch the online players by physically getting within a few metres of their virtual location. Of particular interest was the way in which runners on the ground exploited and manipulated the inaccuracies of GPS in order to ambush and catch online players [8]. For example, runners sometimes relied on 'hiding' in the GPS 'shadows' created by buildings obscuring satellites in order to obfuscate their position from online players until the last moment, when runners would then spring out from the shadows and ambush unsuspecting players. In this example, again, spaces of interference (i.e., GPS shadows) became an exciting and special dynamic within the game, deepening the playing experience rather than being a source of breakdown for runners and players to constantly repair. Here the spatial character was created by the contingencies of GPS coverage; this was experienced for runners as a developing "body of knowledge", informing them of, for example, 'good' times of day for being in particular locations and appropriate places to 'hide'. The movement of players around the space was largely self-managed, whilst being obviously influenced and adapting to the increasingly more exposed and 'visible' structure of the contingencies.

Savannah [3] was a GPS-based educational game that involved (teenage) players assuming the role of 'lions' roaming a virtual savannah (a playing field), and receiving information on PDAs via a simple interface. The savannah was 'contoured' with virtual regions of different terrain, within which might also be some prey to feed on; players needed to traverse this unmarked flat space of the field in order to locate the prey. The game was also collaborative in that in order to fell larger prey (such as wildebeest), several players had to coordinate an attack within the same region. Analysis of the game described how the invisibility of region boundaries (and occasionally the uncertainties of GPS) caused discrepancies between participants' views of the action, and thus their ability to coordinate attacks successfully. Players would typically stop on the boundaries, and, when a cluster of co-players began to form around them, half would be inside the boundary of the region, and the other half, outside. The Savannah environment was 'flat' rather like the environment of the Journey into Space; whereas the Journey into Space's environment was shaped and given spatial character by the qualities of the camera and torch, Savannah's space was shaped by the combined qualities of GPS and prescribed regions as experienced via the PDAs. Whilst the space of manipulation for Savannah players was largely all-pervasive and consistent (unlike the previous examples of sensor technology such as Wifi and GPS in use), players' appreciation for their whereabouts within this manipulation space was problematic. Players encountered difficulties in this featureless environment precisely because the boundaries between regions were exposed to the player only in one dimension, i.e., as a point. This vastly reduced the resources available to the player and co-players in their coordination of attacks. The design implications drawn from Savannah eschewed a design that revealed the terrain of the manipulation space (i.e., exposing the region boundaries to players) in favour of invisibly extending the region around players when performing a collaborative attack, thus shielding them from the effects of differing views due to standing on the edge of regions problems. Movement about the field with these envisioned changes would be managed in a large part by this hiding. In contrast to the exposing of structure and self-managed play of Treasure described above, players' actions here instead are somewhat modified by the obscured structure.

The examples so far have all been games, whereas the Journey into Space was a storytelling event. At this point we consider MIT Media Lab's KidsRoom [4]. This was a vision-driven experience in which children were guided through an adventure story by computer-generated characters projected onto the walls of a large room. This room was furnished with a bed, a chest of drawers, rugs and so forth. During the story, the children were required to perform actions (such as pretending to use a bed as a boat, hiding behind a piece of the furniture, or dancing on a rug) in the space that were then detected by the vision system. There were several points in the story when participants had to be guided into particular spaces of interaction for the purposes of detection, such as being directed towards particular rugs, or all moving onto the bed that was in the room. Due to the need to detect the participants performing certain actions (such as dancing), the manipulation spaces were mutable, sometimes covering a small mat, at other times covering a bed and again at other times the whole room (in the case of hiding away from any camera). These moments were managed automatically by coaxing children, as part of the narrative of the story, to the appropriate manipulation spaces and away from the interference spaces that might obstruct detection by the system. For example, care was taken when creating the script for the projected creatures guiding the children through the experience, such that instructions about these spatial requirements were woven into the sense of the story. The spatial character of the room created by the sensor technology was thus not revealed to participants but was rather worked into the narrative in an endogenous fashion so that the children could be guided into the correct places. Movement around the room was thus directly managed by the system's projected interactive characters, meaning that, rather than involving a human actor as in the Journey into space, the system's program provided instruction and structured interaction within the space.

Finally, there are many existing examples of designs and implementations of performance-oriented uses of sensor technology, particularly those involving the capture of bodily movements for dance or music-related applications. The Theremin, in which the movements of hands in proximity to a metal antennae are converted to an audio signal, is perhaps the most well-known antecedent to more recent sensor-based work. There are two main ways in which performance-oriented systems may capture the performer: sensors located locally to the performer (e.g., those worn on the body), or sensors embedded in the environment.

There are also many examples of systems employing wearable sensors that are attached to performers. Artists such as Pamela Z [20] and Michel Waisvisz [9] instrument their own bodies (arms or hands, for instance), and techniques such as these have received increasing interest within HCI. Examples include instrumented footwear to control the creation of sound [16], wearable sensors for members of an audience to participate within a performance (e.g., light sensors, accelerometers, joint angle, temperature, touch) [15], or similar kinds of wearable sensors instead for professional dancers controlling a preprogrammed sequence of visuals and sound [17]. Other kinds of performances may reject registration located on performers themselves in favour of environmentally-registered approaches, often using computer vision techniques. There are various interactive dance environments, such as DanceSpace [19], that track bodily conduct and map it to sound and visuals. Some applications have used similar environments in slightly different contexts, as in the case of an augmented martial arts performance where, via computer vision, a practitioner is embedded in a martial arts game [14]. In this particular example an audience watched the game as well as the martial artist themselves as their moves are tracked by the system and used on their virtual counterpart.

In these two sets of examples of performance and performance-like scenarios (such as performative public spaces like nightclubs), potential spatial interference is either managed and limited through using locally-situated personal sensors for selectively controlling and collecting the data that is of interest (e.g., light and touch sensors). This is particularly true in the 'sensorially noisy' environment of a nightclub. An alternate strategy present in these scenarios is to entirely deny interference through configuring the performer(s) in purposefully distant spatial relationship to spectators (here, audience members), i.e., avoiding having participants at all.

These varied examples illustrate a range of approaches to the ways in which manipulation and interference spaces are handled and presented (or not presented) to actors or participants as well as the way in which they influence and shape movement around the environment. Treasure was designed to fully exploit these spaces, meaning that breakdown was from inception employed as purposeful and valid game feature. Runners' work in CYSMN also exploited the spatial aspects of sensor technology, however this was not designed as part of the game or particularly exposed, but was rather an emergent feature of the practical outworking of the game and the runners' work. Similarly, in Savannah, the exact spatial character of the field was only partially exposed and yet suggested solutions indicated that this character could in fact be hidden from participants, with an approach that guided players through the contingencies of the spatial character being most appropriate. For the Journey into Space event the boundaries of manipulation and interference space were partly exposed in breakdown during the storytelling, and yet partly hidden by Rachel's adaptations made in order to manage these breakdowns. Thus it occupies some ground between Savannah and KidsRoom. For KidsRoom, participants were very much guided around manipulation and interference spaces by the system, in order to hide the spatial character of the room from them. This 'hiding' was achieved through designers accounting for spaces of interference, using the system to guide children to spaces of manipulation and the 'sweet spots' within them.

It has been established] that a key feature of the actor's work in the Journey into Space is guiding participants. In the design of each of these examples the level and form of guidance offered to those within the space—either by actors or by the

Fig. 5.13 A spectrum of
spatial character. [Image
reproduced from [18]]

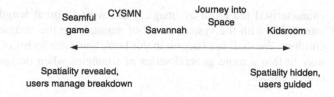

interactive system itself—varies, and correspondingly, the design decisions to hide
or expose the spaces in which manipulations and interference are possible. Figure 5.13 simply illustrates these and positions some of the examples discussed in
these terms. At one extreme end of the axis, manipulation and interference spaces
are revealed to users who are expected to fully guide themselves and manage breakdown as part of their interaction, whereas at the opposing end, such manipulation
and interference spaces are hidden from the them, and they are guided through the
spatial arrangement by the system in some way or perhaps by actors. Towards the
centre are systems in which spatial aspects of manipulation and interference are partially revealed, however users are provided with some support to resolve breakdown.
(It is of note that this spectrum places systems involving younger children towards
the right, whereas the left features systems involving adults or older children. It is
possible that this fact has implications for the use of the different strategies.)

The design spectrum axis here admittedly does not point in any particular way to
the times when revealed or hidden design strategies will be most appropriate. The
analysis of the Journey into Space, for example, has shown how a performance-like
environment can suffer from breakdown induced by a structure that is not revealed to
the actor, and yet at the same time has illustrated how repair and adaptation of conduct in the space to the mostly-invisible spatial character can develop. This results in
(at least) limited management of breakdown. As such a redesign of the Journey into
Space could conceivably take either design route; the spatial character could be further revealed by barriers to stop participants getting too close to the wall, or on the
other hand the spatial character could be further hidden, perhaps by providing the
actor with a more developed understanding of the space that enabled them to manage its spatial character and thus guide the storytelling and the group experiencing
it in a more graceful manner.

In addition to this, there is the issue of differing abilities actors or participants
may have in comprehending spatial character, should they need to. In the case of the
Journey into Space and KidsRoom, the participants were young children and furthermore, guided strongly in their interactions either by an actor or by the system.
In other examples cited teenagers or adults were involved. It is possible that different
actor strategies of 'guiding and hiding' or revealing will be appropriate for different
demographic groups. For children, for instance, a designer may wish to intentionally
hide spatial character for pedagogical reasons, or perhaps in order to create certain
forms of experience, such as a 'magical' system where the effects produced by manipulations of the interface are exposed, but the underlying manipulation space is
hidden from users (in contrast to the Telescope's 'intriguing' interface). Indeed, it
is no coincidence that, in spite of the sometimes problematic nature of interaction
with the Journey into Space's sensor environment, we saw the way in which Rachel

characterised the torch as 'magic', and went to great lengths in order to smooth interaction with the system in aid of maintaining the 'magical' experience for the children. We shall see later on in this book how such forms of interactive experience may fit into a more general series of strategies when designing manipulation and effects spaces.

5.4 Summary

In this chapter we have seen the ways in which a digital interface was embedded both within interactions between actors and participants as well as the performance of the storytelling itself. Whilst the data that has been examined has primarily highlighted instances of technological breakdown, it is within these troubles that the observations of the previous chapter—the roles of participant and audience—have been extended to include the work of the *actor*. The role of actor here has been described through the vignettes as being a professional guide for participants, instructing them, physically structuring interaction, organising turns and managing the story's trajectory. The actor's work involves competence in repairing breakdowns and adapting to the contingencies of the technology, and as part of this, coming to understand and take account of the spatial character of the system. It is through this understanding that the actor may successfully perform the necessary work in guiding participants through the space and the story itself.

This spatial character has been elaborated through examining various instances of technological breakdown, repair and adaptation to contingencies. As part of this we have also seen how notions of manipulations and effects may be extended conceptually to be thought of in terms of manipulation *spaces* and interference *spaces* (or, a spatial character of interaction).

Finally, this chapter has considered various other systems in which the spatial characteristics of sensor or sensor-like equipment play a central part. This contrasted the 'hiding and guiding' strategy of the Journey into Space event with systems in which spatial character is revealed to actors or participants, suggesting a spectrum of possibilities for design.

Next we shall see how, in the following chapter, the roles presented so far may be expanded even further with the introduction of distinct performative settings in which particular roles—such as that of actors and orchestrators—may operate. In addition to this, the next chapter also builds upon the professional audience management and guiding work conducted by the actor in this chapter, developing an analysis which involves multiple actors and orchestrators, who collaboratively maintain the smooth running of the performance, the transition of audience members to participants, and so on.

References

1. Benford, S., Giannachi, G.: Temporal trajectories in shared interactive narratives. In: CHI'08: Proceeding of the Twenty-sixth Annual SIGCHI Conference on Human Factors in Computing Systems, pp. 73–82. ACM, New York (2008). doi:10.1145/1357054.1357067

2. Benford, S., Giannachi, G., Koleva, B., Rodden, T.: From interaction to trajectories: designing coherent journeys through user experiences. In: CHI'09: Proceedings of the 27th International Conference on Human Factors in Computing Systems, pp. 709–718. ACM, New York (2009). doi:10.1145/1518701.1518812

3. Benford, S., Rowland, D., Flintham, M., Drozd, A., Hull, R., Reid, J., Morrison, J., Facer, K.: Life on the edge: supporting collaboration in location-based experiences. In: CHI'05: Proceedings of the SIGCHI Conference on Human Factors in Computing Systems, pp. 721–730. ACM, New York (2005). doi:10.1145/1054972.1055072

4. Bobick, A., Intille, S., Davis, J., Baird, F., Pinhanez, C., Campbell, L., Ivanov, Y., Schütte, A., Wilson, A.: The KidsRoom: a perceptually-based interactive and immersive story environment. Presence: Teleoperators and Virtual Environments 8(4), 367–391 (1999)

5. Chalmers, M., Barkhuus, L., Bell, M., Brown, B., Hall, M., Sherwood, S., Tennent, P.: Gaming on the edge: using seams in pervasive games. In: Proceedings of the Second International Workshop on Gaming Applications in Pervasive Computing Environments at Pervasive 2005. Springer, Berlin (2005)

6. Chalmers, M., Galani, A.: Seamful interweaving: heterogeneity in the theory and design of interactive systems. In: DIS'04: Proceedings of the 2004 Conference on Designing Interactive Systems, pp. 243–252. ACM, New York (2004). doi:10.1145/1013115.1013149

7. Cobb, S., Mallett, A., Pridmore, T., Benford, S.: Interactive flashlights in special needs education. Dig. Creat. 18(2), 69–78 (2007)

8. Crabtree, A., Benford, S., Rodden, T., Greenhalgh, C., Flintham, M., Anastasi, R., Drozd, A., Adams, M., Row-Farr, J., Tandavanitj, N., Steed, A.: Orchestrating a mixed reality game 'on the ground'. In: Proceedings of the SIGCHI Conference on Human Factors in Computing Systems, pp. 391–398. ACM, New York (2004). doi:10.1145/985692.985742

9. Dykstra-Erickson, E., Arnowitz, J.: Michel Waisvisz: the man and the hands. Interactions 12(5), 63–67 (2005). http://doi.acm.org/10.1145/1082369.1082416

10. Fraser, M., Stanton, D., Ng, K.H., Benford, S., O'Malley, C., Bowers, J., Taxén, G., Ferris, K., Hindmarsh, J.: Assembling history: achieving coherent experiences with diverse technologies. In: Proceedings of European Conference on Computer Supported Cooperative Work (ECSCW), pp. 179–198. Oulu University Press, Oulu (2003)

11. Ghali, A., Boumi, S., Benford, S., Green, J., Pridmore, T.: Visually tracked flashlights as interaction devices. In: Proceedings of 9th IFIP TC13 International Conference on Human-Computer Interaction (INTERACT). IFIP (2003). http://www.equator.ac.uk/PublicationStore/Interactfinal.pdf

12. Green, J., Schnädelbach, H., Koleva, B., Benford, S., Pridmore, T., Medina, K., Harris, E., Smith, H.: Camping in the digital wilderness: tents and flashlights as interfaces to virtual worlds. In: Extended Abstracts on Human Factors in Computing Systems (CHI), pp. 780–781. ACM, New York (2002). doi:10.1145/506443.506594

13. Grimson, W.E.L.: Object Recognition by Computer: The Role of Geometric Constraints. MIT Press, Cambridge (1990). Chap. 1

14. Hämäläinen, P., Ilmonen, T., Höysniemi, J., Lindholm, M., Nykänen, A.: Martial arts in artificial reality. In: Proceedings of the SIGCHI Conference on Human Factors in Computing Systems, pp. 781–790. ACM, New York (2005). doi:10.1145/1054972.1055081

15. Hromin, D., Chladil, M., Vanatta, N., Naumann, D., Wetzel, S., Anjum, F., Jain, R.: CodeBLUE: a Bluetooth interactive dance club system. In: IEEE Global Telecommunications Conference (GLOBECOM), vol. 5, pp. 2814–2818 (2003). doi:10.1109/GLOCOM.2003.1258748

16. Paradiso, J., Hu, E., yuh Hsiao, K.: Instrumented footwear for interactive dance. In: Proceedings of the XII Colloquium on Musical Informatics (AIMI), pp. 89–92 (1998)

17. Park, C., Chou, P.H., Sun, Y.: A wearable wireless sensor platform for interactive art performance. In: Proceedings of Fourth Annual IEEE International Conference on Pervasive Computing and Communications (PerCom), pp. 52–59 (2006)

18. Reeves, S., Benford, S., Crabtree, A., Green, J., O'Malley, C., Pridmore, T.: The spatial character of sensor technology. In: Proceedings of ACM Conference on Designing Interactive Systems, pp. 31–40 (2006). doi:10.1145/1142405.1142413
19. Sparacino, F., Wren, C., Davenport, G., Pentland, A.: Augmented performance in dance and theater. In: International Dance and Technology 99 (IDAT99) (1999)
20. Z, P.: Audible image/visible sound: Donald Swearingen's Living Off The List. 21st Century Music 8(1) (2000)

Chapter 6
Orchestration and Staging: Fairground: Thrill Laboratory

The settings explored in the previous two chapters were relatively simple, consisting of one main space in which interaction with technology took place. Similarly, the technology in use was quite self-contained, with only one or two main components that formed the core of the interface. In this chapter, and the next, the focus is switched to systems that are more complex and distributed, involving greater numbers of technical and performance team members, and arguably more challenging situations.

In exploring these larger-scale settings, this chapter will explore notional subdivisions of the settings in which interaction takes place, introducing a basic distinction between them. Through this we will explore (following a dramaturgical perspective) *centre-stage* areas, where actors conduct themselves, generally construct the event's 'atmosphere', and make legible a participant's activities for a watching audience. Contrasting with this is *behind-the-scenes* areas, where the role of the *orchestrator* becomes important in collaborating with actors in order to weave together a performance from distributed and disparate elements, as well as supporting the transition of audience members into participants (contrasting with the self-led transitions we have seen in Chap. 4). Such transitions, as we shall see, can also be transitions through subdivisions of the setting.

Fairground: Thrill Laboratory (F:TL) was a series of six theatrical events pioneered by Brendan Walker of Aerial, and staged at the Dana Centre (Science Museum, London) in three weeks during October and November 2006.[1] The events were designed to explore the nature of 'thrill' through a combination of science and entertainment, involving talks by experts (for example, in biometrics and theme park ride engineering), projections of physiological and video data streamed from a selection of participants on theme park rides, and the opportunity to go on the ride at the end of the evening.

---

[1]Fuller details of the technical design of the events can be found in [11], since these details are only briefly summarised in this chapter. Since the initial study of this project [10], a further iteration of the system was deployed in 2007 [1], as well as subsequent, related experiments involving 'adaptive rides' that actually respond to captured rider physiological data [7].

S. Reeves, *Designing Interfaces in Public Settings*, Human-Computer Interaction Series, 93
DOI 10.1007/978-0-85729-265-0_6, © Springer-Verlag London Limited 2011

Fig. 6.1 The Booster (*left*), and rider seated on it (*right*). [Images used with permission; ©Mixed Reality Lab]

After a set of introductory talks, the audience was presented with a visualisation of live telemetry streamed directly from the ride. Firstly a member of the production team rode, providing a commentary of his experience. Secondly, a 'lottery' was used to select an audience member whose telemetry would be transmitted next. During the final stage of F:TL, all other audience members were free to ride, with volunteers using the telemetry equipment as often as the technical and organisational infrastructure could support.

Each week featured a different amusement ride that was set up outside so that it was visible from the various spaces used within the venue. This chapter's data is drawn mostly from the experience surrounding the last and most extreme of the three, the Booster, a pure white-knuckle ride that relies mainly upon fear and on extreme accelerations to elicit a sense of thrill in the rider (see Fig. 6.1 left and right). The Booster features a central tower supporting a 40m-long rotating arm, similar to a windmill. Freely rotating carriages are attached at either end of the arm and hold two pairs of riders seated back-to-back. The speed and direction of the rotating arm can be controlled, with riders experiencing accelerations reaching up to around 4.0 g.

A custom-built wearable telemetry system captured four sources of data from riders: video of their face, audio as a means of self-reporting, electrocardiogram

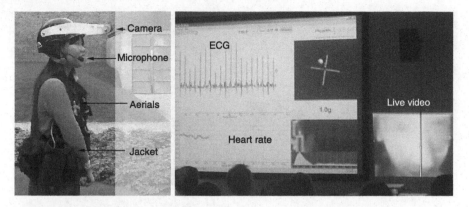

Fig. 6.2 The wearable telemetry technology (*left*), and visualising the data (*right*). [Images used with permission; ©Mixed Reality Lab]

(ECG) and acceleration. This equipment was integrated into a jacket as shown in Fig. 6.2, left. The design of the jacket had to meet several challenges, including fitting the passenger restraint system of each of the rides, being comfortable to wear and remaining easily serviceable. In addition to this, the design had to address the physical strain of wearing head-mounted equipment at high G-forces.

The audience experience of the telemetry data was supported by the so-called 'expert' visualisation, shown in Fig. 6.2, right, which was projected in the main auditorium (other more impressionistic visualisations were projected into the bar and onto the side of the building as ambient displays). This visualisation included the ECG and heart rate graphs, numerical heart rate data, a 3D visualisation of the gravitational forces experienced by the rider and live video from the helmet camera in addition to the audio stream broadcast over speakers. During transmission, experts were at hand who introduced the data to help the audience understand what to expect and how to make sense of it.

Some appreciation of the spatial and organisational setup of audience members, ride orchestrators and those participating in riding as well as their various lines of communication is critical for the understanding of the vignettes that are presented later. The following therefore provides a brief overview. Overall the event was staged across multiple spaces inside and outside the venue, while the discussion here concentrates on those spaces that are directly necessary.

Data from a single rider sitting on the ride outside was transmitted to the *main auditorium* (2nd *floor*), visualised and discussed. Event hosts guided the theatrical part and explained the data so that the group of 50–90 spectators had good access to the information. In addition, the main telemetry control area was set up on one side in the same space (as shown in Fig. 6.3), physically overlooking the ride outside. From here, the technical team ensured the availability of the live data streams at the right times during the event.

On the ride, set up outside approximately 40 m away from the auditorium, riders experienced the (approx.) two minute ride program. As part of the telemetry equip-

Fig. 6.3 The control area (*top*), in detail (*bottom*). [Images used with permission; ©Mixed Reality Lab]

ment, the rider had a one-way audio link to the control room, which was sometimes (but not always) broadcast to the audience in the auditorium.

Outside in front of the ride (ground floor), from which professional ride opera-tors controlled the speed, direction and duration of the ride, in collaboration with a member of the technical team, who was in two-way radio contact with the con-trol room and fellow team members upstairs. At the right times during the event, the telemetry data, operation of the ride and verbal commentary by the rider were coordinated via this link. The team had remote access to a laptop situated in the ride operator's booth which collected and passed on the telemetry data. It is important to clarify at this stage that the technical team, largely consisting of researchers who developed the technology deployed at the event, ran the event in collaboration with ride operators working in their capacity as fairground professionals (i.e., the techni-cal team were not responsible for the running of the ride itself, only the technology on the ride).

6.1   Running and Experiencing the Laboratory

F:TL initially differs from both One Rock and the Journey into Space studies in that the experience consisted of a discrete series of events which were spread over the course of several weeks, as opposed to an event that ran daily. It also provided a larger-scale performance environment in which greater numbers of the public took part, supported by more complex arrangements of technology. Furthermore, F:TL required continual work done by a large number of team members both in front of an audience as hosts, and as a technical team in order to equip riders, capture their telemetry data successfully in order for hosts to present it in real-time to that audience. As such F:TL provides a quite radical expansion of study scope in terms of people, technologies and spaces.

Data collection by researchers involved in the development and running of the telemetry system took place on most of these evenings, with later events tending to have more data available for analysis. This data included video recordings and the telemetry data from eighteen different riders (i.e., helmet camera, heart rate and acceleration data). The video recordings totalled approximately fifteen hours in length. As well as this video and log data, some key points were followed up by researchers through five semi-structured phone interviews with members of the public who participated. Two further semi-structured interviews with ride operators at the events were also conducted (by the author).

In order to study the video and log data from the event, the videos recorded from hand-held cameras, the video of the rider's face, and graph plots of acceleration and heart rate were visualised using the Digital Replay System (DRS) [8]. This analytic tool enables the study of multiple concurrent data streams alongside one another and in a synchronous manner (shown in Fig. 6.4), as well as supporting the repeated viewing of segments of action which are of interest. In some senses similar to the simulation tool constructed for One Rock, DRS was used here to recreate the visualisation that would have been visible to audience members as well as reconstructing for the analyst the different perspectives on the action (the rider's helmet camera and any hand-held camera work) and the physiological situation of the rider.

An analysis of this data set has been published previously, examining in particular the ways in which existing relationships between riders, ride operators and those watching the ride are 'perturbed' by the introduction of interactive technologies [10]. This chapter builds upon these observations but also introduces extensive new material expanding focus to include preparation for the event. Four segments from the data set have been worked into vignettes, such that they provide exhibits of observations made over the data set at large. Whilst selection was informed by the ongoing development of the framework, the vignettes have also been selected to provide as broad an overview as possible of the event as it happened, reflecting the different perspectives of various members of the event. It is of note that with the exception of the first, the vignettes presented in this chapter are drawn from the final night of F:TL when the event structure and technology were at their most stable and well-developed.

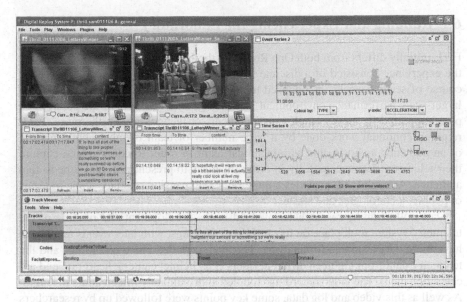

Fig. 6.4 The Digital Replay System (DRS) analysis tool. Two videos are playing along with various plots of physiological data. [Image used with permission; courtesy of Digital Replay System (DRS), ESRC e-Social Science Research Node 'Digital Records for e-Social Science', grants RES-149-25-0035, RES-149-25-1067]

The first vignette shows some of the initial orchestration work required in setting up the system for its use later on that day. The following three vignettes in turn exhibit the experiences of different roles of members of the event—actors, participants and orchestrators respectively—however the focus upon orchestration is retained for each. The second vignette follows a 'professional rider', a member of the production team who gave an initial public demonstration at the start of the event, and details the performative work actors engaged in with orchestrators to collaboratively produce the performance. The third follows the relatively routine experience of Sally, a member of the public audience who became a rider by virtue of winning the ticket-lottery, and covers the variety of orchestration work involved in assisting her transition to participant. The fourth vignette then returns the focus to the orchestrators, exploring the activities of the technical team and ride operators as they decide how to deal with a moment of crisis in which one of the equipped riders appears to be in difficulty. In each of the vignettes, members of the technical team are referred to as Orchestrator ⟨X⟩.

6.1.1 Setting up for Orchestration (Vignette 1)

This first vignette details an instance of the setting-up procedure for the Ghost Train, which was a ride featuring in some of the earlier performances before the events where the Booster was featured. Essentially the Ghost Train is a covered roller coaster. As with each instance of the event, regardless of the particular ride that

Fig. 6.5 Orchestrator H wearing the jacket and helmet camera during setup (*left*), standing in front of the ride (*right*). [Images used with permission; ©Mixed Reality Lab]

week, ride operators deployed the Ghost Train on the morning of the event, readying it for the members of the technical team to begin setting up and testing the telemetry technology.

The setting up involves a number of stages. Firstly the technical team must deploy some basic equipment: laptops, projectors and cabling inside the auditorium; equipment such as aerials outside in front of the ride, a laptop in the ride operators' booth beside the ride, and a network link from there to the auditorium. This approximately took an hour. Secondly, the team must ensure the jacket, when located in front of the ride, communicates at a basic Internet Protocol (IP) packet level with the control area (using 'ping'[2]). Thirdly, the team attempts to get the various data streams transmitting from the position in front of the ride, and then fourthly attempt this on the ride itself. While the exact details of this process differed between rides to some extent, general problems encountered were more similar. The second to fourth stages of the setup process took several hours, often leading right up to the evening event.

It is in the second stage of basic network functionality that we join the action. A member of the technical team, Orchestrator H, is fitted with the jacket and goes to stand on the lawn in front of the ride (Fig. 6.5). The team members in the control area upstairs are at first attempting to receive video data from the jacket's video transmitter. The video transmitter streams data to the control area via a machine situated in the ride operator's booth next to the ride. The orchestrators have begun by 'pinging' the transmitter using this machine.

Orchestrator S: ((explaining to camera operator)) so we're just trying to connect to the video transmitter now (0.8) so that transmits over (.) over IP over TCP/IP so at present it's turned off err we can't ping it at the minute

After a series of timed-out pings, the console window on one of the screens in the control area visible to the orchestrators indicates that two packets have been

---

[2]The command 'ping' tests the connectivity between two computers on a network, indicating transmission latency (i.e., round-trip time), data loss and so on.

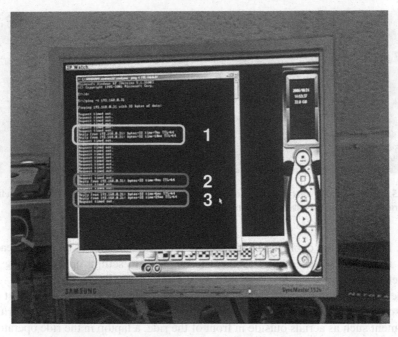

Fig. 6.6 Intermittent ping responses. Earlier responses (1) are towards the top of the window, later ones towards the bottom (2 and 3). [Image used with permission; ©Mixed Reality Lab]

received (Fig. 6.6, (1)). Orchestrator S (in the control area) communicates this to Orchestrator H (on the ground) via radio.

> Orchestrator S: ((to Orchestrator H)) okay no yeah we can ping it now (.) did you change something?
> Orchestrator H: no I didn't
> (3.0)
> Orchestrator S: so yeah (.) so we couldn't ping it for a while and then it came back on again (1.0) it comes on and off (.) on for a couple of seconds and off again
> ((a successful ping appears, Fig. 6.6, (2)))
> Orchestrator H: is that ping?
> Orchestrator S: that that's ping yeah
> (...)
> Orchestrator M: yeah no it's just dying isn't it ((inaudible)) I think it's gotta be (0.6) it's the battery
> ((two more successful pings appear on the console, Fig. 6.6, (3)))
> Orchestrator C: oh no it's (0.4) got
> Orchestrator M: got two
> rchestrator C: yeah
> Orchestrator M: then got time-out ((ping time-outs on console, Fig. 6.6, below (3))) (0.4) yeah (0.4) no change the battery and see whether that ((inaudible))
> Orchestrator S: so when (0.6) when were those batteries charged up then
> Orchestrator A: just today

Having spent some time achieving basic network connectivity, the team turn their attention to the other data streams, namely ECG data and accelerometer data. At this point the team are examining the ECG data being transmitted.

Orchestrator M: it's just getting all the (0.4) crappy static
(13.0)
Unknown: we're getting a proper (.) ECG type shape I'm just holding it with my fingers at the moment to get something like ((inaudible))

Once these data streams have been established as working to an adequate level the orchestrators attempt to establish a reliable audiovisual stream.

Orchestrator S: ((to Orchestrator H)) ((mumble)) the angle on the antenna so that it points further upwards (2.0) the video's pretty much perfect actually oh no (.) no it's gone again now
Orchestrator H: can you ping it ((inaudible))
Orchestrator M: it's pinging and I can hear him and can see him quite well now (.) really well
Orchestrator S: ((to Orchestrator H)) okay so the video's actually really good now

Establishing this audiovisual stream is more problematic than the others (i.e., ECG and acceleration) due to the higher bandwidth required for continuous unbroken transmission (therefore avoiding the problems of rejoining dropped-out streams), and unreliable transmitter hardware/software in general. The alignments and positionings of aerials attached to the wifi access point are crucial as well, and the team can be seen here experimenting with this, moving an antenna further "upwards" and then probing its connectivity with ping from the control room.

Having established the system as being at an acceptable level of functionality in the basic case (i.e., the jacket's wearer situated on the lawn), we now join the action some time later, where the orchestrator on-the-ground (Orchestrator H) is walking around the Ghost Train ride's various platforms, whilst the team in the control area monitor the signal (via inspecting the video output, as seen in Fig. 6.7, top left and right) and direct his movements (Fig. 6.7, bottom left and right).

Orchestrator T: ((to Orchestrator H)) to your right ((Orchestrator H walks right a few metres; Fig. 6.7, top right, shows the 'good' signal that results)) (2.4) wait till we get him back
(1.0)
Orchestrator S: so the on- the only thing so (0.4) the possibilities I can see=
Orchestrator T: =is he back?
Orchestrator M: um (.) yeah
Orchestrator T: ((to Orchestrator H)) you're now back=
Orchestrator M: =and (.) really good
Orchestrator T: ((to Orchestrator H)) and really good (1.2) on your right side the bloomin aerial at the back of you aren't you?
(4.0)
Orchestrator H: ((inaudible)) keep walking now

After a short while Orchestrator T updates Orchestrator H on the progress in the control area.

Orchestrator T: ((to Orchestrator H)) um you're still timing out (1.2) hold on a minute you're now (1.0) we're now getting some video (.) from somewhere (2.4) we're now back ((Fig. 6.7, bottom, with Orchestrator H moving along the ride's platform))

Orchestrator T instructs Orchestrator H to move, with Orchestrator M relaying the current 'status' of resources that indicate signal, such as ping time-outs, and

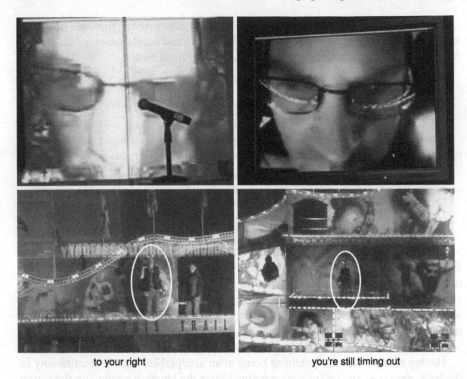

to your right   you're still timing out

Fig. 6.7 Frozen signal (*top left*) and 'good' signal from Orchestrator H's helmet camera (*top right*); Orchestrator H (*circled*) moving on the ride's various platforms in order to assist the mapping out of the ride's path and corresponding signal quality (*bottom left* and *right*). [Images used with permission; ©Mixed Reality Lab]

the visible video image. Reasoning about the quality of the signal and the moments when it drops out relate the alignments of aerials in the jacket and on the ground in front of the ride. Compounding this is the fact that the ground-based aerials are highly directional in order to focus the signal.

6.1.1.1 Developing Spatial Working Knowledge

This vignette exhibits how the orchestrators conducted their setting-up procedure as a gradual, *layered* build-up, starting with basic network functionality (such as pinging the video transmitter) and working towards higher level, qualitatively-assessed functions (such as the signal quality of ECG and later, the quality of video). Eventually the stages of this layered build-up became increasingly similar to the actual deployment and running of the system during the performance. This culminated in attempting to 'map out' the rider's experience either by physically moving to those locations where the ride would run (as in Orchestrator H's moving around on Ghost Train platforms, guided by Orchestrator T) or repeatedly riding the ride itself (a procedure for testing the Booster).

This progressively layered build-up enables the orchestrators to work within a complex space of technical contingencies in a systematic manner. For instance, in the first half of the vignette the team constantly ping the video transmitter, attempting to analyse what causes the IP packets being sent to the video transmitter to time-out (i.e., they never get there). The first possibility identified is that the equipment state has recently changed in some way and that something recently "changed" may account for the packets that have unexpectedly been received. Orchestrator S suggests this to Orchestrator H (asking if he has "change[d] something"). Orchestrator H indicates this isn't the case, and so the team reorient their enquiry, resolving amongst a field of possible problems what the most likely troubles are with the transmitter, i.e., that the pattern of pings 'looks like' and has 'got to be' indicative of battery problems. Past experience in the field of possibilities informs the team's navigation through it, and informs how this sequence of packets is interpreted.

This vignette has only exhibited a few of these paths through the problem space, however interviews with the orchestrators who were present at the events revealed a number of further contingencies that had to be factored into the running of the system. For example, there was the known reliability and tolerances of the hardware/software in use, such as the video transmitter, which turned out to be highly unreliable in practice and posed considerable problems when setting up the system. Orchestrators also drew on the known number of points of failure in the system such as the jacket wiring, batteries and the network connection, as well as factoring in the relative ease of diagnosis of those failures, along with an understanding of how those failures would manifest themselves (e.g., ping time-outs or static-laced ECG signals). Finally there were also 'dependencies' that existed between elements of the system (e.g., a non-working accelerometer generally implied that no other part of the system would be functional either). The layered strategy orchestrators employed helped them rationalise this potentially confusing space of possibilities through creating stability with a simple technique of building-up individual working components.

The layered strategy is thus intended to mitigate the effects of each systems' contingent character. Less problematic systems, meaning systems with fewer possible points of failure, with known higher reliability, and easier diagnosis of problems, are set up first. In the first vignette, one of these is the ECG, such as when orchestrators attempt to get a clean signal. Subsequently upon the foundations of these systems, more problematic systems, i.e., with more points of failure, more fragile hardware/software, less reliability, those that present more difficulty in diagnosing problems, are brought online. In this first vignette this is the audiovisual stream.

As we have seen in this vignette, one of the main resources for the orchestrator throughout the setting-up and running of F:TL was the ping command, which provides for much of the continuous basic status enquiries orchestrators have of the networked elements of the system such as the video transmitter. Response times from ping came to be used to interpret and predict video performance. For example, according to members of the team, a ping response of one to two milliseconds implied that the audiovisual quality would be high, ten to twenty milliseconds implying a possibility of video failure (i.e., video dropout), and latency values of greater than twenty milliseconds increasing the likelihood of failure further. It is also worth noting that orchestrators in this vignette make sense of each resource together, 'cross-referencing' between resources in order to determine the extent of troubles, what underlies them and how they might be mitigated or solved, such as how orchestrators here cross-referenced ping data with audiovisual data.

This working knowledge is a *spatial working knowledge*. We have previously seen knowledge of this kind in the Journey into Space, where the actor through experience with the interactive system and advice given to her came to develop an appreciation for the spatial contingencies of manipulations of the interface. As a result she was better able to guide participants around the space. Here the team of orchestrators develop an accomplished understanding (or "mental map" as one orchestrator puts it below) of the behaviour of the system through engaging in activities that 'map out' the ride. In this vignette this involved Orchestrator H setting the aerial positionings and alignments, and then walking the path of the ride (or some approximation thereof). The process furnishes orchestrators with information about areas in which loss of data is to be expected, and those in which signals are strong, thus informing later determinations of the status of the equipment. In the words of one orchestrator, they could then work out based upon this spatial knowledge whether they would be "looking to fade out the video and audio at particular point during the ride based on a mental map from the testing" or could trust the system to run on its own.

This point is also relevant for the general running of the system; that is, there is a level of 'acceptable error'. This is particularly visible at the beginning of the final vignette (see p. 114), where orchestrators are quickly satisfied that the system is working despite problems (such as dropouts) through identifying the causes of those problems as tolerable rather than catastrophic or fundamental.

6.1.2 Orchestrating with Actors (Vignette 2)

The event is in the format of a performance in front of an audience, and in many ways builds upon the existing practices of fairground ride operators. One of the ride operators who was interviewed highlighted how the ride itself must be operated in order to "play to the audience", particularly for rides such as the Booster where "you get five riders and you might get an audience of fifty people watching them". It is into this existing performative environment that the interactive technologies of F:TL are situated. Thus, a crucial job for the orchestrators is in applying their working knowledge of the technology (as seen extensively in the previous vignette), and, working together with actors, ensure that they keep the event running smoothly for the audience as well as the riders.

The opening sequence of this vignette begins with Alan, the 'professional rider', waiting on the ride outside having already been presented to the audience downstairs. The audience is moving upstairs and getting seated. Two of the orchestrators are outside on the main platform of the Booster ride (one of whom is Orchestrator H). Two more orchestrators are in the control area upstairs and are in radio

it's very variable

Fig. 6.8 Trevor physically annotating the visualisation. [Image used with permission; ©Mixed Reality Lab]

contact with one of the orchestrators on the ground. As the audience settles, a host at the front of the room provides a very brief introduction for the audience, introducing Trevor (Fig. 6.8), an expert in the sensing technology whose role it is to explain its operation and the nature of the visualisations. Once standing by the projection, Trevor goes on to describe the individual components of the visualisation.

Trevor: on the ECG ((pointing at the ECG display again)) we see the peak ((flattens hand and raises further into air)) when the heart is beat (0.4) we analyse it (.) and calculate ((points at heart rate display at bottom)) (0.2) the heart rate (0.6) we see Alan is still (1.2) ((moves hand horizontally)) sitting there and waiting (0.4) so his heart rate is not big ((inaudible)) seventy or ((inaudible)) we see it changes all the time ((waves left hand along the heart rate line)) it's very variable

Trevor's conduct with his hands at the visualisation highlights how variable the visualisation is and thus how to make sense of and 'read' what is a 'reasonable' or 'expected' level of variability in heart rate, ECG and so on (Fig. 6.8). He attempts to animate and augment what is on the display by translating trends into larger-scale physical movements. As his description comes to a close, Brian, another host, who is at the back of the room begins speaking.

Brian: I think (1.0) we'll see we'll um I'll cut to alan now and see what he's got to say what he's got to say just before we start the ride (1.0) ((beeping radio sound, Brian talks into radio)) right tim could you get alan to start speaking please?

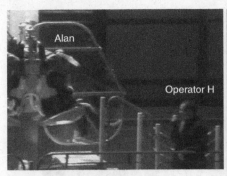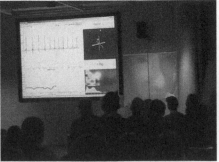

Fig. 6.9 Alan waiting on the ride with Orchestrator H on radio (*left*); Alan starts reporting (*right*). [Images used with permission; ©Mixed Reality Lab]

Alan is silent for approximately three seconds during which time the ride starts moving relatively slowly.

Alan: uh okay I'm assuming you can hear me (0.4) and it's pretty cold out here ((audience laughs)) (...) it's going to be an interesting ride and ((inaudible)) get spun around and it's actually quite (.) a pleasant (.) pleasant sensation (0.2) the view (.) up here (0.2) is phenomenal (1.0) and (0.2) the ground (.) comes rushing towards you pretty quickly here I'm not really going fast yet so

It is notable that Alan mentions the ride's slowness. The ride was, in fact, intentionally run slowly at the beginning as experience had shown that this increased the reliability of wireless communications, providing stability during the moments when Brian 'hands over' to Alan. As a professional rider, Alan has already been on the ride many times, but each time he must describe his experience anew. Although he can talk to his audience he cannot see or hear them in return and so must broadcast himself to unseen-but-assumed audience (Fig. 6.9).

Alan now continues his reportage. However, as the ride speeds up so his talk begins to feature more exclamation than description.

Alan: and I've (.) started to rotate oh here it goes and I'M UPSIDE DOWN (.) O:::H! ((audience laughs))
(2.0)
Brian: brian to tim ((an orchestrator outside)) can you go faster please?
((audience laughs))
(1.0)
Alan: the ground's ((inaudible)) vE::RY QUICKLY
((audience laughs))

Although it is in the planned schedule of events that the ride will indeed speed up after a short period, Brian theatrically highlights this moment to the audience. Brian's statement transforms what might normally be a private coordination between the technical team into a public one.

At this point there is sudden silence as the video freezes and audio drops out. The audience laughs and starts talking amongst itself, with some audience members at the back looking out the small windows to the ride itself.

Host: have we lost him?
Brian: are we (0.2) I think we've lost alan ((laughs))
(3.6)
((video resumes and Alan can be heard laughing))
Host: no he's back=
Brian: =oh no he's back
((audience laugh))
(3.0)
Alan: WO:HO::
(4.6)
((Video and audio freeze again))
Brian: o::h

Brian and the host comment on what is observable to the audience, such as "losing" Alan (i.e., the audiovisual stream freezing), getting him "back" (i.e., resumption of the audiovisual stream) and finally "losing" him yet again. It is part of the performative work of Brian and the Host to weave Alan's broadcast into the ongoing trajectory of the performance, highlighting his comments, covering during disconnections, and fading him in and out as necessary.

Brian: okay I'll get him off the ride now I think he's had enough (0.8) okay can we let err let alan off please?
((video and audio begin to work again))
Alan: I can't really talk ((fades out))

As we saw earlier, Alan's more sober description became more interspersed with laughter and exclamation. Here Alan states as he is faded out that he is finding it difficult to talk. Even though Alan is a 'professional rider', there are times when he may 'lose control' to some extent due to the extreme physical nature of the experience.

Finally, Trevor returns to briefly describe Alan's heart rate, explaining that he can "start to relax now", highlighting the decrease with his hand once again. Brian then closes the performance.

Brian: brilliant that was alan on the booster! ((claps))
((audience claps))
(7.0)
Host: lovely (0.4) so we're in operations as you can see (0.4) lots going on lot of scientists (0.2) a lot of equipment ((large projection switches to a blue screen. Host presses buzzer, audience laughs, goes over to centre and picks up phone)) (7.0) control ((puts down phone)) apparently we're going to send some of you into space

6.1.2.1 Actors and Orchestrators, Legibility and Visibility

The actors here—particularly Brian, the host and Trevor—must make *visible* and *legible* to the audience the various components of the presentation. In this second vignette, Trevor describes the various components of the visualisation as well as annotating them with gestures in order to provide information about how to make sense of the various graphs and also what the expected behaviour of the various traces will be. In order to do this he verbally describes as well as indicating trends and patterns with his hands. Later on in the vignette when Brian thinks that Alan has "had enough" and requests that the ride end, Trevor then accounts for Alan's heart rate is decreasing, suggesting he is "relax[ing]". Trevor thus makes legible for the audience the meaning of the display and its sometimes subtle changes. He does this through description and physically augmenting changes and trends by tracing them out with his hands.

Conversely, orchestrators deliberately ensure that their activities are not legible or visible. Orchestrators in F:TL run the technology in a location at the very back of the room along a series of desks (Fig. 6.3). The audience members face away from them, seated towards the projection area in which actors run the performance through talks, presentation of the data, and interludes. The orchestrator's activities are shrouded in darkness, their manipulations of the various pieces of technology are small and illegible to the audience, whereas the actors make use of a large projected display, and as we have just seen, make its contents legible to the audience through animated gesture and talk. The differing spaces in which actors and orchestrators perform their work is sometimes used by the actors, characterising this orchestration work as "equipment" and "scientists" and—although not demonstrated in this vignette however occurring in others—often annotated by indicating this work of running the event happens "over there" whilst pointing towards the back of the auditorium. Thus the contrasting spaces, legibilities, visibilities, and bodily and talk activities that orchestrators and actors engage in may characterised respectively as 'behind-the-scenes' and 'centre-stage' settings.

6.1.2.2 Weaving the Performance Together

Actors and orchestrators operate within different spaces, with different mandates and in different capacities. However, the actors and orchestrators must *collaboratively weave* the various components of the performance together. In this vignette, Alan has his ride experience presented to the waiting audience. The data transmission is approached by the other actors in the auditorium with a number of strategies to manage contingencies as well as to integrate the presentation into the trajectory of the performance at large. This begins with an actor, Brian, 'bookending' the presentation of the data by transforming a private 'orchestration communication' into a public one by asking Tim, an orchestrator in front of the ride, to cue Alan. Alan's broadcast is performed for an audience he cannot see, with Brian highlighting the moment of the ride's speeding up with another public moment of orchestration-like work. During moments of audiovisual dropout, the actors (Brian and the host) then theatrically highlight and emphasise the failures to the audience as part of their work of accounting for data loss. Brian performs some final 'bookending' in deciding when Alan has "had enough", ensuring that the length of the broadcast is woven into the pacing of the performance in general.

Fig. 6.10 Orchestrator F attaches the ECG electrodes to Sally. [Image used with permission; ©Mixed Reality Lab]

6.1.3 Orchestrating Participation (Vignette 3)

In the third vignette, a member of the public, Sally, has won an opportunity to ride the Booster in the public lottery. After Alan has been on the ride, the host explains that a member of the audience with a winning ticket (which they purchased to attend the event) will go on the ride, and begins to pick ticket numbers which she then calls out. When the number that matches the one on her ticket is called, Sally indicates she has won, and two actors guide her from the audience, along with her friend, Anne. They exit the auditorium and go down the stairs, then exit the building and walk towards the ride. Sally must now put on the necessary equipment. Also present are Orchestrator H, J (filming), T, and F, who in this case is female so as to avoid potential embarrassment when fitting sensors to Sally's torso. Standing near the ride, and after a short moment of discussion about the cold and "nerves", Sally begins to don the equipment, the first element of which is the heart monitor.

> Orchestrator F: we need we need to attach these ((holding up patch)) (.) here and here on your skin so I'll do that over here

At this point Sally and Orchestrator F, who step away from the main group, creating a more private area in which Sally is facing away from the group as the sensors are placed on her torso (Fig. 6.10). The setup procedure continues as Orchestrator H now helps Sally into the jacket and helmet (Fig. 6.11).

> Sally: do I need to take my glasses off=
> Orchestrator H: =not the glasses but I think the (.) the ((holds hand to back of his head)) ponytail

it's a bit loose   now let me see

Fig. 6.11   Orchestrator H fitting the jacket and helmet (*left*), and appraising the equipment (*right*). [Images used with permission; ©Mixed Reality Lab]

((Sally undoes her ponytail))
(40.0)
Orchestrator H: ((moves around to the side of Sally, holding the helmet's camera)) is that relatively even? (2.0) does that fit? ((Orchestrator H moves round the back again))
Sally: yeah yeah it's a bit (.) it's a bit (.) loose
Orchestrator H: ((moves helmet left and right with hands)) is that ok ((inaudible))
(…)
(14.0)
Orchestrator H: now we need ((takes wires to the left of him)) to attach these to the sensors ((inaudible)) the other one goes over here ((points at Sally's right side)) ((inaudible)) ((to Orchestrator F)) you put those just here ((places palms on side of his torso)) yeah? ((inaudible))

Shortly after this is done, Orchestrator H then inspects the equipment.

Orchestrator H: ((stands up straight now, steps back from the jacket)) now let me see (0.4) we've got everything

As the first part of the donning procedure comes to a close, Orchestrator H physically steps back to appraise the situation. Setting up thus far required the removal of Sally's pony tail, getting the fit of the helmet correct so that Sally's face will be in view, and is comfortable for her. The equipment must be 'just right' in preparedness for the ready signal as well as being relatively comfortable for the rider. This takes a significant amount of time and Orchestrator H has at this point already spent several minutes getting to the moment at which it is possible perform the next task, marked by his physical appraisal of the state of the equipment (Fig. 6.11, right). This second phase of readying involves testing the various functions of the equipment, which Orchestrator H now does, taking a couple of minutes to do so.

Orchestrator H: ((walks back away from Sally, grabs her jumper and guides her into a position)) could you stand here for a second and just stand this way exactly that way and ((camera operator)) if you could just hold it back (.) a bit so we can get the
((Orchestrator H goes to pick up radio))
(6.0)
Orchestrator H: ((speaking into radio, oriented towards main building)) hello er we've got everything switched on are you getting data? (10.0) you getting er the video as well? (3.0)

just count again

Fig. 6.12   Orchestrator H tests the equipment (*left*), Sally and Anne are seated on the ride (*right*). [Images used with permission; ©Mixed Reality Lab]

shall we test audio (. . .) ((Orients body halfway between building and Sally, glances at Sally))
so the err (.) just count or something ((glances back up to building, back down the Sally again))
((Orchestrator H glances between tho building and Sally frequently for the next section))
Sally: ((looking at Orchestrator H)) one two three four five six seven I'm really scared at the moment I might actually crap myself any minute now (.) so is that ((inaudible))
Orchestrator H: just count again
Sally: okay one two three four five six seven
((Sally continues counting several times whilst Orchestrator H talks with upstairs))
Orchestrator H: confirmed (.) okay that's fine thanks ((turns towards Sally, nodding)) s'alright

The equipment is now designated as working. Sally, Orchestrator H and the others must wait in readiness for the signal to start the ride.

Unknown: how long have we got before everyone gets on it?
Orchestrator H: ((to Sally)) we've got about ten minutes but lu- yesterday it varied by quite a lot so I hope it will be ten minutes

This sequence shows the considerable time and work required to get the rider and equipment to a state of readiness. The rider must stand at particular orientations so as to align aerials ("stand this way exactly") for lengthy periods conducting tests in concert with Orchestrator H (Fig. 6.12, left).

After further waiting, the signal is given to Orchestrator H who then suggests they "go on" the ride. Trailing wires, battery levels and so on then are checked again. Sally and Anne wait for the ride to begin, chatting (Fig. 6.12, right).

Sally: it's really cold isn't it brrr is this all part of the thing to like proper heighten our senses or something so we're really screwed up before we go on it? Do you offer post-traumatic stress counselling sessions?

Finally the signal is given that the presentations upstairs have come to a close and that the audience is ready. Sally begins talking as the ride's steps retract, with the ground staff present on the lawn watching.

Sally: um: hello:: um I'm sitting on the ride slightly scared but um really really excited so it should be cool (1.0) if I die I love you all (3.0) shall I just keep talking? oh the ride's about to start! okay we're currently going up oh this is so cool! we're kinda hanging forwards and um we're coming down to the ground we're going quite slow at the moment (1.0) I'm absolutely fine at the moment (7.0) okay yeah they're speeding up a bit now this is absolutely brilliant (2.0) um yeah quite high O::H ((screams)) okay that was cool oh my go::d wow! ((screams))

After the ride comes to a stop, Sally and Anne are helped off by Orchestrator H. Like Alan in the previous vignette, Sally is broadcasting to the unseen-but-assumed audience. Similarly to Alan she also begins by providing a running-commentary of her experience until she breaks into less controlled screaming and exclaiming as the ride speeds up.

6.1.3.1 Orchestrating in a Distributed Environment

One of the key features of this vignette is how orchestration work is *distributed* across sites, with orchestrators maintaining *mutual awareness* and *synchrony* with the performance as it progresses. These three aspects together are important for ensuring the smooth orchestration of participation.

Firstly this vignette provides an interesting complement to the first. Here the orchestrators maintain a shared awareness of the amount of time left till the participant, Sally, ideally should get on the ride and when the ride itself must begin for the audience. Their run-up to this moment is taken up with repeatedly testing and checking the system to ensure that the critical data is broadcast successfully so that the actors in the auditorium may smoothly conduct the presentation.

However, Orchestrator H is located in front of the ride, sometimes with a number of other orchestrators and actors, whereas the other orchestrators are located at the back of the auditorium along with all the technology required for presentation of the data streams. Furthermore, Orchestrator H's relationship with fellow orchestrators is somewhat asymmetric, in terms of physical and digital access. Each party has access to different sets of these resources. Orchestrator H can modify the positionings and orientations of the aerials on the ground; he has access to the jacket and can change its state in various ways (e.g., cycling the power on the video transmitter, realigning aerials, shifting equipment between the jacket's pockets), but is unable to see or hear any output from the sensors in the jacket itself (besides power lights, and checking battery voltage levels with a multi-meter) and so must test the data streams via radio. He also has access to the ride itself via communications with the orchestrator operating the ride booth (which we shall see more of in the next vignette). However, he is unable to see or hear what is occurring in the control area (i.e., where presentations of the data are performed). The orchestrators in the control area upstairs, on the other hand, can see and hear the jacket's sensor outputs (i.e., audiovisual, accelerometer and ECG data), and they have direct access to the activities going on in the auditorium with which they can coordinate their activities.

Being distributed in this asymmetric way means that orchestrators must establish and generally maintain control of the system through continual contact and mutual awareness (via radio) between control area the orchestrator by the ride. It is worth noting that this has been seen in the first vignette already, where orchestrators communicate the current audiovisual quality to Orchestrator H.

This leads into a feature of orchestration that is central to keeping the individual strands of the performance together. Orchestrators must synchronise their distributed activities with actors as part of presenting the performance to the audience. In this third vignette, Orchestrator H and his fellow orchestrators discuss what the likely time to wait will be so that, as mentioned above, Sally's data is broadcast at precisely the right moment. Similarly, as we shall see in the fourth vignette, orchestrators must prepare the jacket and its data transmission, consult ride operators for an 'opening' in the ride, and get the participant on, as well as dealing with the resolution of a moment of crisis. Thus synchrony becomes a major concern for Orchestrator H as he must get the participant onto the ride at the right time.

6.1.3.2 Orchestrating Transition

The other central feature of orchestrating participation that this vignette provides an instance of is audience-participant transition. The vignette exposes the role of the actor in that transition, the way in which participation becomes manifest for an audience member, and most importantly for this chapter's study, exposes the part orchestrators play in running that audience-participant transition behind-the-scenes. Transition between audience and participant within One Rock was an ad-hoc affair managed and negotiated between two visitors around the physical arrangement of the Telescope and surrounding objects. F:TL is a much larger-scale performance and employs carefully crafted techniques for enabling the transition of a given audience member to participant seated on the ride, broadcasting their experience to other members of the audience. This transition is achieved through a number of methods.

Immediately of interest within this vignette's end is the *orientation of the participant* to the nature of the performance, developed by the collaborative work of the actors and orchestrators in running the performance. This orientation is, in essence, the expectation on the participant (here, it is Sally) to provide some kind of talk when on the ride, which itself is vital to her transition from audience member to participant. This orientation is achieved both through the way in which participation is framed by the 'professional rider', Alan, as seen in the previous vignette, and the elicitations of the orchestrators and actors as they come into contact with Sally here in this vignette. When Alan is presented to the audience in the second vignette, hits delivery—i.e., one of continuous description of his experience as it happens— provides a frame for Sally's own participation here. This initial framing, coupled with information from the orchestration team gives Sally a particular framework with which to participate in the lottery, the ride experience, and leads to the character of her commentary presented here. We also saw framings of participation in docent-visitor engagements with the Telescope device in Chap. 4, although over a much smaller interactional timescale.

A more detailed observation within this is that the transition is achieved via *performative routine* of the lottery. This special moment of chance selection by the actors is used to begin the transition period for a member of the audience as they are whisked away by actors to the ride.

As we have seen, an *equipment-donning* procedure is commenced by orchestrators. This moment is lengthy and must be carefully followed. In the vignette this involves various stages before Sally may even step onto the ride: Sally has the ECG electrodes placed on her in a private space; she then has her ponytail removed so that the helmet fits; the jacket and the helmet are adjusted so as to be comfortable; Orchestrator H appraises the situation; next Sally must stand with a particular orientation and in a particular location in order to be ready for the test; Orchestrator H asks Sally to count continuously whilst he discusses with the orchestrators in the control area whether the equipment is working; then there is a long wait until the audience in the auditorium is ready for Sally during which time she gets on the ride; there is some final checking of wires and battery levels; Sally and her friend wait for some time longer whilst sitting on the ride; and finally, the ride runs. This involved process forms part of the way that transition is achieved, serving both an entirely practical purpose and, as Sally reflects (she wonders out loud whether the process is to "heighten [their] senses"), to increase anticipation before the ride itself.

The *location of the participant* in the environment is also of importance. At first Sally is made visible to the audience through the lottery routine, however subsequently is taken behind-the-scenes in order to engage in equipment-donning and testing whilst the audience are presented with some further talks. Sally is then is subsequently broadcast to the audience as part of the 'centre-stage' of the performance in the auditorium, where she performs remotely for them.

Although we have already seen transitions before in this book, this chapter has introduced transitions which involve greater physical change (e.g., donning equipment, moving to a different location), and, crucially, significant amounts of orchestration work in managing the technology employed during those moments of transition. We can connect Sally's transitional journey from audience member to participant with notions of trajectory introduced in the previous chapter. Benford and Giannachi fit transitions such as these within a larger framework of multiple interactional trajectories that may be traced through an experience [3]. In their framework, these transitions are critical moments in trajectories where "users must cross between spaces, rub up against schedules, take on new roles, or engage with interfaces" [3, p. 350].

6.1.4 Managing Intervention (Vignette 4)

This final vignette focusses upon the control area upstairs (see Fig. 6.3, bottom), during a time after both Alan and Sally have been on the Booster. The audience are now on the lawn in front of the ride, either queuing, on the ride itself, or spectating. Also on the lawn is Orchestrator H, helping a (female) rider who has volunteered herself from the queue to don the equipment (Fig. 6.14, right). Orchestrators A, S, T and J are in the control area (Fig. 6.14, left). The orchestrators have in front of them on one screen the feed from the rider's helmet camera, and on another they have the visualisation that was presented to the audience in Fig. 6.8. This can be

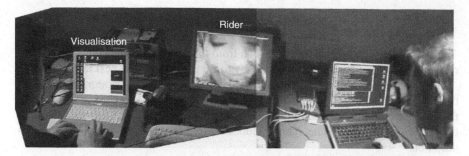

Fig. 6.13 The control area in detail. [Image used with permission; ©Mixed Reality Lab]

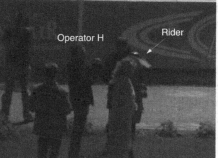

hello there what's the reception like?

Fig. 6.14 The control area (*left*), Orchestrator H preparing the rider (*right*). [Images used with permission; ©Mixed Reality Lab]

seen in Fig. 6.13. The audio from the rider's helmet camera is available using a pair of headphones attached to one of the machines, and the orchestrators are able to see the ride from afar through the windows either side of the control area.

> Orchestrator S: yeah (.) I can hear audio
> (1.4)
> Orchestrator A: we have (0.4) err audio (0.8) do we have ECG and (.) accelerometer?=
> Orchestrator S: =no not yet
> (1.0)
> Orchestrator A: not even accelerometer cos I don't think he turned that off

Shortly after this, Orchestrator H radios in to Orchestrator A.

> Orchestrator H: hello there what's the reception like?
> (...)
> Orchestrator H: is the video working though?
> Orchestrator S: video's working fine=
> Orchestrator A: ((to Orchestrator H) =yeah the video's working fine and audio ((inaudible))
> Orchestrator H: okay so can we go on the next ride yeah?
> (1.0)
> Orchestrator A: ((to Orchestrator H)) having having said that video has just closed but I think once you oh it's back again (.) I think once you go on the ride it'll be okay

Orchestrator J: I think there's somebody (.) somebody standing in front of her so probably she's blocking the transmission

Once Orchestrator H has the go-ahead from the control area he consults with the ride operator to indicate that they are ready to get the rider on the next available ride.

This sequence exhibits the counterpart perspective to Orchestrator H's work in the previous vignette. Here we see the extensive work of the team upstairs in getting the ECG, accelerometer and audiovisual streams functioning to such a degree that they are in a 'rideable' state. This includes reasoning about the causes of wireless drop outs.

In addition to this, the challenges posed by distribution of the orchestrators comes into play here once again, since there is the potential of sensor interference from audience in front of and milling around the ride. Here this requires that orchestrators monitor the space around the ride as well in order to fully determine the source of problems.

Now that the system is in a readied state and the last ride has come to a stop the rider and her co-rider are taken by Orchestrator H to the front of the queue, where they walk onto the Booster platform together. Shortly after this point, when the other carriage is being loaded, the rider attempts to contact the ground (Fig. 6.15). In fact, her audio is not generally audible but is channelled into some headphones which Orchestrator S has in his hands. However, she probably does not know this.

Rider: scuse me can you hear me?[3]
Orchestrator S: she's saying can we hear her
(1.0)
Orchestrator A: ((to Orchestrator H)) she's saying can we hear her (.) wave to her or something
Rider: scuse me
(1.0)
Orchestrator H: yeah I don't ((inaudible)) forward (0.8) she sounded quite scared
Rider: are you sure nick? ((Nick is sitting next to her))
(2.0)
Orchestrator A: ((laughs)) (1.4) excellent that's what we want to hear
Rider: hello control?
(3.0)
Orchestrator S: she thinks we can hear us
Rider: control please
(1.0)
Orchestrator A: she thinks we can hear her (1.0) her heart rate's gone down a bit now (…)
Rider: okay control room can we please turn it off for Nick?
Orchestrator A: I can't quite see her eyes but
Rider: he's really scared
Orchestrator S: she said she's really scared
Rider: please can you get the ride off?
Orchestrator S: she said she's really scared can we take her down
Orchestrator A: ((to Orchestrator H)) apparently apparently the ((inaudible)) on the top says she's really scared can we take her down

---

[3]Note that the rider's talk in this and later transcripts has been 'artificially' integrated into the discussions occurring in the control area, and that members of the team can only hear rider talk via a single pair of headphones.

she really is saying that she wants down?

Fig. 6.15 The rider communicates with the control area and members of the control area glance at one another. [Image used with permission; ©Mixed Reality Lab]

Orchestrator H: sorry?
Orchestrator S: I think we should (.) I think we should pretend we haven't heard
Orchestrator H: sorry could you repeat
Orchestrator T: do you think it seriously or?
Orchestrator A: ((to Orchestrator H)) ap apparently the girl on the top is really scared can we take her down
Rider: there's nothing to be scared hey
(8.0)
Orchestrator A: how how how scared do you think she is (.) she's not looking too=
Orchestrator J: =I think it's natural reaction though
Orchestrator H: she really is saying that she wants down?
Rider: hello control can you please hear me?
((Orchestrator A looks at Orchestrator S, who has the headphones to one ear during this))
(3.0)
Orchestrator S: s'ye yeah ((takes headphones away from ear)) she keeps saying (1.4) can she come down=
Rider: hello ple::ase
Orchestrator A: =she does keep saying that I mean we might ((inaudible)) actually so maybe bring her down if you can
Rider: hello::

As the ride proper begins, what is a critical moment for the technical team arrives.

Orchestrator A: how how's she looking is she still=
Rider: stop stop please stop please stop no::
Orchestrator H: =((inaudible))
Orchestrator S: yeah she keeps she keeps shouting out stop
(0.4)

Orchestrator A: ((to Orchestrator H)) she she keeps shouting out stop (.) go go and see the
ride operators ((inaudible))

At this point, Orchestrator H can be seen moving towards the booth in order to
instruct the ride operator to slow or stop the ride. Shortly after this the ride is slowed
down, but not stopped, which appears to resolve the crisis.

Rider: are you okay? nick are you okay you okay you okay? nick are you okay? look look it's
((inaudible)) no it's okay
Orchestrator S: no she says it's okay she says it's [okay]
Orchestrator A: [oh   ] (.) sorry (.) Orchestrator H she
says it's okay now (.) she says it's okay

6.1.4.1 Monitoring and Intervening

Orchestrators manage the crisis in this vignette through careful *monitoring and intervention* [9]. In a sense there is nothing 'new' about such orchestrator activities.
Indeed, as one ride operator who was interviewed stated, part of their work practice
involves developing a sensitivity towards "spot[ting] somebody who's a little bit on
the timid side" within the queue, verbally checking with them "if they're okay to
go on [...] the ride" once they get to the head of the queue, and thus providing
an opportunity for an unprepared rider to opt-out of the ride. However, the use of
the physiological data and video stream introduces the possibility of monitoring the
state of the riders in ways beyond the normal practices of professional ride operators
in attending to the riders' demeanours as they wait in line.

As we have seen in this vignette, the orchestrators engage in continuous monitoring, drawing on a multiplicity of resources (the rider's appearance, their talk,
physiological data, the experiences of Orchestrator H). This monitoring is also coupled with the coordination of a distributed, disjointed team. The main work for the
technical team in this episode, both on-the-ground and in the control area—like the
professional ride operator's job—is in determining the 'seriousness' of the situation
for the rider, and then acting appropriately. Experiencing fear is a presumed possibility (if not an expectation) with a ride like the Booster, and the technical team must be
sensitive to 'normal' or 'expected' levels of fear, as opposed to 'serious' fear which
calls for a different course of action for the team (i.e., intervention). Playing a further
part in this determination work is the nature of the relationship between the technical
team and the professional ride operators, namely that the technical team are not in
direct control of the ride and therefore must also decide whether they will intervene,
and how that intervention might take place in the context of a professionally-run fairground ride. For the technical team, as the situation progresses, a variety of methods
come into play in determining the seriousness of the unfolding situation: Orchestrator H observes: "she sounded quite scared"; Orchestrator A considers her heart rate
and facial expression ("how's she looking"); Orchestrator T explicitly introduces
the issue of seriousness ("do you think it seriously or?"); and finally Orchestrator S
reflects on her persistence ("she keeps saying", "she keeps shouting out stop").

Initially the rider's communication attempts are woven into a joke ("wave to her
or something"), and the team "pretend [they] haven't heard", relying on plausible

deniability. This plausible deniability can only be sustained for so long, however, due to the determined level of seriousness, and as such the team must begin to consider stopping the ride. This strategy, however, carries with it a number of significant overheads. Stopping the ride or slowing it down just for one person obviously disrupts the experience for co-riders and requires intervention by the orchestrators. The orchestrators are responsible for generating and maintaining the 'thrillfulness' of the event for those taking part in it, yet at the same time must sensitive to their individual experiences and how those experiences may impact other riders. The difficulty in maintaining this balance is revealed by the detailed consideration the team make using the various displays and sensors at their disposal. Thus the overheads of intervention—i.e., stopping the ride—are weighed by orchestrators against interpretations of the heart rate of the participant, the looks of her eyes and the content of her talk. After discussion between the orchestrators around topics of whether to "think it seriously" that she is scared enough to perform the intervention, or whether it is a "natural reaction", a decision is made and the intervention gets underway. The critical factor in intervention is this trade-off between the growing need for action to be taken and the overheads involved in that action.

6.2 Discussion

In these four vignettes we have seen how the role of the *orchestrator* plays an important part in many aspects of running interactive technologies in public performance environments. The issues surrounding orchestration are often a key concern for designers of public technologies more broadly. This section summarises the basic attributes of orchestration, and surveys some existing literature on orchestration with respect to the action exhibited in F:TL. It also summarises key orchestrator relationships to other roles, such as *actors, participants* and *audience*, highlighting a simple division of the setting into *behind-the-scenes* and *centre-stage*. Finally, the key aspects involved in *transition* between audience and participant are reviewed.

Previous studies have explored orchestration activities in a range of performance and gaming environments, the findings of which this chapter's analysis has often drawn upon. The first of these is Desert Rain [9]. This was a performance in which a small group of players drawn from the general public explored a virtual world, each with individual objectives to achieve, against the backdrop of the 1991 Gulf War. In order to run this experience, a number of orchestrators engaged in behind-the-scenes activities, monitoring players as they navigated the virtual world (ensuring player engagement was not endangered, such as players getting 'lost'), and intervening when and as necessary in order to sustain player engagement. Koleva et al. unpack the variety of orchestration activities that are produced behind-the-scenes. These include use of a monitoring interface that provided an audio link with players, along with controls for modifying the virtual environment; orchestrators also had physical access to players' individual cubicles from which they were playing. Interventions were either entirely virtual and performed without player awareness (for example, orchestrators subtly 'nudging' the virtual position of players when 'stuck'), or could be more invasive and perceptible to the player, ranging "off-face" (less invasive, performed via audio link) to full face-to-face interventions (where orchestrators stepped into the cubicles with players) [9].

This approach was similar to that employed in Avatar Farm, an interactive drama conducted in a virtual environment [6], in which 'invisible' technical team members performed behind-the-scenes tasks in order to move the drama forward. The performance art game we have seen already, Can You See Me Now?, is also relevant here. In this, orchestration was distributed between performers on the streets and those running the game in a control room. Here orchestration required mutual awareness between those on the city streets and those elsewhere, as well as developing a working knowledge of 'good' and 'bad' areas in which the game might be played [5]. Other related work has examined how the production of a narrative is collaboratively constructed between those running a mobile SMS-based game and those playing it [4].

The vignettes that have been presented in this chapter have either contributed to or built upon observations developed in this existing literature. Throughout the vignettes the technical team members have been referred to as orchestrators. They had to navigate a complex set of technical contingencies and dependencies from the assemblies of technology that were involved in the running of F:TL. In doing so, orchestrators developed a spatial working knowledge of these contingencies, employing this understanding as part of a layered approach to set-up. This builds upon notions of working knowledge by detailing the process of setting-up as well as exploring how that working knowledge is employed during the performance. Orchestrators also worked closely with actors in order to ensure the smooth running of the performance. Whilst both being members of a 'professional' team, the orchestrators and the actors involved in F:TL worked in substantively different roles. As we have seen in the previous chapter, actors run the performance, guiding participants and/or audience through some experience. The orchestrators work alongside actors in order to support their performance. To this end, actors purposefully made their activities highly visible and legible to the audience, whilst orchestrator activities were purposefully hidden and illegible. This division in terms of the contrasting way performance activities are done has been characterised in the vignettes simply as 'behind-the-scenes'—i.e., where orchestrators conduct their activities—and 'centre-stage'—where actors do their corresponding work, developing existing notions within the literature outlined above regarding how these different settings are actually established. Whilst this division is maintained, we saw how orchestrators and actors collaboratively weaved together the elements of the performance for the audience.

Orchestrators were also involved in orchestrating the activities of audience members as they transitioned to participants. Like some of the previous studies on orchestration, orchestrators in F:TL conducted their work in a distributed manner, overcoming potential problems through establishing and maintaining mutual awareness across sites, and crucially, ensuring synchrony between their own activities and the trajectory of the performance in collaboration with actors. In transitioning to participants, orchestrators were involved with actors in orienting the audience member to the features of participation (e.g., the professional rider's framing of their partic-ipation, conducting performative routines like the lottery). Transition also involved equipment-donning, relocating the participant behind-the-scenes and sychronising their participation with the actors presenting to the audience.

Finally orchestrators were also responsible for intervention, a key activity also for orchestrators in Desert Rain, Avatar Farm, and, as we shall see in the next chap-ter, the performance art game Uncle Roy All Around You [2]. This required care-ful management of the needs of maintaining a thrilling experience for participants, whilst being sensitive to the potential for 'expected' fear to turn into 'serious' fear that needed to be acted upon. This aspect of balance is in many ways similar to the problems facing Desert Rain orchestrators, who had to perform intervention to help players whilst ensuring this did not damage the players' engagement with the experience. As we saw in the final vignette, these responsibilities over intervention may also have an ethical dimension, such as having to consider the welfare of other members of the performance, particularly participants and audience.

6.3 Summary

In this chapter we have seen, via a series of vignettes, how the role of the *orchestra-tor* featured in running the F:TL events. In addition to presenting this new concept, this chapter has built upon the studies of One Rock and the Journey into Space and elaborated on the roles of *participants* and *actors*, and *audience-participant tran-sitions*. Examining the roles of orchestrator and actor together has in turn exposed two broad performative settings in which they do their work: *behind-the-scenes* and *centre-stage*.

Orchestration was deconstructed through considering a number of facets of behind-the-scenes work, as exposed by the vignettes and the study of F:TL in gen-eral. These facets were the orchestrator's layered and spatial working knowledge of the system employed in the course of navigating a complex problem space; physi-cal distribution of the orchestrators and ensuring mutual awareness across sites as a strategy for tackling this; performing interventions depending upon the trade-off between the necessity to act and overheads involved in acting; and finally working to support actors' activities through operating in synchrony with them in their work to weave together strands of the performance.

The job of orchestrators was also set in contrast with actors' work; orchestrators operate behind-the-scenes whereas actors operate centre-stage, contrasting between more public and more private spaces, and opposite levels of perceptual legibility for the audience. Orchestrators' relationship to participants was also presented through discussing audience-participant transition in greater depth. In this form of transition some key stages were identified: the performative routine of the lottery, donning the equipment, being taken behind-the-scenes, and being oriented to the nature of participation in F:TL.

The next chapter will expand this even further, both through elaborating upon framework concepts covered previously, but also circumscribing the roles themselves, developing concepts of transition and piecing together a more complete picture of the different settings explored so far. In introducing Goffman's notion of a 'frame' delimiting the experience, the next chapter presents an analysis of a performance that purposefully plays with the boundaries of that performance, and in doing so provides an interesting breach that exposes how frames are constructed, managed, and exploited by artists.

References

1. BBC 1 News (Live), interview with Brendan Walker on Oblivion: Thrill Laboratory, broadcast 19/09/07
2. Benford, S., Crabtree, A., Reeves, S., Flintham, M., Drozd, A., Sheridan, J.G., Dix, A.: The frame of the game: Blurring the boundary between fiction and reality in mobile experiences. In: Proceedings of SIGCHI Conference on Human Factors in Computing Systems (CHI), pp. 427–436. ACM, New York (2006). doi:10.1145/1124772.1124836
3. Benford, S., Giannachi, G.: Performing Mixed Reality. MIT Press, Cambridge (2011, in press)
4. Crabtree, A., Benford, S., Capra, M., Flintham, M., Drozd, A., Tandavanitj, N., Adams, M., Row-Farr, J.: The cooperative work of gaming: orchestrating a mobile SMS game. Comput. Support. Coop. Work J. Collab. Comput. (JCSCW) (2007). Special Issue on Leisure Technologies
5. Crabtree, A., Benford, S., Rodden, T., Greenhalgh, C., Flintham, M., Anastasi, R., Drozd, A., Adams, M., Row-Farr, J., Tandavanitj, N., Steed, A.: Orchestrating a mixed reality game 'on the ground'. In: Proceedings of the SIGCHI Conference on Human Factors in Computing Systems, pp. 391–398. ACM, New York (2004). doi:10.1145/985692.985742
6. Drozd, A., Bowers, J., Benford, S., Greenhalgh, C., Fraser, M.: Collaboratively improvising magic: an approach to managing participation in an on-line drama. In: Proceedings of European Conference on Computer-Supported Cooperative Work (ECSCW), pp. 159–178. Kluwer Academic, Dordrecht (2001)
7. Egglestone, S.R., Marshall, J., Walker, B., Rowland, D., Benford, S., Rodden, T.: The Bronco: A proof-of-concept adaptive fairground ride. In: ACE'09: Proceedings of the International Conference on Advances in Computer Entertainment Technology, pp. 371–374. ACM, New York (2009). doi:10.1145/1690388.1690463
8. Greenhalgh, C., French, A., Tennant, P., Humble, J., Crabtree, A.: From replaytool to digital replay system. In: Online Proceedings of the 3rd International Conference on e-Social Science (2007)
9. Koleva, B., Taylor, I., Benford, S., Fraser, M., Greenhalgh, C., Schnädelbach, H., vom Lehn, D., Heath, C., Row-Farr, J., Adams, M.: Orchestrating a mixed reality performance. In: Proceedings of SIGCHI Conference on Human Factors in Computing Systems (CHI), pp. 38–45. ACM, New York (2001). doi:10.1145/365024.365033
10. Schnädelbach, H., Egglestone, S.R., Reeves, S., Benford, S., Walker, B.: Performing thrill: designing telemetry systems and spectator interfaces for amusement rides. In: Proceedings of SIGCHI Conference on Human Factors in Computing Systems (CHI), pp. 1167–1176. ACM, New York (2008). doi:10.1145/1357054.1357238
11. Walker, B., Schnädelbach, H., Egglestone, S.R., Clark, A., Orbach, T., Wright, M., Ng, K.H., French, A., Rodden, T., Benford, S.: Augmenting amusement rides with telemetry. In: ACE'07: Proceedings of the International Conference on Advances in Computer Entertainment Technology, pp. 115–122. ACM, New York (2007). doi:10.1145/1255047.1255070

Chapter 7
Frames and Bystanders: Uncle Roy All Around You

Building on the complex distributed performance of Fairground: Thrill Laboratory, this chapter turns to the final study, which expands the concerns of the book to consider the boundaries of the interactive experience in which orchestrators, actors, participants and audience interact via technology. This expansion comes from examining mobile-based interactions on city streets as part of a performance art game, where distinctions between the real and the fictional are deliberately blurred. The ambiguity of this environment forces us to consider the *framing* of interaction with technology in public settings, and how this becomes a crucial part of systems design. A byproduct of analysing the work of establishing and maintaining a framed 'game world' is, particularly for experiences taking place on city streets, the increased relevance *bystanders*, who become unwittingly drawn into the digitally-mediated interactions of players.

The game which helps reveal these interesting aspects of interaction with technology in public settings is Uncle Roy All Around You (URAAY), an interactive mobile experience designed by the performance art group Blast Theory. In URAAY, members of the public, equipped with hand-held devices (PDAs), undertake a journey through a city in search of a shadowy and mysterious character called Uncle Roy. These 'street players' are introduced to the game through a scripted briefing in which they are asked to hand over all of their personal possessions, bags, phones, money and identification in return for the PDA that they will use to play the game. Thus prepared, they are sent out into the city (Fig. 7.1, left) to follow a series of often ambiguous textual clues that respond to their current location and lead them on a convoluted journey through the city streets in search of Uncle Roy's office. Their progress is monitored throughout by remote online players (Fig. 7.1, right) who are able to track their position and can communicate with them via text messages (street players respond with short audio messages), and who may provide them with additional guidance or hindrance, for example steering them towards or away from the office.

As they travel through the city's streets and parks, street players are invited to engage in various activities that increasingly demand interaction with their surroundings and introduce elements of 'live action'. Firstly, online players may ask them to

Fig. 7.1 Following clues on the streets (*left*); the online player's view (*right*). [Images used with permission; ©Mixed Reality Lab (*left*) ©Blast Theory (*right*)]

Fig. 7.2 Completing the postcard in Uncle Roy's office (*left*); receiving a call (*centre*); getting into the car (*right*). [Images use with permission; ©Blast Theory (*left, right*) ©Mixed Reality Lab (*centre*)]

retrieve a postcard from a key location such as the saddlebag of a chained up bicycle (their online experience informs them of the existence of the postcard and that they need to ask a street player to retrieve it). On reaching Uncle Roy's office, they are asked to step inside and explore and also to complete the postcard at an empty desk (Fig. 7.2, left), moving from the public environment of the city streets to the apparently private environment of someone's personal office.

Having left the office, they are then instructed to wait in a nearby phone box (Fig. 7.2, centre). The phone rings and they receive a call that asks them to cross the road and get into a waiting car (Fig. 7.2, right) where they experience the climax of the game, an interview with a live performer who questions them about their trust in strangers and whether they would commit to enter a year long contract to help a stranger—another player somewhere in the game—if ever called upon. Online players who have helped guide them to the office receive the pay-off of seeing them inside over a surveillance camera and are asked the same questions about trust and commitment.

The game is staged over a period of about ten days in each city it has visited, typically being played continuously for six to eight hours each day. Each street player's experience last for a maximum of one hour and up to twelve street players are active at any one time, with new players being added as current ones complete the experience. Up to twenty online players may be present at a time. The 'game zone' consists of around one square kilometre of city streets. Finally, live performers played

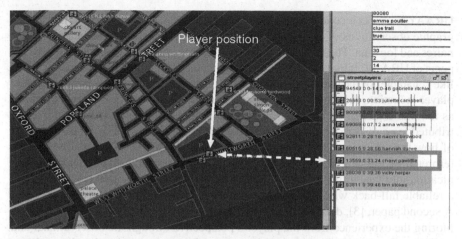

Fig. 7.3 A section of the orchestration interface. Player positions, connectivity status and game state are displayed on the map, along with corresponding connection history on the *right* (the bar indicates game time remaining). One player has been indicated with an *arrow*, along with their corresponding history data, which has been marked with a *box*. [Image used with permission; ©Blast Theory]

several significant roles in the experience, ranging from planned and rehearsed performances (the initial briefing, phone call and interview in the car) to more general orchestration duties on the streets, including monitoring players' progress and occasionally improvising interactions with them (e.g., fixing technical problems as is presented below).

The orchestration team running the game performed monitoring of players via radio contact with team members on the streets, who sought out and maintained visual contact with players of relevance (which itself was often a difficult task [5]). Orchestrators also used special control room interfaces that displayed player information such as last known GPS-derived location, connectivity status and state in terms of progression along the clue trail (see Fig. 7.3). Using both digital information on the player's state (such as a loss of connection) and observation data from team members on the streets, orchestrators were able to determine whether to intervene, assisting 'confused' players, players with crashed devices, and so on.

7.1 Performing Uncle Roy

URAAY had a wider physical scope than the other studies presented in this book. Not only did it involve a larger-scale performance, but the work has also toured: London in 2003 (at the Institute of Contemporary Arts—the ICA), and Manchester (at The Cornerhouse) and West Bromwich (at The Public) in 2004. The game has been experienced by many hundreds of street players (between approximately 200 and 350 per city) as well as over one-and-a-half thousand online players.

With URAAY having been run in three separate cities over the course of a year, a large quantity of data has been gathered by research teams. Previous studies of

URAAY have been conducted on the basis of this data, which consisted of ethnographic observations of the various parties to the game, player feedback questionnaires and log data. These earlier studies have documented and examined various aspects of URAAY. Initial work included a detailed ethnographic report on the "worklike" character of the game—explicating the practices of artists in running the game, player induction, the interpretation of clues and navigation work by players, as well as familiar topics of orchestrator monitoring, intervention, and working with a distributed team of performers [5]. Benford et al. [4] present an in-depth examination of how the self-reported positioning mechanism within URAAY was used and interpreted by online and street players. By coding online and street player communication into categories, the paper demonstrates how self-reported position can be a reliable fall-back when automatic positioning fails or is unreliable in some way. A second paper, [3], details the technical implementation of URAAY, as well as exploring the experience from the player's perspective through the observational and questionnaire data, and brings together some of the conversational coding scheme results from [4]. Through this a number of design strategies for location-based performances and games are formulated, such as being "realistic about positioning and networking technologies", and "exploit[ing] ambiguity" of information, context and relationship to others in order to create a compelling (but safe) experience.

Benford et al. [2], upon which this chapter draws and builds some of its observations (coupled with [5]), look at the work of orchestration in URAAY, as well as presenting URAAY as a 'framed' experience in which ambiguity is a key feature in constructing the game world for the player. It also offers a couple of strategies for designing the frame of the game. Finally, whilst not being a direct study of URAAY, this chapter also draws heavily on a paper that identifies ambiguity as a key resource for design [8]. In this work, Gaver et al. catalogue three forms of ambiguity that may feature in design (which are also referred to in [2]): informational ambiguity in which invitations to multiple interpretations of information are made; contextual ambiguity in which the context an interface is situated in is out-of-place in some way with the nature of the interface itself; and relational ambiguity in which the role of the interface's user is left open to interpretation or destabilised in some way. These different forms of ambiguity will be touched on in the foregoing discussion of URAAY.

The body of data this chapter presents is drawn mainly from video recordings captured by Andy Crabtree during ethnographic work conducted at runs of the URAAY game in Manchester and West Bromwich. This video-based data was recorded from a variety of perspectives, with ethnographers shadowing street players, observing the control room and front of house, and shadowing street performers. This chapter also uses player feedback via a short exit questionnaire (collected by members of the research team involved in the performance), which probed their general attitudes to the game, and especially features they liked and disliked about their experience. Like the previous chapter, the selection of video and questionnaire data and the way in which it was approached analytically was informed by the development of the framework. A number of short vignettes, coupled with quotations from the questionnaires are presented here in order to demonstrate how ambiguity features in the game, which in turn develop in later discussion into framework issues such as performance 'frames', and the role of the 'bystander'. In slight contrast with previous chapters, however, this study has less emphasis upon video data, drawing on more secondary material such as participant feedback.

In this chapter we are interested in the ways in which the ambiguity of the game world was crafted by its designers, particularly in the way the design trades on the ambiguity inherent in everyday situations on the streets. Being described nebulously as a 'game', URAAY's ambiguity contrasts strongly with previous chapters' studies in which the organisation of the experience was decidedly unambiguous and quite well-defined to members of the public attending them. As such it provides fertile ground for expanding upon the environment occupied by people in roles we have already explored—that of actors, orchestrators and participants. However, in this instance, the ambiguous design of the game's features create a form of 'breaching experiment' [7] where the boundaries of normal everyday conduct are disrupted in some way (as we shall see), and through this breaching, reveals for analysis the routine work that orchestrators, actors and participants perform in order to both construct and interpret URAAY's game world. Thus, although URAAY presents conscious attempt to destabilise the nature of performance, potentially 'breaking' many of the concepts developed thus far in this book, this chapter's study of URAAY instead demonstrates the robust ways in which roles, transitions and the framings around these roles may be applied even to such performance contexts.

This chapter's analysis addresses three main aspects of URAAY's play that are of particular interest in developing the more major concepts of framing and by-standers. Each of these three sheds a different light on some of the ways in which the experience in general was presented to the player. There is some sense in which the separation of these aspects is artificial—URAAY is in general an ambiguous experience—however for the purposes of analysis some broad distinctions must be made. The first aspect is the ambiguous status of objects players interact with in some way or places players visit, with the game's design leaving open the question of to what context those objects 'belong' or under what mandate players enter a certain building. Secondly of interest is the ambiguous status of street performers in the game, again with the design of the game potentially implicating members of the public at large through this ambiguity. Thirdly, and finally, there is the work of running the game, part of which involves the street performers maintaining the game world for the player through monitoring and carefully timed intervention.

These three aspects are presented below with short vignettes drawn from video footage of players and street performers, and elaborated upon with quotations from player feedback. Before this, however, some brief comments must be made on how members of the public actually became players.

7.1.1 Joining the Game

As mentioned before, members of the public who take part in the game firstly undergo a process of induction through a short briefing, during which they are asked

Fig. 7.4 Players being inducted (*left*); leaving possessions behind (*centre*); on to the streets with the device (*right*). [Images used with permission; ©Andy Crabtree]

to leave all their possessions behind in a box which remains with the performers. After this players are handed the PDA they are to use during the game and sent off onto the streets of the city. The combination of a (sometimes long) wait, followed by scripted briefing, the depositing of possessions (Fig. 7.4 left and centre), handing over of the device they are to use, along with some brief instructions on using it (Fig. 7.4, right) completes the transition of the member of public into an active player of URAAY game. Some comments left in feedback reveal the reported effect this induction sequence had on players:

> "The bit of anxiety that accrued during the hour-long wait for my turn was minor compared to the state I found myself in next: stripped of all belongings, on my own in central London, with 45 minutes and counting to complete a task whose magnitude I could only imagine."

> "Players were asked to leave all possessions at the ICA so I had no watch, mobile or map. This worried me because I didn't know the area and when directed to Pall Mall or other places, I had no idea where these were and unfortunately, the people I asked for directions got it wrong resulting in me heading in the wrong direction. This, however, didn't detract from the experience."

The peculiarities of this induction orient the player to the nature of the game and set a precedent for the ways in which their later experiences on the streets are interpreted and made sense of.

7.1.2 Ambiguous Status of Objects and Places

During the game itself, the clues and instructions given to players often involve objects or places in their local environment and draw them into the activities the player undertakes in order to find Uncle Roy. In this short sequence, a player, Kelly, is standing in a car park and requests further instruction from the online player who is helping her. Having received an answer, Kelly reads out the message:

> Kelly: oh (0.4) please look for a yellow kiosk by the car park exit
> ((Kelly turns left to see the kiosk and runs towards it. She opens the door and walks in. See Fig. 7.5.))
> Kelly: ((recording a message for the online player)) I'm at the kiosk now I've just picked up a postcard and it says go to the nearest phone box and call the number (1.0) so I'm going to go do that right now

Fig. 7.5 Kelly opens the kiosk door (*left*), and retrieves the postcard (*right*). [Images used with permission; ©Andy Crabtree]

Fig. 7.6 Arriving at the hotel (*left*), and opening the door of a room (*right*). [Images used with permission; ©Andy Crabtree]

Later on in the game, Kelly is instructed to head towards a hotel (Fig. 7.6, left). On entering she finds is then directed towards a certain room, and having found the right number, enters through the door (Fig. 7.6, right).

There are other examples of such use of objects and places as part of the game. In some instances the postcard was located not in a kiosk but in the saddlebag of a chained-up bicycle. Again, in other runs of the game, players entered an office building or got into a car they had been directed to (in which strangers were sitting).

In each of these examples the objects or places were deliberately introduced by and under the control of the game's designers (i.e., were 'props' and 'sets' within the performance). For example, objects like the postcard or bike were carefully placed in certain spots, and the player's presence in locations like the office building or hotel room were arranged for.

Players' comments in feedback further illuminate some of these moments; one reported that they "enjoyed going into the building", whereas another commented:

"At one point near the end you were directed to get into a car. I felt uneasy about this because you 'never get in a car with a stranger' but you assume it must be part of the game because of the sequence of events that lead you to that point. I probably wouldn't have got in the car if there weren't this sequence of events leading up to it."

This feeling of trust and safety was repeated by another player:

"You're given enough to feel safe, but not too safe. Great sense of anticipation. Loved seeing someone approach the car."

These quotations particularly exhibit the main issue at work here. Whilst players understood that they were in a performance, and were still able to make a judgement as to what was appropriate and safe conduct; the ambiguity and instability over the game world's objects (i.e., what was a 'prop' and what was not) and places (i.e., where was permissible to enter and where was not) meant that the player was required at times to cross some of the usual boundaries of public behaviour. In the sequences above, for example, Kelly enters a kiosk that is part of the car park and a hotel room subsequently, however although she herself displays no apparent questioning, it is clear from feedback that such activities can tend to carry with them a level of uncertainty over the appropriateness of conduct. It can be said then that these objects and places are 'implicated' by the game and that there may be some uncertainty whether they are implied to be 'within' the game or implied to be 'outside' the bounds of the game.

7.1.3 Ambiguous Status of People on-the-Streets

Uncertainty over the status of objects or places the player visited also extended to members of the public around them as they navigated their way through streets. A key tactic employed by the designers of URAAY in achieving this ambiguity was to give players clues that appeared to potentially implicate passers-by in the game without ever explicitly stating that they were actually involved or not. As an example, one clue, delivered to players who were near a busy footbridge, instructed them to turn and follow an approaching stranger who was wearing a white T-shirt. By sheer serendipity a passer-by might pass wearing a white T-shirt and even if not, players could still believe that there *should be* such a person nearby. Some players noted that this tactic could lead to a powerful experience, especially when the game was played in busy environments such as central London:

"I liked the instructions to follow people."
"The area it was played in gave you the feeling of everyone in London passing being involved."
"Not knowing who at first was a performer and who was not a performer—everyone is a performer."
"The sense of looking at everyone and thinking that they were part of this."

This ambiguous design resulted in some player's actions occasionally extending to actually involving, rather than just implicating, passers-by either through simply asking for directions or seeking to involve bystanders more directly in the fictional world of the game:

"I asked a bunch of strangers if they were Uncle Roy."

In actuality, the urban area in which the players were experiencing the URAAY game contained street performers who perhaps would be playing the part of Uncle Roy or interact with the player in some other way. Such deliberate and explicit interactions with street performers were, due to the construction of the game, also shrouded in uncertainty by virtue of them occurring within the same context as implicated passers-by. Breakdown in the boundaries of typical behaviour in public enabled players to engage in those interactions. For example, the player noted previously reported being "uneasy" about entering a car, due to their orientation to their consideration of "never get[ting] in a car with a stranger", and yet nevertheless, by virtue of the established game context, did indeed step into the car.

Of course, the context in which people engaged in the game as players also contributed to the crossing of these boundaries:

"The last bit was very odd—but u didn't feel too uncomfortable. The set up is lightly connected—it is not blind trust as I have some institutional trust in Blast Theory and the Institute of Contemporary Arts."

7.1.4 Maintaining the Game World

Finally we turn to the topic of the work street performers (for an extensive analysis of this work, see [5]). These were members of the production team who roamed the streets in order to observe and possibly assist players. A large technical and support crew occupies the control room, providing instruction and assistance to the street performers, who operate around the areas in which players will be taking part in the game. In this short sequence Sarah and James are monitoring the various players. Sarah comments via radio to James (who is outside on the streets):

Sarah: the woman with the black plastic coat has just walked off the game area (0.6) um:: she just c- ah no she's coming back (0.4) um:: (0.4) but she's heading the wrong way up oxford street (0.2) away from the red spots

(Locating a "red spot" is an introductory task for players; they are asked to find the red spot presented to them on their device's map.) Here James and Sarah are attempting to ensure that the player stays within a prescribed zone of the game world so that they will be able to complete the game within time, and not get lost in the process. Finding key locations, such as the whereabouts of the postcard, phone box or office are essential for the player; street performers and control room staff are monitoring to ensure interactions with the game's relevant objects and places.

At another point, the same street performer, James, has been covertly monitoring a female player who is walking along a street. James is performing this activity by standing to one side near some trees that are some distance down the street from the player (Fig. 7.7, left). As she approaches he maintains his position.

James: ((to camera operator)) looks like she's a bit (.) confused

Fig. 7.7 The player walking down the street (*circled, top* and *bottom left*) whilst being monitored by James (*top*), and subsequently turning back (*bottom right*). [Images used with permission; ©Andy Crabtree]

And, shortly after:

James: right I'm I'm gonna ((participant pauses and reverses direction back down the street, Fig. 7.7 centre and right)) (2.0) oh no (.) she's not (1.0) okay ((laughs))

James later notes to the camera operator the difficulties in staying invisible to the player:

Pete: uncle roy needs your pda   Matt: how very sinister   Pete: you may continue now

Fig. 7.8 Pete taking the device (*left*), 'adjusting' it (*centre*), and handing it back (*right*). [Images used with permission; ©Andy Crabtree]

"See the thing is the nearer you get to the corner house the less spaces there are to hide and watch ... it's easier said than done to say to someone stay there and not get heard or saw when you're on the main crossing where everyone's coming past you."

For the final sequence, we join a player, Matt, who has encountered some trouble with his device. One of the street performers, Pete, approaches and intervenes. (See Fig. 7.8.)

Pete: ((approaching Matt)) uncle roy needs your pda ((whilst holding out hand for device))
(1.0)
Matt: right okay ((Pete takes the PDA from Matt's hands and carries on walking)) ((laughs)) it's still not err ((Pete stops by a wall, facing away from Matt))
(4.0)
Matt: ((to camera operator)) how very sinister
(12.0)
Matt: there's quite a big team working behind (.) behind the scenes (10.0) that was bizarre a total stranger's come up to me (1.6) seems to know my pda (.) needs adjusting (1.4) ran up behind me give me quite a shock really (.) err dunno where he came from

After a short time Pete turns around and walks up to Matt, handing back the device.

Pete: you may continue now ((Pete immediately walks away from Matt))
(2.0)
Matt: ((to camera operator)) I may continue

Such intervention assumes a particular character dictated by the design of the game and the maintenance of the character of the game world. Pete states "Uncle Roy needs your PDA" whilst requesting the device with an open hand, and upon receiving it, creates a private space in which to conduct his activities by turning away from Matt, and walking a little further to face the wall. Matt characterises Pete as a "total stranger" and his actions as "sinister". In addition to this Matt comments to the camera operator that he received "quite a shock", and revealing he didn't know where Pete "came from"; clearly Matt was up to this point unaware of Pete's status as being more than 'just another passer-by' until Pete chose to conduct his intervention and reveal himself to Matt.

Finally, it is worth returning to some post-game feedback. One player remarked that "the physical intervention of street players was great" as well as another noting their "feelings of uncertainty and mistrust [they] experienced when facing [the]

street actors". Players also commented on the belief that they were being monitored impacted their play, thanks to "not knowing who was involved and who was watching":

> "My initial feelings were of slight paranoia because you knew you were probably being watched and certainly monitored. I felt very much on my own with no one to confer with or discuss how to do it, or if it was the right way. This was accentuated by the thought that people may be watching you 'doing it wrong'. I couldn't help but look around me to see whom else might be in on it."
>
> "I don't think I saw any mad people in the street as I was expecting—although I suspected everyone."

7.2 Discussion

The four aspects of URAAY that have been presented in the previous section obviously do not cover the entire experience comprehensively (see [5]), however they have been picked in order to point towards some key elaborations on the observations of previous study chapters. In keeping with previous study chapters, we can now begin to assign labels to the various parties present in URAAY. The members of the public that are drawn into the game (described as 'players') are made participants through an induction process performed by actors. Operating behind-the-scenes in a control room and out of sight on the streets are a team of orchestrators (described as 'control room staff' and 'street performers' respectively in the analysis). Finally some of the orchestrators operating on the streets ('street performers') also intervene as actors either to assist confused/lost participants or to fix problems with their device. As mentioned in a previous study of URAAY, orchestrators and actors must engage in a variety of activities such as being able to recognise confused or lost participants through visual inspection from a distance and via orchestration tools enabling remote monitoring of the participant's position and the state of their game [2].

Initially we can address some of the simpler issues presented in the foregoing analysis. Firstly, within URAAY, there are familiar behind-the-scenes and centre-stage settings: orchestrators stay hidden behind-the-scenes either through being situated in a remote control room or by 'blending in' with the general members of the public on the streets; 'centre-stage' becomes relevant when intervention occurs and, as we have seen, orchestrators become revealed to the participant as actors. In URAAY, however, a third general setting occurs, which complements these two others: *front-of-house*. Members of the public arriving to play the game become participants through a performative induction routine within this front-of-house setting, performed by actors. A similar induction process can be seen Desert Rain, mentioned previously, in which participants were given a military-style briefing before they engaged in the experience itself. In this sense, the front-of-house area in URAAY configures participation in the game, 'bookending' or framing the experience. This 'setting of the scene' informs the action that takes place centre-stage,

Fig. 7.9 James's position on the bench, 'blending in', as the player walks by along the street. [Image used with permission; ©Andy Crabtree]

emphasised through the comments from participants that the process of induction heightened their feelings of anxiety.

The next feature to examine is how interventions reveal a new transition: from *orchestrator to actor*. Orchestrators' work involves staying behind-the-scenes by 'blending in', perhaps through occupying crowded locations (see Fig. 7.9), yet at the same time closely monitoring participants. The orchestrators must maintain control over how they are seen by participants (i.e., whether they are 'read' as being part of the game—i.e., actors, or are merely members of the public who have no relationship to it), as illustrated in James's comments on the difficulty in 'blending in'. Orchestrators must also carefully gauge the moment of transition to actor, avoiding unnecessary intervention (as seen when James watches a participant, is about to intervene but then corrects himself), and when performing the transition that reveals themselves, modify their conduct to be oriented to the character of the game (as in Pete's conduct).

The ambiguity of presentation of the game world to the participant leads this discussion to two further concepts: the notion of the *frame* and the role of the *bystander*. The 'frame' of the performance is broadly used to mean the context within which the performance takes place. This concept of a frame is taken from Goffman (introduced in earlier chapters), who explains the process of framing as being how "definitions of a situation are built up in accordance with principals of organization which govern events ... and our subjective involvement in them" [9, p. 10]. In other words, "principals of organization" help make a performance intelligible to those engaged in and observing it. Goffman also describes how the status of such a frame may be ambiguous for those attempting to interpret how to perform their conduct:

"A driver wiggling his hand out the window can cause other drivers to be uncertain for a moment as to whether he means to signal a turn or to greet a friend." [9, p. 304]

Uncertainties and ambiguities over framings are well-documented within a range of literature. For example, Sacks describes the skilled police-work involved in determining the status (or "moral character") of activities on the streets [13], whereas Goodwin explains how contesting interpretations of the frame of activity may be deployed by defence or prosecution within trials when examining video evidence [10]. Similarly, Levine shows the sense-making process bystanders undertake in accounting for their lack of intervention when interpreting the framing within which others are encountered on the streets [11].

One performance art game that is worth revisiting here in more detail here is Can You See Me Now?, discussed in previous chapters. To reiterate, this is a game in which members of the public, navigating a virtual model of a city online with their avatar, are chased through this model by performers. These performers, equipped with handheld computers with GPS and WiFi (subsequently GPRS), had to run through the actual city streets (with their position mapped to the virtual model of the city) in order to catch the online players [1]. Due to their unusual appearance and actions (for example, zigzag running patterns and the performative routine of taking photographs of empty spaces—the locations where they caught online players), performers attracted considerable attention from passers by. When CYSMN toured to Cologne and Toyko this interest spilled over to more active involvement as groups of children ran alongside the performers (see Fig. 7.10). The legibility of these actions to bystanders as being part of a frame of a performance is of particular interest here. Within CYSMN, the frame 'spills out' into the real world, and the other activities that ensure that frame's legibility (an introduction to the game, the presence of online players, etc.) are not necessarily available to the bystander. The frame's status is thus (intentionally) made somewhat 'unstable' by revealing only certain parts of the performance, and then deploying those parts on the streets.

Returning to Goffman, an example is reported of a casino robbery that was misinterpreted. This example is particularly relevant for understanding URAAY:

"Miss Healy [an actor], staging an impersonation of Hildegarde, was dragging [Mr] Hayes [another actor] from a ringside table when a masked man wearing a green GI fatigue uniform entered from the kitchen.
The masked man was carrying a machine-pistol, and he fired a volley into the ceiling. The audience roared with laughter at this 'realistic' bit of play-acting. Miss Healy, realizing the shooting wasn't part of the act, ran into the rest room and remained there.
Three more hooded men entered. One wore a gray hat and appeared to be the leader. The audience applauded, still assuming it was part of the entertainment that made the loss of their memory less painful. Another volley into the ceiling ended the laughter." [9, p. 313]

It is precisely this kind of ambiguity between what is apparently part of the frame and what is not that the design of URAAY exploits. The frame in URAAY is thus constructed in a particular way by the game's very organisation and configuration

Fig. 7.10 Bystanders become involved in Can You See Me Now? [Image used with permission; ©Blast Theory]

as well as the active work by actors and orchestrators in maintaining, repairing and developing the construction of the frame as the game progresses.

This has been demonstrated through the ambiguous status of objects and places (the first section of analysis)—i.e., whether it is the case that objects and places are part of the frame (e.g., props) or whether they belong outside the frame. In the context of the examples provided in this chapter, this creates uncertainty over whether the bike belongs to someone outside the frame of the game, uncertainty over whether the participant has a mandate to enter the office or hotel room, or uncertainty over entry to the car park kiosk (whether it is or is not permitted).

By using the frame to delimit the setting in which action occurs, we also generate possibilities for being outside the frame. This phenomenon is visible in the second section within the analysis, where members of the public on the streets in which the participant plays the game became implicated in the frame primarily via ambiguous clues sent to the participant, who then interpreted these messages as having relevance for those people passing them by. Participants reported feeling that those surrounding them could be part of the game, and that "everyone is a performer". The way in which the game was presented to the participant, and the conduct of orchestrators when they did take part in interventions as actors further reinforced this sense of implication. Matt, for example, displays some level of bewilderment when a "total stranger" comes from 'nowhere' and takes his device. There are two cases to consider here: firstly the case of the passer-by *outside of the frame* being implicated as an actor within the frame by the participant; and secondly the case of the actor who is within the frame but is not implicated as an actor by the participant. We will call members of the public in the first case *bystanders*, and an essential component of this role is that the bystander is *unwittingly* [14, 15] implicated, or in other words that they are unaware and ignorant of the frame.[1]

There is a sense in which framing, ambiguity over distinctions between the game world and the real world, and the largely blurry nature of the experience for players, is what distinctively defines so-galled pervasive games such as URAAY and CYSMN. Indeed, Montola, Stenros and Waern, in their book on the theory and design of pervasive games, suggest that a salient feature of pervasive games is the way in which they "expand the contractual magic circle of play spatially, temporally, or socially" [12]. Thus we can see concepts of bystander roles, wittingness and the boundaries of the frame in terms of Montola et al.'s framework; i.e., reminding ourselves that these concepts are often highly contingent upon the interplay of three aspects, namely the time, place and the social context in which conduct with and around digital interfaces is produced.

The final issue developed by introducing the frame is that the broadly-categorised 'settings' of behind-the-scenes, centre-stage and front-of-house, may be thought of as *subdivisions* of the frame itself. These settings are often spatial in character in URAAY: front-of-house induction is conducted in a relatively private space physically separate from other areas; behind-the-scenes activity is obviously performed in a space physically hidden from participant access; and centre-stage corresponds essentially to the streets, being readily accessible and revealed to the participant who plays the game. Intervention by orchestrators, and their transition to actors is managed through their control over how the settings of behind-the-scenes and centre-stage are navigated. Orchestrators reveal themselves as actors and conduct activities with the participant in this revealed setting. Subsequently to such intervention they quickly 'blend in' and become hidden once again behind-the-scenes.

7.3 Summary

The analysis in this chapter has focussed primarily upon how implication of other members of the public in the *frame* of the game takes place through an ambiguous design of the boundaries of that frame. This ambiguity extended to objects within the game world and places the participant visits as well as the level of collusion by members of the public implied in suggestive clues delivered to them. This concept of the frame circumscribes all the roles we have seen up till now, with the roles of participant, actor, orchestrator or audience being inside the frame. It has also produced the possibility of being outside the frame, which has introduced the new role of the *bystander*, a unwittingly implicated person who is not part of the frame of performance.

In examining URAAY, and developing previous chapters' observations, we have also seen how the frame is subdivided into various performative settings: behind-the-scenes, centre-stage and *front-of-house* areas. This chapter has also explored

---

[1]The use of the concept of 'wittingness' in performance frameworks was jointly developed with Jenn Sheridan, see [6].

how orchestrators conduct *orchestrator-actor transitions* during intervention in the ongoing activities of the participant.

Having explored each study in detail, the concepts introduced along the way can now be pieced together, along with new ideas drawn from the various literatures explored in Chap. 2. Thus, the next chapter synthesises this into a framework for designing interfaces in public settings.

References

1. Benford, S., Crabtree, A., Flintham, M., Drozd, A., Anastasi, R., Paxton, M., Tandavanitj, N., Adams, M., Row-Farr, J.: Can you see me now? ACM Trans. Comput.-Hum. Interact. **13**(1), 100–133 (2006). doi:10.1145/1143518.1143522
2. Benford, S., Crabtree, A., Reeves, S., Flintham, M., Drozd, A., Sheridan, J.G., Dix, A.: The frame of the game: Blurring the boundary between fiction and reality in mobile experiences. In: Proceedings of SIGCHI Conference on Human Factors in Computing Systems (CHI), pp. 427–436. ACM, New York (2006). doi:10.1145/1124772.1124836
3. Benford, S., Flintham, M., Drozd, A., Anastasi, R., Rowland, D., Tandavanitj, N., Adams, M., Row-Farr, J., Oldroyd, A., Sutton, J.: Uncle Roy All Around You: Implicating the city in a location-based performance. In: Proceedings of Conference on Advanced Computer Entertainment (ACE) (2004)
4. Benford, S., Seager, W., Flintham, M., Anastasi, R., Rowland, D., Humble, J., Stanton, D., Bowers, J., Tandavanitj, N., Adams, M., Farr, J.R., Oldroyd, A.: Sutton: The error of our ways: the experience of self-reported position in a location-based game. In: Proc. of the 6th International Conference on Ubiquitous Computing, UbiComp, 2004, pp. 70–87. Springer/ACM, New York (2004)
5. Crabtree, A., Benford, S., Rodden, T., Greenhalgh, C., Flintham, M., Anastasi, R., Drozd, A., Adams, M., Row-Farr, J., Tandavanitj, N., Steed, A.: Orchestrating a mixed reality game 'on the ground'. In: Proceedings of the SIGCHI Conference on Human Factors in Computing Systems, pp. 391–398. ACM, New York (2004). doi:10.1145/985692.985742
6. Dix, A., Sheridan, J.G., Reeves, S., Benford, S., O'Malley, C.: Formalising performative interactions. In: Proceedings of 12th International Workshop on Design, Specification and Verification of Interactive Systems (DSVIS), pp. 15–25 (2005). doi:10.1007/11752707_2
7. Garfinkel, H.: Studies in Ethnomethodology. Prentice-Hall, New York (1967)
8. Gaver, W., Beaver, J., Benford, S.: Ambiguity as a resource for design. In: Proceedings of Conference on Human Factors in Computing Systems (CHI), pp. 233–240. ACM, New York (2003). doi:10.1145/642611.642653
9. Goffman, E.: Frame Analysis: An Essay on the Organization of Experience. Harper & Row, New York (1974)
10. Goodwin, C.: Professional vision. Am. Anthropol. **96**(3), 606–633 (1994)
11. Levine, M.R.: Rethinking bystander non-intervention: social categorisation and the evidence of witnesses at the James Bulger murder trial. Hum. Relat. **52**(9), 1133–1155 (1999)
12. Montola, M., Stenros, J., Waern, A.: Pervasive Games: Theory and Design. Morgan Kaufmann, San Mateo (2010)
13. Sacks, H.: Notes on police assessment of moral character. In: Sudnow, D.N. (ed.) Studies in Social Interaction, pp. 280–293. Free Press, New York (1972)
14. Sheridan, J.G.: Digital Live Art: Mediating wittingness in playful arenas. Ph.D. thesis, Department of Computing, Lancaster University (2006)
15. Sheridan, J.G., Bryan-Kinns, N., Bayliss, A.: Encouraging witting participation and performance in digital live art. In: BCS-HCI'07: Proceedings of the 21st British HCI Group Annual Conference on People and Computers, pp. 13–23. British Computer Society, Swinton (2007)

Chapter 8
A Framework for Designing Interfaces in Public Settings

This core chapter develops an analytic framework for public interfaces that shows how many current design approaches can be related to one another through a few underlying concepts. In doing so, it draws on studies presented in previous chapters as well as a range of example interfaces and studies of interaction, especially from interactive art and performance. In addition, these observations are developed from collected experiences within the Mixed Reality Laboratory (University of Nottingham, UK) of working with external artists and performers to stage a series of installations, performances and games over the past decade (including, but not limited to, the events detailed in this book). Although this framework is presented in an analytic and reflective form for the most part within this chapter, it is worth recalling at this point Chap. 1, noting the framework as a way of mapping out a design space, and as a series of constraints and strategies for a variety of different design communities. Moving beyond the analytic nature of the framework, however, will be a topic of discussion within the final chapter.

The framework is introduced in this chapter in an incremental manner. The first section (8.1) will develop the observations of Chap. 4, considering interaction with and around the Telescope device in the context of a wider examination of HCI and art literature by performers or about performance and performance-like settings. The discussion thus purposefully moves away from a generic conception of the 'user', at first considering the general roles of *performer* and *spectator* through a basic separation of public and private within such settings. (The relevance of 'participant' and 'audience' roles discussed in Chap. 4 as specialisms of 'performer' and 'spectator' roles respectively will be addressed shortly.) Of interest is how a performer can express their interactions with an interface, and how a spectator might experience these interactions. This section also breaks down performative action into a performer's manipulations (including gestures around an interface) and effects of those manipulations (including effects reflected back upon the performer).

The second section (8.2) revisits the division of public and private, and reviews a wide variety of interactive systems, from mobile devices to interactive installations and performances, in addition to those studies presented earlier. In each system, the section examines how manipulations and effects are variously hidden, partially-

S. Reeves, *Designing Interfaces in Public Settings*, Human-Computer Interaction Series, 141
DOI 10.1007/978-0-85729-265-0_8, © Springer-Verlag London Limited 2011

hidden, revealed or even augmented in particular combinations in order to engender different forms of interaction and thus spectator experience. Following on from this, the section builds upon the observations on manipulations and effects developed in Chap. 4 particularly, as well as the review of different systems. This is developed into a taxonomy. This taxonomy is further extended to explore how its quadrants may be thought of in terms of four characterisations of broad design strategies: 'secretive' interfaces, 'expressive' interfaces, 'magical' interfaces and 'intriguing' interfaces. These design strategies are also present in some of the systems presented within the study chapters and, once again, these are reviewed.

Developing from the analysis presented in Chap. 7, the third section (8.3) of this chapter then discusses how a performance is *framed* within a given setting, leading to the consideration of a simple distinction in how spectators may be 'inside' or 'outside' of the frame, introducing notions of 'witting' and 'unwitting' spectators in their experience of performer interactions. This introduces two different specialisms of the spectator role—*bystanders* (unwitting spectators) and *audience* (witting spectators)—as well as presenting two strategies for constructing the frame. The section also discusses framing strategies through designing the way in which ambiguity is deployed in the frame, such as deliberately blurring the distinctions between the roles of actor, audience, participant and bystander.

The fourth section (8.4), again examining exemplars within the literature and, drawing on studies presented in previous chapters, turns to focus on how spectators or performers may *transition* between roles, as well as considering the nature of two further spectator and performer specialisms; respectively, non-professional *participant* spectators and professional *orchestrator* performer roles. Two key kinds of transition are also explored. Firstly the section examines transitions between the 'non-professional' roles of bystanders, audience and participants. Then, introducing a further specialism of the performer role—the *actor*—considers how the more 'professional' roles of actors and orchestrators may feature in transition.

The final substantive section brings together in a summarised form each of the components presented in previous sections, most notably introducing a diagrammatic representation of the various elements of the framework and definitional statements about each component. It also highlights how the frame itself has been subdivided into the settings *behind-the-scenes* (areas less exposed to participants and audience members, and being where orchestrators work typically, covered most comprehensively in Chap. 6), *centre-stage* (where the majority of the performative action takes place, the major domain of actors and participants) and *front-of-house* (where bystanders may be inducted into the frame, becoming audience).

8.1 Performers and Spectators, Manipulations and Effects

This section lays down a number of basic terms and concepts that will be referred to throughout this chapter as examples of technology deployed in various performance and performance-like scenarios are discussed.

8.1.1 Users as Performers

We have previously seen in Chap. 4's study of One Rock how conduct around the interface was conceptually divided into two main roles: those visitors acting with the device (participants) and those observing that interaction (audience). Subsequently these roles were enriched with more professional roles of actors and orchestrators (Chaps. 5 and 6) as well as the role of the bystander. For the first half of this chapter we will be considering a variety of systems which may involve orchestrators, participants or actors, the distinctions between which we will gloss over at this point as each being a form of 'performer'. Similarly, audience and bystanders will in turn be glossed as being a form of 'spectator'. This simple division will drive this section's analysis and be used to illuminate a number of issues before the roles developed over the course of the studies are re-introduced.

So, with this gloss in mind, we can begin by considering the user of an interface as a 'performer'. This is defined as follows:

A *performer* is the primary user of an interface.

In order to explain the use of this term, the discussion must be prefaced with three points about performer, interface and performance. The first point is that the use of the term 'primary' is intended to mean that other participants, for example members of an audience at an artistic performance, may also be able to interact with the interface, as secondary users. In this section, however, it is the performer's interactions that are most central to the performance, as such interactions are usually the main focus of attention for others. Secondly, the 'interface' is not viewed here as a monolithic component, but rather as consisting of potentially disparate arrangements of different interactive technologies [22]. We have previously seen such arrangements in Chaps. 6 and 7, which both featured complex, distributed interfaces that various members of the performance employed. In other examples, musicians might use synthesisers, a laptop computer and acoustic instruments in the course of a performance, or a dancer might trigger a series of sound and lighting effects by interacting with an array of movement sensors. This follows on from Bowers' ethnographic studies of electroacoustic musical performances, where he uses the term "performance ecologies" to describe how collections of technologies, instruments and devices are spatially organised in some "local arena for action" with which the performer works [8, p. 47]. In such cases, the concept of 'the interface' is very much about an 'ecology' of disparate technologies that is formed into a coherent assembly (see [13, 45]).

The third and final key point concerns the extent to which the performance is deliberately staged. Although much of the focus of this book has been upon more explicitly staged performances in which artists deliberately set out to engage an audience (such as in each of the study chapters), the framework here also includes incidental, accidental or what has previously been generically called 'opportunistic' performances. These opportunistic performances involve interaction in a public setting in which a user becomes of particular interest to others and thereby becomes a performer, typical examples being users of interactive museum or gallery exhibits. Chapter 4 explored use of the Telescope device in such a setting, and the ways in which the physical features of the device such as its size and a user's 'performance' with it, involving the manipulations required to operate the device, were experienced by other visitors in the exhibition. This led to some visitors becoming engaged with the device by way of this highly visible and potentially 'intriguing' conduct by the user of the device. Developing this further, there are some museum and gallery exhibits that meld these two senses of performance together more explicitly, such as in the "Brain Opera" [34], which enabled members of the public to interact with a set of touring new musical instruments, helping an untrained audience to intuitively compose music. It is worth noting at this point, however, that situations such as these differ in artistic 'intent'. This means that although the broad view presented here covers many forms of performance, at the same time it is acknowledged that there is an inherent 'intentional' difference in staged performance and 'performance' present in public social interactions.

In addressing this question of deliberate and opportunistic stagings of performance or performance-like activity, Goffman's well-known dramaturgical approach to social interaction is important for consideration. Returning to the discussion presented in Chap. 3, Goffman's assertion that social interaction in general can be thought of as performance [20, p. 17] is appealed to throughout this chapter, along with his technique of frame analysis as in [21]. Whilst Goffman's metaphor has its critics (e.g., [47]), using this simple formalism for approaching social interaction as performance (and vice versa) can perhaps illuminate the foregoing analysis of people's interaction with interfaces in public settings and provide some basis for design. An understanding of the implicit performative characteristics of such use may have broader implications for HCI and CSCW, a topic which is covered in the final chapter. For the purposes of discussion, however, the focus of this chapter will remain on more explicit performances, be they planned or more opportunistic.

It was also discussed in some depth within Chap. 2 how the relationship between an interface and its primary user has been the main focus of HCI for many years. There is wealth of literature on how to design this interaction, addressing a very wide range of concerns, many of which are grouped under the umbrella of usability (covering issues such as time to learn, task performance, error rate and satisfaction, e.g., [35]). More recently, CSCW has brought considerations of social groupings to the study of the interface, and has broadened its original analytical focus (which initially centred around private settings such as the workplace) to increasingly include public settings. This growing interest in public settings is encompasses artistic and playful interfaces, and has been addressing issues such as playability, immersion, and the potential use of ambiguity in interface design (see [18]).

8.1.2 Manipulations and Effects

Considering the relationship between a performer and their interface leads to focussing on the specific issue of performative gestures and movements that take place 'around' an interface. Performers often gesture artistically around their direct manipulations of the interface, performing distinctive movements prior to or following on from the actual moment of interaction. This can be seen in traditional performance contexts such as musicians playing conventional musical instruments or sportspeople striking balls. Indeed, in Chap. 4 we saw how Telescope users performed such preparatory and follow-through activities, crafting their approach to and disengagement from the device with respect to those standing near-by. Such gestures play two important roles. Firstly, interactions consist of more than the moment of contact with the interface technology (e.g., pressing key); preparation and follow-through are essential components of a skilfully performed physical action, perhaps best seen in a golfer's swing. Preparatory gestures may also form some element of communication between performers themselves, as described, for example, in Bowers' report of his "noticeable sprawl" of readiness in a musical performance in which is then picked up on by his co-performer [8, p. 31]. Secondly, such gestures are an essential element of deliberately performing interactions for others to see and appreciate, expressing skill and control and introducing an aesthetic component to the use of technology. Rosen [37], for example, describes how performers' gestures at the piano fundamentally influence spectator appreciation of the skill and emotion involved in the performance of a piece of music, and Sudnow [44] describes how seemingly extraneous gestures become part of the practice of productions at the keyboard. Previous work in HCI has discussed the role of performative gestures in playing electronic instruments, using the term "expressive latitude" to refer to performance gestures that are not directly sensed by the instrument [7].

Performers' actions around their interfaces may also be more functional. The Telescope in Chap. 4 demonstrated how performers might have to do some work engaging with and disengaging from interactive technologies. In other scenarios when approaching an interface, this might also involve picking up an interaction device or donning a wearable technology, like a head-mounted display for instance. The movements and gestures involved in approaching the technology, such as moving into sensor range or putting on an interface, may be publicly visible (again, noted in the study of the Telescope) and hence part of the performance even though they may not directly result in intentional input to the system. Indeed, there is a danger that such actions will cause input to the system anyway, accidentally triggering unintended interactions and making the performer appear to be clumsy or inept. This was seen extensively in Chap. 5, where the storyteller rapidly adapted to the contingencies of such manipulation environments in order to manage participants' input to the system over the course of the performance, avoiding practical problems such as accidental triggering.

Further to this, performers may also disengage in order to rest or reposition themselves before resuming a performance, may put down one piece of technology in order to engage with another or may hand over a technology to another performer. These kinds of interactions can be seen in public settings such as museums where visitors hand over technologies as well as in stage managed performances. For example, the studies in Chaps. 4 and 5 both demonstrated how such handing-over of the interface or devices associated with it may have the potential for being problematic, but also can be resolved by performers in their negotiations around the resources that are provided by the interface. In One Rock, this was between visitors using the Telescope whereas in the Journey into Space it involved the storyteller employing instructed handovers as a means of managing interaction with technology in the performance environment (as mentioned above).

A performer's actions with an interface, however, may not necessarily be very intimately tied to the instant of use. For example, interactive technologies may be used to enhance or augment existing forms of performance, such as sensing and responding to the movements of dancers on a stage. Here the technology may occupy a more subordinated or minimal role since the existing form—i.e., dancing—may require interaction only as part of the overall performance, or perhaps be relegated to a supporting role only, for example, providing triggers for certain lighting or sound effects. A dancers' movements in this example have artistic and aesthetic qualities in some sense independent of the moment of contact, for indeed they, not the technology, are the 'main event'.

This discussion is closely related to a framework described by Bellotti et al. [3] for the design of sensing-based interfaces, in which they discuss the serious challenges posed to interface designers including "how to disambiguate signal-to-noise" and "how to not address the system". Each of these directly impacts the ways in which performers operate the interface and how spectators are handled by the interface. For example, designing an interface such that performers can easily and rapidly disengage in order to "not address the system" for a period of time may be vital for its smooth operation in a performance scenario. Previous research into the design of sensing-based interfaces has argued that designers should consider how to support movements that, while integral to a performance, are not sensed by the system. This includes supporting performative gestures around an interface that add expression to an interaction without directly making input to the system—for example, by deliberately providing spaces around an interface where it is possible to move freely without triggering unwanted interactions, or otherwise exploiting the limitations of sensing technologies [6].

8.1.3 Users as Spectators, Public and Private Interactions

The next element of the framework is the spectator of the performer's interactions.

Spectators are a necessary part of the performance, but they are not the primary users of the interface. Rather, their concern is to 'observe' and make sense of the performer's interactions—although they may also sometimes interact with the interface accidentally. (There is also a sense in which a performer themselves is a spectator for their own interactions [14].)

Unlike many examples of CSCW, where several users share an interface on a more or less equal footing, the concern here is with a situation in which there is a distinctive asymmetry; either the performer *deliberately* conducts interactions for spectators to experience and appreciate (as in three of the four studies in this book), or the performer's interactions are perceptible to spectators implicitly (as in users of the Telescope in Chap. 4).

The basic starting point to consider for designing for the spectator experience is a common, but over-simplistic idea: the distinction between public and private interaction. Personal phone calls, for example, are often an essentially private action and might ideally be shielded from others when conducted in public settings, for the benefit of both parties [1]. In the most extreme cases, technologies may be embedded in private booths that are placed in the public setting, such as in interactive photo kiosks. Other interactions are clearly intended to be public, such as those of an electronic musician or performance artist whose use of interactive technologies is a carefully staged spectacle. Other interactions fall somewhere in-between, such as museum installations like the Telescope within One Rock, which, as vom Lehn et al. observe, involve multiple levels of engagement, including those who are directly interacting, those in an immediate co-located group who share the interaction, and bystanders who observe from a distance, learning by watching others and waiting their turn [29] (parallel observations are made in literatures on large screen interactives, e.g., [9]).

Although performers have been defined as being the primary users of the interface, it is possible for spectators to interact as well, either deliberately or accidentally.

In a typical performance (such as theatre, music or stand-up comedy), a performer is highly aware of spectator reaction; indeed, a performer's awareness of spectators in such situations is often fundamental to the flow of the performance, as the performer ongoingly crafts their conduct mutually with that of the audience. Often, for example, street performance will involve quite explicit interaction between performer and audience, since the performer must first attract a crowd (constructing an "edge" [12]), and engage in subtle interactional methods with crowd members in order to maintain and manage the flow of their performance [12]. Even where spectators are more restrained, the manifest presence of an audience is clearly critical to the sense of 'liveness'. One intriguing possibility is to extend spectator feedback by enabling spectators to interact with a performance interface, for example by exerting some degree of control over a common display shared as a large projected interface. In turn, this requires techniques for collecting and aggregating input from potentially many spectators. A range of techniques are available from relatively well established technologies for voting (e.g., dedicated voting handsets in television studios or voting by text messaging from mobile phones) through to more experimental approaches in which computer vision is used to track crowd gestures (e.g., the Cinematrix system in which a large crowd wielded red and green pieces of card in order to play a game of 'Pong' that appeared on a large projected display [11]).

However, spectator interaction may also be accidental and undesirable. Accidental interaction may arise through unintended interference with sensing systems, perhaps most obviously a problem with video-tracking where spectators can unintentionally interfere by moving into camera view, casting shadows or causing changes in ambient lighting (e.g., blocking light sources, opening or closing doors, or switching lights on and off). Chapter 5's study of the Journey into Space noted how the performer's running of the storytelling involved frequent guiding work, structuring children's interactions within the space as a strategy for avoiding interference.

Designers might avoid such interference by careful sensor placement and design of the environment that incorporates somehow the constraints of 'safe' interaction space into the fundamental configuration of that design. In particular sensing technologies need to be carefully designed into the general design of the performance space—the set, stage and seating—so as to encourage or avoid spectator interactions. This aspect is discussed further in a later section, concerning how a performance is 'framed'.

In summary, the argument presented here is suggesting that the basic distinction between 'public' and 'private' is not subtle enough to capture some of the essential features of existing public interfaces. In particular, it is important to consider exactly what aspects of a performer's interaction are made available to spectators and how this is achieved. Therefore, further distinctions must be introduced in order to help express the various possibilities. At this point interaction can now be analysed in terms of manipulations and effects.

8.1.4 Defining Manipulations and Effects

Interaction goes beyond seeing the interface in terms of input and output. Here two fundamental features introduced earlier—manipulations and effects—which have begun to include social aspects of interaction, are stated more definitively for the reader:

Manipulations are defined here as the actions carried out by the performer, including manipulations of physical controls (buttons, mice, joysticks and so forth) as well as gestures, movements and speech that are sensed by the interface. Manipulations have *spatial* attributes, and include actions outside of the interface's sensor scope; i.e., gestures, movements, and utterances that take place around the interface but that do not directly result in input to it. Sometimes these are purely functional, sometimes they are purely artistic, and sometimes a mixture of both. In any case, manipulations correspond to more than just system 'input' since their definition includes non-sensed actions as well.

Effects are the results of manipulations, for example the display of images, graphics and sounds or the actuation of physical objects. Effects include what is identified here as the main 'content' of the performance, but may also include other visible effects of the performer's manipulations of the system, such as the appearance of menus, icons, cursors and so forth that are a necessary part of manipulating the contents. Effects also include the apparent action of the interface on the performer themselves. These may be direct effects, such as when the performer is tethered to the interface in some way, or in more extreme cases where the system is actively (and maybe autonomously) controlling the performer's body. An example of this can be seen in the work of the performance artist Stelarc, in which the interactive system causes his body to move through a series of electrical impulses, triggered in the first instance by spectators interacting with an interface [48, p. 159] (see Fig. 8.1).

Performers may also display a physical and/or emotional reaction to the interface, deliberately or involuntarily, and the resulting gestures, movements and expressions

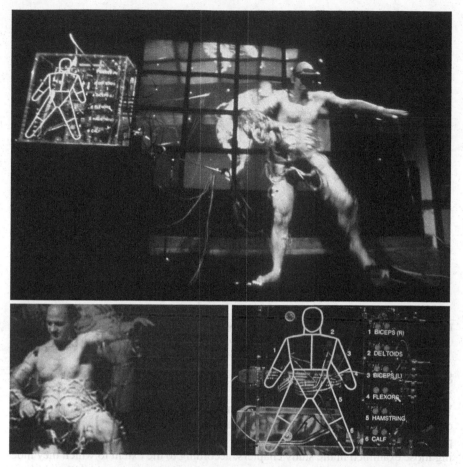

Fig. 8.1 Muscle Stimulation System by Stelarc (*top*); detail of the artist's body attached to muscle stimulators (*bottom left*), and the interface used to trigger them (*bottom, right*). [Images used with permission; Muscle Stimulation System by Stelarc, Melbourne 1994, photographer Stelarc (*top*); Split Body by Stelarc, Galeria Kapelica 1996, photographer Igor Andjelic (*bottom right*)]

around the interface can also be seen as being part of the effect. An example of this may be found in artist Marcel.lí Antúnez Roca's Epizoo performance piece in which the artist's face and body is attached to audience-controllable actuators. When an audience member activates "[p]ressure on the [artist's] forehead" this pressure "is apparently painful because the artist starts screaming loudly" [48, p. 161]. This is, of course, a rather extreme demonstration of a performer's physical reaction to the interface. The definition of effects, therefore, does not correspond to system 'output' since effects are not confined to being located purely in the technology but can also be found in the human elements. Finally, like manipulations, effects also have spatial characteristics; for instance, effects may occur in a space disconnected from the manipulations which created them (as in Chap. 6's telemetry equipment).

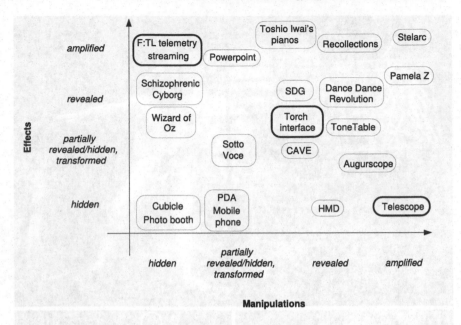

Fig. 8.2 Classifying interfaces according to how they hide or reveal manipulations and effects (systems presented in previous chapters are *highlighted*)

8.2 Revisiting Public and Private Interaction

We are now ready to revisit and expand on basic ideas of public and private, further developing them in terms of the varied ways in which a spectator can experience a performer's interaction. We can classify a wide range of existing interfaces, including those examined in the study chapters, according to the extent to which they hide or reveal a performer's manipulations compared to the extent to which they hide or reveal the corresponding effects. Figure 8.2 shows the resulting taxonomy, populated with a range of example interfaces that shall be referred to throughout the rest of this section. Not all aspects of the studies presented in this book are classifiable according to the following taxonomy, however, since it focusses on a 'device level' of interaction, and thus applies more to the smaller settings of interaction in One Rock and the Journey into Space. Nevertheless, there are some aspects of interaction in Fairground: Thrill Laboratory and Uncle Roy All Around You which have relevance in this taxonomy, although later on in this chapter these studies will play a further role in developing the analysis of orchestration, framings, and so on.

At the bottom-left we see what is traditionally considered to be private interaction in which both manipulations and their effects are hidden from the spectator such that they are exclusively available only to the performer, an example being any interface located in a private booth such as the photo booth mentioned previously.

Towards the top-right we see the most public interactions in which both effects and the manipulations that cause them are revealed to spectators and perhaps even amplified in some way (i.e., in a crude sense, made more obvious). An interactive whiteboard belongs in this general area, as do many conventional examples of single display groupware (SDG) in which people collaborate openly around a shared display [43]. Chapter 5's torch interface also fits into this general area through its mapping between manipulations (including the throw of the torch beam) and (literally) amplified audio effects.

The areas to the top-left and bottom-right are somewhat less conventional. Towards the top-left we see examples of interfaces in which effects are revealed but manipulations, including the performer themselves in extreme cases, are hidden. Here we find interfaces employing magic-like effects, including 'wizard of oz' interfaces—interfaces often used during the early stages of design, perhaps during rapid prototyping (e.g., [17])— that might involve, say, a performer speaking through a real-time animated character from off-stage.

At the bottom-right we have the converse, where manipulations are revealed but effects are hidden. Here spectators might watch a performer using a display or engaging with technology in some fashion, but cannot share in the content of their experience. For example, immersive head-mounted displays used in public settings permit spectators to see only performer manipulations (such as the interactive installation Osmose by Charlotte Davies). A further example from a museum setting is Chap. 4's Telescope device. As discussed, rotating and tilting the Telescope not only involved relatively conspicuous manipulations, but also implicated a physical target within the space (i.e., the Incubator), and having the effect of further amplifying manipulations as the performer would be clearly seen bending over to look into the device. The eye-piece design, however, rendered effects of those manipulations invisible to spectators.

Having explored the four extreme corners of the taxonomy next we may consider, with further exploration of these extremes, other examples of public interfaces that lie more towards the centre of Fig. 8.2 and therefore involve more subtle trade-offs between hiding and revealing manipulations and effects.

8.2.1 Mobile Personal Displays

Due to their small size, many of the fine details of interaction with mobile personal displays such as PDAs and phones may be hidden from most spectators. There are, however, further more subtle distinctions. A spectator who is close by, directly looking over the shoulder of someone who is using a PDA, may be able to observe their manipulations and the resulting effects. This interactional feature has been exploited to interesting effect in a mobile 'Pacman' game in which players use their own PDAs to control 'ghosts' that can appear on other players' PDAs, causing players to dynamically reposition themselves in an attempt to see others' displays or conversely hide their own display from the view of others, often amusingly tying themselves in knots in the process [39].

More distant spectators will miss small manipulations of mobile devices such as key presses, but will probably still be able to see that the device is being used due to characteristic 'phone gestures', such as broader interactions with the device itself (e.g., placing a phone to one's ear) and other characteristic bodily motions, such as physically marking private space by bodily orientation and pose [19, 28]. Mobile phones in particular project some of their manipulations and effects into the surrounding environment, including ring-tones and the performer's talk, which sometimes appears to be at least in part deliberately performed for spectators in the local environment as well as for the distant conversant.

The Sotto Voce museum guide system [2] is especially interesting in this respect, because a spectator can elect to eavesdrop on a fellow participant's audio, choosing whether or not to share the effects that the performer triggers. (This was possible even in the absence of physical proximity.)

Finally we can return briefly to Chap. 7's study of Uncle Roy All Around You, highlighting how its use of PDAs places player interaction with the technology within the taxonomy (i.e., 'PDA' and 'Mobile phone' category in Fig. 8.2). Interestingly, the fact that manipulations of the PDA were 'partially hidden' and its effects where very much hidden, meant that considerable orchestration work was required to monitor players as they progressed through the game. As noted in previous research, orchestrators on-the-streets had to develop skills in recognising players [4] in order to overcome this mostly hidden combination of manipulations and effects.

8.2.2 Interactive Installations

Interactive installations demonstrate a very wide variety of approaches to hiding and revealing manipulations and effects. Some installations rely heavily on spectator comprehension of manipulations and their mapping onto a revealed effect for their entertainment value. Dance Dance Revolution arcade machines, for example, present players with a set of footpads (usually with eight large 'buttons') that must be triggered in specific sequences in time with an accompanying soundtrack. Manipulations of the machine are not hidden from spectators in any way, and are in fact made very obvious by the physical movement required to operate it (a design concept we saw already with the Telescope in Chap. 4). Appreciation of the linkage between a performer's steps and their success in the game (i.e., effects) is central to being a spectator. A testimony to the effectiveness of the game's design can be found in the significant community of players who engage in both organised performances and competitions, and more impromptu demonstrations of ability for onlookers [42].

Projected 3D displays such as Cave Automatic Virtual Environments (CAVEs) reveal both manipulations and effects to co-present spectators, in that the manipulations required to navigate the virtual environment are visible (via the conduct of the user) as well as the effects of those manipulations (via the projected display). Only a single tracked performer, however, receives the full 3D experience that is correct for their physical perspective as they move; in contrast, spectators may receive a 'downgraded' secondary view that is slaved to the performer's movements.

The Tonetable [7], is an interactive table-top display that was exhibited in a science exploratorium and permitted four performers at a time to interact with a simulated physical model of water using trackballs. The Tonetable deliberately sonified the movements of the trackballs in order to draw spectators' attention to their use. At the same time, non-linear algorithms were used to map trackball manipulations onto visible effects on the graphical simulation and sonification, so that whilst it was clear that performers were interacting, the legibility of their interaction—the relationship between manipulations and effects—was not immediately obvious or even ultimately predictable, demanding further reflection. The use of non-linear mappings to partially obscure the relationship between manipulations and effects is common in artistic installations where it introduces a degree of ambiguity in an attempt to provoke curiosity, engagement and exploration (a more detailed discussion of the role of ambiguity in interface design can be found in [18]).

The final example in this section is the Augurscope, a stand-mounted mobile display that can be wheeled around outdoors in order to view 3D models such as historical reconstructions from different physical vantage points [40]. Like the Telescope mentioned previously, this is a large interface that can be rotated and tilted in a highly visible way. Unlike the Telescope, its effects are displayed on a laptop-sized screen that makes them visible to nearby spectators, such as members of a co-visiting group, although not to more distant spectators.

8.2.3 Performances

The final category of public interfaces is those used as part of deliberately staged public performances. Artists who interact with technologies in front of spectators are not always content with revealing manipulations, but may actively seek to amplify them in order to make their performances more expressive. Musician Pamela Z [49] uses gesture controllers in her performances in order to control electronic instruments in tandem with her voice (Fig. 8.3, left and centre). By using more expressive sensing interfaces, she both reveals and then amplifies the manipulations that are normally involved in the playing of electronic instruments. In a further example, Toshio Iwai's work Music Plays Images x Images Play Music [48, p. 767] involves automated lighting effects that visually amplify a pianist's manipulations of a conventional piano keyboard. Some of Stelarc's performance pieces also reflect this sense of augmented manipulations or effects situated in a public performance environment, such as his Muscle Stimulation System piece [48, p. 159]. In this performance, muscle stimulators were attached to the artist's body and were made accessible to the spectators via a touch-screen. In this way, incorporating the performer into the interface itself provided a visceral demonstration of the way in which manipulations of an interface could be amplified to result in highly visible movements of the performer's body.

Amplification is not necessarily involved in all performances however. In Schizophrenic Cyborg [41] a participant plays the role of a 'cyborg' by having

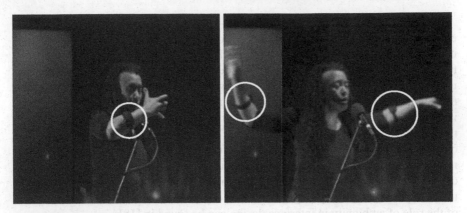

Fig. 8.3 Musician Pamela Z, with gesture controllers indicated. [Images used with permission; ©Donald Swearingen]

a digital display fixed onto their torso. A separate performer, the 'parasite', then anonymously interacts with this display. This is done in such a way that their manipulations are hidden from the cyborg and other spectators, whereas the effects are made clearly visible on the cyborg's body and so became a talking point for spectators.

For Fairground: Thrill Laboratory presented in Chap. 6, aspects of the interface fit within the taxonomy at this point. The streaming telemetry data in particular was highly amplified for the spectators, revealing 'hidden' aspects such as heart rate in a visible, and, thanks to actors, legible fashion. In comparison, the manipulations (i.e., movements of the ride) required to produce the data stream were very much hidden, with the ride only visible through small windows which the audience sat directed away from.

It is also worth briefly drawing attention to a quite different and more everyday kind of performance, that of giving presentations using tools such as Microsoft's Powerpoint or Apple's Keynote software. Some current presentation tools are limited in terms of their ability to support fluid performance in ways that can be explained by the taxonomy. Spectators typically see effects—a slideshow—in an amplified way (i.e., projected onto a large screen). The performer's physical manipulations may be more or less visible depending on the set up. What is interesting—and problematic—is that spectators often see and hear the whole of the computer's output, including alerts, system messages and all of the visible effects of the performer's interactions with the underlying operating system. Ideally, only the performer would see this information so that they could more fluidly orchestrate the show for the spectator and reduce distractions. For example, many presenters will have often wanted to be able to secretly alter later slides as a presentation progresses, perhaps in response to time pressure or questions from audience members, but without this being visible to all. Interestingly, a number of current presentation tools have begun to identify this problem and provide support for hiding manipulations, an example of which is Keynote, which supports two displays—a private display for the presenter and a public one that the audience sees.

Finally we can consider the presentation to the watching audience within Chap. 6's study of Fairground: Thrill Laboratory. Here the broadcast telemetry data was projected onto a large area, which experts further amplified through gesture and description. Whilst the rider could be said to be engaged in manipulations, primarily it was the technical crew and hosts' job to successfully weave this broadcast material together through their collaborative manipulations. It is also of note that this collaborative manipulation required to run the projection often involved activities conducted in the control area, behind-the-scenes, shrouded in darkness and involving small physical manipulations in addition to the more obvious amplified gestures of the hosts.

8.2.4 Interfaces as Secretive, Expressive, Magical and Intriguing

In order to draw out some broader design principles from the various examples that have been reviewed above, the taxonomy presented earlier will be revisited here. There are four general approaches to designing public interfaces proposed here, each of which addresses different concerns, noting however that these strategies should be read primarily as characterisations. The main point here is to identify key strategies and sensitise designers to them.

Secretive interfaces tend towards hiding both manipulations and effects. This may be to protect spectators from knowing about the experience until it is their turn, or to protect performers from interference from spectators.

Expressive interfaces tend towards revealing, even amplifying, both manipulations and effects. For performances, their primary concern is to entertain spectators by enabling them to appreciate how well a performer is interacting with the system, for example admiring the skill of a virtuoso user or being entertained by a new user's attempts to use the interface. For installations, expressive interfaces are concerned with attracting spectators to an exhibit. They may also possibly involve managing flow by controlling the approach to the exhibit at particular times, as well as enabling spectators to learn by watching so that they can prepare themselves for their own turn with the interface.

Magical interfaces tend towards revealing effects while hiding the manipulations that led to them. Lamont and Wiseman [27] discuss the fundamental base of magic as relying on "methods" which lead to "effects". A magician may use many different methods to achieve the same effect, however the magician's skill lies in ensuring the spectator is only aware of the effect. A magical interface may reveal the performer, making clear that they are causing the effects whilst not revealing the manipulations, or alternatively the performer may be completely hidden, in order to impress spectators with the implied capabilities of the interface alone. A 'wizard of oz' interface can be envisaged as an extreme form of magical interface in which even the magician is hidden. Certain forms of interactive technology may also be conducive to the construction of such interfaces; as Marshall, Benford and Pridmore suggest, "the very invisibility of sensor-based systems makes them an ideal candidate for magical interfaces" [31].

Intriguing interfaces[1] tend towards revealing manipulations while hiding effects. While at first sight this may appear to be the most counter-intuitive of the four strategies, it does offer some interesting possibilities. As with expressive interfaces, spectators may be attracted by seeing the interaction and may be able to learn something of what to do by observing, but in this case will not experience the effects until it is their turn. Watching others manipulate and react to the interface without seeing the content may serve to provoke curiosity and increase anticipation, heightening the 'payoff' delivered when it is finally their turn. This particular strategy was evident in the Telescope device, which drew visitors in via its relationship to the environment around it, and through the potentially 'intriguing' way that the effects of user manipulations were hidden from view.

This intriguing strategy might be particularly relevant to theme park design where it can be used to generate mounting suspense, anticipation, excitement and even limited apprehension before a ride. In the extreme, it may be important to convey the feeling that the experience is going to be much 'worse' than it actually turns out to be, perhaps by amplifying some of the revealed manipulations, for example emphasising the imposing physical scale of the technology. It also provides a way of engaging spectators who are queuing for their turn, especially in situations where visitors have to pay for the experience or pay for each piece of content individually, in which case it is important to attract spectators to the interface and entertain them while queuing but without giving away the payoff for free.

Fairground: Thrill Laboratory featured some aspects of this through its design techniques, which are detailed here. Audience members experienced a number of talks on the psychology of thrill, the history of fairground rides, and so on, in a downstairs area before the vignettes seen in Chap. 6. During these talks, the fairground ride for that evening's event was shrouded in darkness. At a particular moment 'commanded' by one of the hosts, the ride's lights were turned on and 'given a spin' by the operator in demonstration. The audience could see the ride through a large plate glass window looking out onto the lawn on which the ride was placed. The ride itself was of course made highly visible by this theatrical moment. After further talks, the audience were taken upstairs for the live telemetry broadcast (as seen in Chap. 6's second vignette). Unlike the room downstairs, this upstairs area had small windows, effectively hiding the ride, in order to reduce distraction and maintain audience focus upon the projected data. As described, this led into the performative routine of the lottery in order to select a participant, ramping up anticipation as noted particularly by the rider (Sally) in the third vignette in Chap. 6. So, in this instance, the design of the experience tried to further amplify the kinds of suspense, excitement and anticipation present within existing rides, through both careful 'grandstanding' of the ride itself via its dramatic unveiling as well as through the subsequent transition routine, donning of equipment and live broadcast to audience.

---

[1]Note that the original paper in which these concepts were first introduced, [36], the label 'suspenseful' was used instead of 'intriguing' (both included in Fig. 8.4).

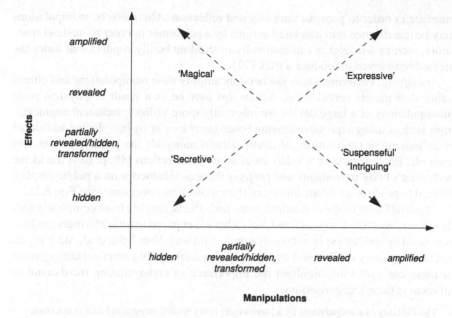

Fig. 8.4 Secretive, expressive, magical and intriguing approaches to designing the spectator's view

Returning to museums and science centres, we can see how such strategies for generating a level of intrigue or anticipation may be important in encouraging visitors to 'have a go', whilst giving them some confidence that they are capable of the interaction required of them and that, even if they take a risk, their actions (and the effects of them) will not be completely public (and therefore risk embarrassment).

Having said this, intriguing strategies—in hiding effects—can potentially cause difficulties as seen in Chap. 4's study of the Telescope and the lack of shared view between participants and sometimes audience. This highlights that the benefits of such a strategy (like other strategies presented here) must be balanced against the possible disadvantages.

Figure 8.4 positions these approaches on the taxonomy.

It is also worth covering in greater detail the further possibilities beyond simply revealing or hiding manipulations and/or effects. Indeed, the example interfaces demonstrate a wide range of possibilities here, including the following, as noted on the axes of Figs. 8.2 and 8.4.

Partially revealing: Effects and manipulations may be partially revealed, either as a result of the scale of the interface combined with distance of the spectators (e.g., PDAs, mobile phones, the Augurscope and the Telescope) or perhaps through more explicit means (e.g., we could redesign presentation tools so that background user interactions were prevented from being projected along with the primary content).

Transforming: We may transform manipulations, for example through non-linear mappings or by aggregating multiple inputs when mapping them onto effects, as employed by artists to introduce an element of unpredictability or ambiguity to an interface in order to provoke curiosity and reflection. Alternatively, manipulations may be transformed into unrelated actions by a performer in order to mislead spectators, such as a magician's intentionally misleading bodily conduct that hides the methods employed to produce a trick [27].

Amplifying: Performers may deliberately amplify their manipulations and effects rather than merely reveal them. Again, this may be as a result of physical scale (manipulations of a large device are inherently more visible), technical augmentations such as using expressive sensing based interfaces, or by introducing additional visualisations or sonifications of manipulations alongside the primary effects. For example, Ed Tannenbaum's video installation Recollections [48, p. 684] tracks the performer's body movements and projects these as silhouettes on a public display, layered to produce a vibrant collage of their movements over time (see Fig. 8.2).

These different forms of manipulations and effects, ranging from completely hidden to very amplified, are not fixed, but rather are engaged in by performers (and experienced by spectators) in a more dynamic, fluid way. Vom Lehn et al., studying an interactive gallery exhibit, and engaging with a earlier publication containing some of these concepts [36], highlight the importance of understanding the dynamism inherent in these categorisations:

> The visibility of manipulations by a [performer] is not readily categorised as it is not static. As individuals explore an exhibit the manipulations of the system by others can begin as 'hidden' but then can become 'revealed'. Indeed once the exaggerated gestural conduct of a participant is recognised as constituting manipulations of the exhibit, there can be a very quick shift from hidden to amplified. Furthermore as we are considering a multi-party public setting, manipulations can be 'hidden' for one spectator but 'revealed' or even 'amplified' for another depending on their knowledge and experience of the exhibit, and on their emerging sensitivity to the conduct of others in relation to the exhibit. Moreover, people can work to hide or reveal manipulations or even effects of technologies (consider the act of turning a mobile phone display to show others). [30]

8.3 Frames, Audience, Bystanders and Wittingness

So far the roles of performer and the spectator have been introduced, setting the two in a simple relationship involving perception of manipulations and effects. In this section the distinction between performer and spectator is extended to describe a more graduated range of roles. As these roles become more graduated it is also important to note that there is no sense in which the designation of roles to particular members of a setting is static; rather, such roles may well be transient, fluid and blurred. Roles instead should be understood as useful abstractions in dealing with this 'messy' reality.

In order to introduce this graduation of roles, Chap. 7's observations on Uncle Roy All Around You and the notion of the 'frame', are drawn into this discussion. To recap this discussion, the frame concept was derived from Goffman, who described the process of framing as being how "definitions of a situation are built up in accordance with principals of organization which govern events . . . and our subjective involvement in them" [21, p. 10]. Broadly framing then means, here, the context within which a performance takes place, with the "principals of organization" helping to make such a performance intelligible to those engaged in and observing it. To some extent similar concepts have been employed in earlier frameworks, such as Sheridan et al.'s performance triad model which integrates context—or the "social, cultural and conceptual placement in which the performance finds itself"—within its framework [41].

So far the perspective on and characterisation of performance in this chapter has to cover everything from explicitly staged interaction to implicit everyday public performance, allying this view with the way that Goffman treats everyday social interaction as performance. However, the distinction between explicit and implicit performances need to be elaborated. For example, staged performances are in some sense 'abnormal' interactions when compared to everyday social interaction as performance. Performers often amplify their manipulations or effects expressively in some way, as seen with examples like Pamela Z and Toshio Iwai. The enhanced legibility of these performances is typically 'designed into' actions, as noted by Rosen [37]. Such staged performance also frequently involves a sense of virtuosity displayed by a performer that is intentionally exposed in this amplified way. Although virtuosity is sometimes displayed in the everyday, and of course, many everyday tasks involve high levels of skill, ability displayed in performance is particular in the manner of its observable amplification. What this means for interfaces (such as Brain Opera's musical instruments) is that the performer—or rather, participant—is 'helped into' a state in which they can perform. In other words, there is a substantive difference between the way professionals stage their virtuosic performances, and how locally-produced performance emerges from everyday social conduct. For example, within the Journey into Space study, much was made of the storyteller's guiding and structuring work employed to help participant children into ('safe') interactions with the interface.

The frame in all cases constitutes an understanding between the performer and spectator that there is a performance, and defines the principles and conventions by which both performers and spectators are able to take part in the performance and interpret what is happening. Unlike many everyday social interactions, performances are usually explicitly and very carefully framed by the performer: the setting is deliberately chosen; various techniques are used to introduce the audience to the performance and to make it clear what action is part of the performance and what is not. For example, conventional western theatre employs all manner of performative routines (ticketing, calls and so forth), a complex spatial structure (the foyer, auditorium, stage, proscenium arch, wings, backstage and so forth), and other technical effects (sound and lighting) to frame a performance. These mechanisms serve to delimit what is part of the performance and what is not, such as in hiding the behind-the-scenes work of stage hands, lighting and sound engineers. This is particularly important when spectators are being asked to 'willingly suspend disbelief' and enter a fictional world. For example, the careful framing of a play enables to audience to understand that a murder that takes place on stage is fictional rather than real, or to still enjoy a story line they know in advance (e.g., a Shakespearian play). Other forms of performance, even relatively impromptu ones, often have their own performative routines and structures which help render the action intelligible to participants. Explicit framing can also be seen in games in the form the "magic circle", which is a kind of theory of framings that identifies the set of conventions, structures and performative routines that delimit what is part of a game and what is not. A player's understanding of this enables them to "play by the rules" [26], [38, pp. 91–98] and furthermore be aware that within "front and back stage areas, ... different rules [may] apply" [32].

Before we begin to explore how the frame impacts spectators, there are two issues that require some remarks. Firstly, it is important to note that performance framings—whether they are impromptu or well-established—are highly dynamic and involve ongoing feedback and negotiation between performer and spectator in the establishment of the frame. This basic observation is consonant with an ethnomethodological perspective on social interaction as an ongoing, collaboratively-produced phenomenon [16, p. 166]. Secondly, the way in which the terms 'public' and 'private' have been used so far (particularly in situating the concerns of this book in terms of public settings) may also be thought of with a sense of their 'framing'. For example, visibly hiding bodily and especially verbal conduct from third parties may be interpreted by spectators as a private frame, whereas revealing conduct may instead frame the activities as being in some way public. Public and private space is thus framed via various "principals of organization" which help make the public or private status of events intelligible to those engaged in them as well as to those observing them. This builds upon the concepts presented earlier of hiding and revealing manipulations and effects, as well as the strategies provided for by different combinations of hiding and revealing. Designing with strategies of, say, 'secretive', 'expressive', 'magical' or 'intriguing' means designing the public/private framing of manipulations and effects.

8.3.1 Spectator as Audience and Bystander

The concept of framing leads to an extending of the definition of performers and spectators. Performers can now be seen as frame 'constructors' whereas spectators are largely frame 'interpreters'. It is also important to note that this distinction between performers and spectators also bears a strong correspondence, respectively, to 'professionals' and 'members of the public'. Introducing the idea of a performance frame also enables us to distinguish between two different types of spectators:

Audience: Those spectators who are within the frame of the performance. They are aware that a performance is taking place and are able to interpret the performer's actions as part of a performance. This particular role was discussed at length both in Chap. 4's study of One Rock and then in Chap. 6's examination of Fairground: Thrill Laboratory.

Bystanders: Spectators who are outside of the frame. Although they may observe the performer's interactions, they may struggle to interpret them as a performance.

Indeed, they may not even be aware that a performance is taking place. They can be said to be 'unwitting' bystanders. Chapter 7 explored the bystander as a fundamental feature of player experience in Uncle Roy All Around You.

This distinction can be a subtle one. Spectators may have varying knowledge of different aspects of the performance frame. Some may be aware that a performance is happening but may not be able to interpret the subtle intended meanings of the performer's actions and have difficulty identifying aspects of the performance as part of the performance, whereas others may have a detailed appreciation of how the performer has set up the frame (perhaps even as a reference or reaction to previous performances), leading them to different and overlapping interpretations. This may be particularly true for performance events in which performative routines are ritualised—such as religious ceremonies—which assume a high level of knowledge on the part of the audience.

The distinction between 'witting' audience and 'unwitting' bystanders is an important one, especially as the spread of mobile and personal technologies is leading to an increasing number of implicit performances taking place in museums, galleries, on the streets and in similar highly public spaces that are shared by many people and involve many different activities. In settings such as these, the performer cannot rely on the traditional mechanisms that are used to separate audience from bystanders. Instead they have to recognise that bystanders are likely to be present and have to carefully consider their experience, as well as that of the intended audience. For example, performers might consider whether the performance will negatively affect bystanders and vice versa, or perhaps how the very presence of unwitting bystanders could enhance the performance.

8.3.2 Designing for the Frame

This section considers how we might design for the frame of the experience, detailing two relevant strategies for this design, as described first in Benford et al. [4]. These strategies are informed by the study of Uncle Roy All Around You and Can You See Me Now?, both presented previously in Chap. 7. For both of these mobile performances, the framing of the experience was particularly important. They each reveal some key 'frame' issues to be considered when designing the bystander's experience and more generally the frame itself.

A number of features of Uncle Roy All Around You that were explored in Chap. 7 are of relevance here. The game was designed as a conscious exploration of the boundaries of public interaction, leading to the player's ambiguous experience of the real and the fictional (such as 'crossing boundaries' by getting into a car with a stranger). Besides discussing the performative routine of joining the game, Chap. 7 showed how the status of objects, places and people are destabilised through the game's design, being presented in a deliberately ambiguous way to the player with a level of uncertainty over whether something is 'inside' or 'outside' of the frame (e.g., what was a 'prop' and what was not), simultaneously constructing that frame through these design choices. A quotation that perhaps encapsulates this most well was the report by one player in the post-game feedback of "not knowing who at first was a performer[2] and who was not a performer".

There are two major perspectives when designing these elements for the frame. The first is the performer's frame, i.e., the 'actual' frame of the performance as understood by the professionals running the performance. The second perspective is the audience and/or participants' frame, i.e., the 'perceived' frame of the performance as constructed by performers and then understood and interpreted by audience or participants. At this point we can now consider two different strategies for crafting these perspectives, and, therefore, designing the frame itself.

8.3.2.1 Strategy 1: Extending the Frame

Benford et al. [4] discuss one framing strategy, in which the fictional world of the performance is made to appear as if extended outside of the limits of the actual performer's frame by directly or indirectly implicating or even involving bystanders. Objects and people outside the actual frame of the performance assume the status of being inside the perceived frame, thus the fictional world is perceived to be more extensive than it really is. This may be achieved in a number of ways. Direct implication of bystanders as content for a performance may be seen in some street performances, such as when mime artists mimic passers-by. Alternatively, the performance may support a more general structure in which indirect implication of bystanders is possible, either by implying them as fellow performers or as witting audience members (ambiguous clues in Uncle Roy All Around You perform this function). Places and objects that are not 'controlled props' (i.e., those under the direct control and ownership of the performers, such as the hotel or car park kiosk) may also be exploited for this purpose. There are two risks arising from this implicated involvement, however. Firstly, there is a risk of humiliation of bystanders if they suddenly become witting when the construction of the frame relies upon their being unwitting (such as in the mime example); alternatively through this wittingness a bystander's privacy may be violated in some way (e.g., by tracking them and then displaying this information publicly). Secondly, and depending upon the intent behind the frame's construction, the implication of the bystander may spill over into forms of involvement that are undesirable for the performance, for example where audience members interact inappropriately and unaccountably with bystanders assuming that they are part of the performance, or perhaps violate the privacy of the bystander (see [33]). This latter risk obviously covers implicated locations as well,

---

[2]In this quotation and indeed in the following description of Uncle Roy All Around You the term 'performer' refers to the professional actors and artists who designed and acted in the performance. However, it is the players who are the primary users of the interface and so should be classed as the 'performers' under a strict interpretation of the initial definitions in this chapter. This issue will be resolved later on when introducing the roles of participant and orchestrator. For now the term 'performer' is used to describe the actors in Uncle Roy All Around You and players to describe the members of the public who used the PDAs on the streets.

such as the player attempting entry to places for which they have no mandate (e.g., attempting to enter the 'wrong' car park kiosk).

The perceived frame of a performance may also be extended by creating a situation in which the audience or participants appear or feel to be exceptionally exposed to the scrutiny of bystanders. This might involve the use of novel or valuable technologies in unusual contexts or where technologies demand a notable behaviour, such as the zigzag running motions of the performers in Can You See Me Now? as they attempt to use GPS to catch an online player. Such a design might involve revealing or amplifying manipulations of an interface in order to attract spectators' (or bystanders') attention. It is also interesting to note that the key manipulations mentioned specifically for Can You See Me Now? are whole-body movements (distinctive to and fro, zigzagging movements) rather than the details of particular key presses, and that such actions become significant because they are unusual in the surrounding context, and in a sense do not 'fit' the frame as perceived by bystanders.

8.3.2.2 Strategy 2: Shrinking the Frame

Correspondingly, a second general strategy is the reverse of the first, in which frame as it is perceived by audience and participants is shrunk in comparison to the actual performer's frame. Thus, while the first strategy implicates people and objects that are outside of the frame in order to extend its apparent extent, this second strategy instead presents people and objects that are in reality part of the performance frame as being outside of that frame. Framing objects and people as though they are not strictly part of the performance can thus have the effect of making the real world be perceived as more extensive than it actually is. In order to achieve this, the performance might require performers to act the part of bystanders and become involved in the performance, as well as somehow suggesting that controlled props and places may in fact belong to other people. These tactics were seen in Uncle Roy All Around You in the form of controlled props and spaces (such as the postcard in the saddle-bag) 'planted' by the performers. These tactics generate excitement by encouraging audience or participants to apparently cross the normal boundaries of behaviour in a given setting. Technology mediated communication can be especially powerful for this as the participant can be placed in a position to make the decision on their own, without the performer being directly present, which might otherwise imply tacit approval (at least if the performer did not step in to stop them). The risk here is, however, that audience members or participants may cross other boundaries that weren't intended by the performer, potentially getting themselves into trouble.

8.3.2.3 Summary

The primary tool exploited by both these strategies is mainly that of ambiguity over the status of objects and people, or in other words, ambiguity in the way the frame and its components are presented to audience and participants. Objects may either be planted props or actually belong to others entirely outside the frame of performance altogether. People, on the other hand, may be professional performers who are well aware of the nature of the frame, or bystanders, completely unaware of the frame and their relationship to it. This ambiguous blurring of the frame can be seen as an example of 'ambiguity of relationship' between the 'viewer' and an 'interface' as discussed by Gaver et al. in a general review of the role of ambiguity in interface design [18].

Several issues derive from this discussion of the framing of a performance and the separation of audience or participants from bystanders. For the examples of Uncle Roy All Around You and Can You See Me Now?, whether and how to attract by-standers to a performance, how to manage admission to a performance, and the ma-jor challenge of orchestrating a smooth and safe experience from behind-the-scenes were pertinent design problems. The next section explores these issues, focusing on some common transitions between roles that occur in performance.

8.4 Dynamism in Performance: Transitions

In the previous section, we have seen how framings have described how bystanders may become implicated in a performance and engage in varying levels of participa-tion. The framework presented thus far is not static, however—it also can reflect on the inherent dynamism in performance, and the fluidity of the roles of its members. In this section the discussion is briefly opened out to consider some key forms of 'transition' that may occur. (As referred to in previous chapters, readers wishing to explore further how concepts of transition introduced in this book fit within a wider context of multiple interactional trajectories in performative events should see [5].)

8.4.1 Bystander to Audience to Participant

The first transition between roles that may be considered is how bystanders are inducted into an experience to become members of an audience, often via some 'front-of-house' work such as ticketing, and then later on perhaps transition further to become actual participants in some performance.

A number of examples illustrate how these transitions may occur in a variety of scenarios. Firstly we can revisit Chap. 4's Telescope device. The study of the Tele-scope and its local surroundings highlighted the way in which visitors engaged in examining objects physically near to the Telescope device were drawn to the Tele-scope by way of its relationship to its surroundings as well as the conduct of any vis-itors using the Telescope. These visitors were an audience to other fellow visitor's interactions with the device, and later themselves also became direct participants through having had the device 'handed over' to them. A key aspect of understand-ing how such transitions occur has been appreciating the importance of the physical features of the design (as with the Telescope's handlebars and eyepiece construction). This issue is further confirmed in Capra et al.'s discussions of an interface for the slow narrative SMS-based game Day of the Figurines [10]. In this game, the physical interface (a large table-based game board containing figurine representations of each player) was purposefully lit, set at a specific height, and oriented in the gallery space so that it was attractive for curious unwitting bystanders, encouraged the growth of an audience, and subsequent participation in the game.

Brignull and Rogers' discussions of a large screen interactives also reflects these observations on transitions between bystanders, audience and participants [9]. They note the presence of what they term the "honey-pot effect", in which those interacting with or located in proximity of the interface attract other people. Like Clark and Pinch's discussion of market traders [12], who rely on attracting a small number of onlookers in order to build up a crowd (using the principle of the honey-pot effect), so the nature of designing transition involves a sensitivity to such phenomena. Further, Brignull and Rogers categorise groups around interactive displays into three "spaces of activity": peripheral awareness of the display, focal awareness (spectating), and direct interaction with the display (see also [46]). Key in this discussion is the notion of "thresholds" which determine the ease with which members of the setting may transition from one state to another (for instance, ensuring the interface supports lightweight forms of initial interaction, and high perceptual visibility).

A further example of audience-participant transition was provided in Chap. 6, via the lottery mechanism of Fairground: Thrill Laboratory, which led to an extended period of transition (managed by orchestrators, discussed below) involving donning and readying equipment, as well as being oriented to the nature of the role (through elicitations from actors and orchestrators and the framing provided by the 'professional rider'), before the audience member became a participant performing for the audience they were drawn from.

Developing from notions of wittingness, other examples from the literature may be drawn on to provide demonstrations of bystanders transitioning into audience to some activity, or becoming participants in that activity. One such example is Deus Oculi [24], an interactive installation at a public arts and crafts festival. It consisted of a large renaissance-style painted scene featuring two figures whose faces were painted on small doors. Behind the doors were small CCTV screens that were linked directly to two hand-held mirrors situated on either side of the painting. When a visitor picked a mirror and looked into it, an image of their face was captured on a hidden video camera and then displayed on one of the screens in the painting. Heath et al. reported how passers-by first acted as an audience to others' humorous interactions with the exhibit, and subsequently by way of this observation came to participate in and engage with the exhibit themselves.[3]

Reflecting particularly upon more traditional artworks such as Deus Oculi, it is essential to appreciate the tradition of artists incorporating transition within their

---

[3] For further analytic detail see [15].

work. Historically, artists have increasingly drawn members of the public into their work as participants rather than conceptualising them as mere spectators of it. As Huhtamo observes, artists in the early 20th century began to "activate" the viewer through techniques such as immersing them or integrating functional buttons into a piece [25].

Returning to further examples of transition, a particularly striking demonstration of induction into participating in an experience is found in Desert Rain (discussed initially in Chap. 6). To reiterate, players in Desert Rain explored a virtual world, attempting to achieve various objectives as part of the game. Before entering the cubicles in which they would navigate this virtual world, and as part of their transition to direct participation in the game, the 'front-of-house' induction work involved giving the group special uniforms to wear and a military-style briefing that provided vital information about their interaction in the experience as well as forming part of the aesthetic of the piece (i.e., informing them of their 'targets'). Transitions to participation in Uncle Roy All Around You also included a performative "ritualized briefing" at the beginning of the game during which players were asked to leave behind all their possessions.

In the foregoing discussion, a number of further refinements to roles present in the frame have been implicitly introduced over the course of this and the previous section. Whilst bystanders and audience have been encountered already, participation is a concept that needs to be clarified here:

Participants: Wittingly engaged in activity beyond what is normally understood as typical audience behaviour, possibly in collaboration with actors, orchestrators or other participants. Participants are normally non-professionals (i.e., members of the public), for whom participation is usually a temporary transition that forms one part of their whole journey through the performance.

In some sense, participants appear to be rather similar to the 'performers' that have been discussed thus far. Here the differences between participation and the roles of performers must be differentiated, which may be done by introducing the role of 'actors' (explored in more depth in the next section).

Actors: Performers who are directly perceptible to audience and/or participants. Actors are usually skilled, employed professionals, however it is their ongoing engagement with the performance as a job of work, as well as typically structuring interactions by participants (see Chap. 5) which separates them from the participants themselves.

8.4.2 Actors and Orchestrators

A second transition to examine here occurs between those conducting orchestration duties behind-the-scenes during a performance, and those who they support, who have been named 'actors' in order to distinguish them both from participants and performers who conduct orchestration duties. Actors characteristically occupy a more obviously perceptible, visible 'centre-stage' position. Some examples may flesh out this concept. The control room that featured in Chap. 7's discussion of Uncle Roy All Around You, for example, communicated with number of orchestrators on the streets who were responsible for monitoring different areas of the game zone as players navigated their way through the game's various clues. As we saw, these orchestrators would discretely monitor the progress of participants from a distance, watching for apparent signs of difficulty, and would locate those who were of concern to other orchestrators in the control room (as exhibited in the vignettes, these included participants who experienced technical troubles with their device or perhaps began walking outside the game zone entirely). Whilst at all times attempting to avoiding unnecessary disruption of game, Chap. 7 examined how orchestrators on-the-ground sometimes needed to 'step out' from their cover 'behind-the-scenes' (no longer 'blending in') and transition to the role of actor and stage interventions in order to fix breakdowns. Indeed, if a participant was reached before they themselves knew they had a problem (as in the intervention experienced by Matt when having his device fixed in the Chap. 7's analysis), these interventions could even enhance the experience, being reported as a positive factor by some players (as demonstrated in the comment noting, for example, "the feelings of uncertainty and mistrust ... experienced when facing [the] street actors").

A second example of this transition is demonstrated by Desert Rain in which a control room was present to help orchestrate the experience for players. Desert Rain's players were constantly monitored both via orchestrative interfaces and by manual observation; this inspection was achieved thanks to a 'rain curtain', which was a fine water spray onto which images of the virtual world were back-projected (see Fig. 8.5, left). The properties of the rain curtain were such that players could be monitored behind-the-scenes by orchestrators without being visible (rather like a two-way mirror). Interestingly, there was a moment during the experience when these monitoring orchestrators stepped through the rain curtain in order to hand an item to the player (Fig. 8.5, right). This clear moment of transition from orchestrator to actor was a powerful event for the participants, and was enabled by careful monitoring and intervention procedures.

Orchestration itself has also been presented in more detail in Chap. 6's study of Fairground: Thrill Laboratory. This examination covered not only the work of intervention (in this case, intervention did not result in orchestrator-actor transition), but also explored how orchestrators developed a working knowledge of the system in order to navigate a complex problem space. Like Uncle Roy All Around You, the orchestrators in Fairground: Thrill Laboratory were distributed physically across sites, and a further job of work for them was ensuring mutual awareness via continual communication. Orchestrators also worked to support actors' activities through weaving together the various strands of the performance, as well as supporting the transition of the audience member to participant through equipment donning and performing this sensitively with respect to actors' work.

This brings us to now define the role of orchestration:

Orchestrators: Professional performers who conduct behind-the-scenes work (such as monitoring, communicating with actors, weaving the performance together

Fig. 8.5 Desert Rain's rain curtain (*left*), and an intervention in which an orchestrator steps through the curtain to face the player (*right*). [Images used with permission; ©Blast Theory]

with those actors and performing interventions) and are not directly perceptible perhaps even to actors. Orchestrators also gain knowledge of and manage trajectories through the experience, particularly for participants and audience [5, pp. 296–297].

In this whole section the framework has been broadened by reflecting upon the dynamic nature of performance, and the fluidity of the way in which members of a framing may transition between roles. Some further refinements to roles present in the frame have also been introduced implicitly. A key challenge presented in this section, then, is in developing an understanding of how to design for transitions between bystanders, audience and participants, and between orchestrators and actors.

8.5 Summary

Since this is the largest and perhaps most complex chapter of this book, it is useful now to draw together what has been presented into a general analytic framework that summarises the key elements involved in interfaces deployed within public spaces, and the relationships that exist between those elements. Some of the main design strategies that can be employed in the design of such interfaces will also be highlighted here.

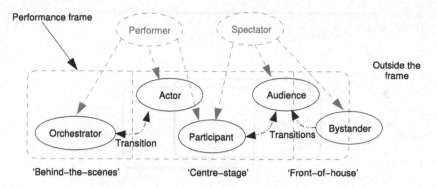

Fig. 8.6 Organisation of components within the frame

8.5.1 The Elements Involved in a Spectator Interface

Broadly speaking, the argument and analysis that has been developed over the course of this book is that the design of a publicly situated interface can be considered in terms of a performance frame that establishes different roles between the participants in and around an interaction. This frame also supports various transitions between these roles. (The range and extent of this framework's applicability beyond public settings, such as for HCI in general, is addressed in the final chapter. Further, there are a variety of ways that it may be 'read' and put into use, which will also be addressed in the concluding chapter.) These basic features of the framework are summarised by Fig. 8.6. At this point we can also recap the relationship between the framework model as depicted here and each of the studies. This is shown in Fig. 8.7.

Initially, the two core roles of performer, the primary user of an interface in a public setting, and spectator, another member of the setting who witnesses the performer's use of the interface, are distinguished between. The relationship between these is created by a performance frame, which is a set of conventions and structures that establish that a performance is taking place and shape how it is interpreted by either party. In this case, performers act as 'frame constructors' and spectators as 'frame interpreters' [15]. The framing of the performance may be highly explicit—as is the case with staged theatrical performances which may involve quite formalised structures for managing who is involved—or more implicit—as is the case with everyday use of interfaces in public settings, which are framed by a set of more or less well-understood social conventions.

Introducing a performance frame leads to distinguishing further roles, separating those who are inside the frame and who therefore understand the nature of the performance to some extent versus those who are out of the frame and who remain unwitting of the performance. More specifically, this chapter has identified the roles of:

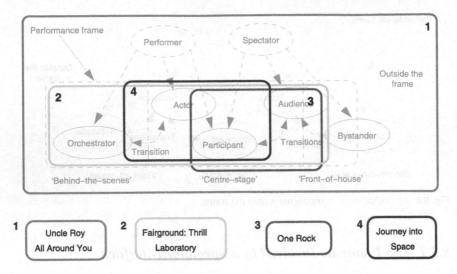

Fig. 8.7 The relationship of the studies to the framework

- *Bystander*: A spectator who is outside the performance frame, but who can be engaged in unwitting observation of or even unwitting participation in the performance.
- *Audience*: A spectator who is inside the performance frame and who is 'witting', that is aware of and able to interpret the performance that is taking place.

Reflections on studies of earlier chapters and other performances within the literature further led to the identifying of other specific sub-roles within the overall performance frame. These were:

- *Actor*: A specialism of the performer role who is directly visible to spectators within the performance frame.
- *Orchestrator*: Another specialism of the performer role that steers what happens within the performance, but in this case without being generally visible to spectators.
- *Participant*: An audience member who temporarily takes on the role of a performer, for example taking their turn with an interface in a public exhibition or being placed in a performance role. However, performance is not their 'core business' as it is for actors and orchestrators.

Implicit in the definition of these more specialised roles is a sub-division of the performance frame into different settings:

- *Behind-the-scenes*: Enables orchestrators to conduct activities such as monitoring and intervening (e.g., in a control room) without being exposed to participants, audience and to some extent, actors.
- *Centre-stage*: Where the majority of performative action takes place.

- *Front-of-house*: The fringes of the performance frame, typically where the audience and some bystanders are situated enabling them to witness the performers while being separated from it.

Very often these settings take the form of distinct physical spaces. For example, in a conventional Western theatre, spaces are clearly physically separated and demarcated by structures such as a proscenium arch, that separates front-of-house from centre-stage, and 'the wings' which separate centre-stage from behind-the-scenes. However, these settings are not just spaces, but are 'places', to use the terminology in [23]. In this way they may also be established more through common understandings, conventions and routines as with street theatre or even through distributed and mobile technologies as seen in performance projects like Uncle Roy All Around You.

The various roles that the performance frame defines are not static structures, but rather facilitate a set of dynamic transitions that define the different experiences of those involved in a performance. The discussion identified two common trajectories, each involving a sequence of transitions, corresponding to common routes through a performance for spectators and performers alike.

Bystander to audience and audience to participant: These are transitions between spectator roles. Bystanders enter into the performance via some front-of-house induction process in order to become audience members. Audience members may in turn transition to a participant role (e.g., being picked out from fellow audience members in some way, or perhaps called up to centre-stage), and possibly return again to the audience.

Orchestrator to actor: These are also common transitions between performer roles. Specifically, performers may alternate between behind-the-scenes duties (orchestration) and centre-stage acting duties (actors).

Finally, it is also important to be sensitive to the boundaries presented diagrammatically in this chapter (i.e., in Fig. 8.6). For example, the frame boundary which the bystander straddles is important when considering transitions between 'unwitting bystander' and 'witting audience member'. Similarly, the boundaries between settings of 'behind-the-scenes', 'centre-stage' and 'front-of-house' are key in the production of the spectator experience; we have seen repeatedly, for instance, how moving some performer activity behind-the-scenes can be crucial for the smooth running of a performance (e.g., in Chap. 7) as well as creating the potential for dramatic interventions (e.g., again, as in Chap. 7, and also Desert Rain, discussed earlier).

8.5.2 Strategies

This framework not only provides a resource for understanding what is happening in different kinds of performance involving interactive technologies, but also points towards key issues that interface designers should consider when designing performative interfaces. In broad terms, designers need to consider how to establish a performance frame including the extent to which their designs support centre-stage, behind-the-scenes and front-of-house activities. They also need to consider the impact of their design on the different roles involved—including any bystanders—and how they are supported, and how transitions between them are to be managed.

More specifically, two interesting strategies that artists and designers frequently adopt in order to deal with these issues have been discussed. When seen from the standpoint of more tradition HCI, they represent unusual and novel approaches to interface design.

The first strategy concerns the extent to which a performer's manipulations of an interface and their subsequent effects can be revealed to or hidden from different classes of spectators. We have seen the ways in which designers choose to hide, partially reveal, reveal and even amplify manipulations and effects. We have also seen how a simple taxonomy of comparing the treatment of manipulations with effects reveals four key designs:

- *Expressive*: In which both manipulations and effects are revealed or even highlighted;
- *Secretive*: In which both manipulations and effects are hidden;
- *Magical*: In which effects are revealed by the manipulations that cause them, however those manipulations remain hidden; and
- *Intriguing*: In which manipulations are revealed to waiting spectators in order to attract them to an interface, but the effects (or, the 'payoff') are hidden until it is their turn to interact.

The second strategy, developed from [4], involves the deliberate blurring of the performance frame leading to a degree of ambiguity between the roles of actor, audience, participant and bystander, building on work in HCI concerned with the general role of ambiguity in interface design [18]. We have seen how designers, particularly within the implementation of Uncle Roy All Around You, can appear to extend the frame of the performance beyond its actual boundaries by implicating bystanders in the performance or can appear to shrink the frame by drawing on props and actors. Both of these can generate considerable excitement for participants, playing with the boundaries between fiction and reality and deliberately challenging the conventions of traditional theatre. However, such strategies also involve potential risks and require careful and professional orchestration in order to carry them out successfully.

The next chapter will step back to consider this framework and set of strategies in light of the opening questions presented in the introduction. It will also discuss the role of the framework for different audiences, and explore ways in which this work may be extended and developed in the future.

References

1. Agre, P.E.: Changing places: contexts of awareness in computing. Hum.-Comput. Interact. **16**(2–4), 177–192 (2001)

2. Aoki, P.M., Grinter, R.E., Hurst, A., Szymanski, M.H., Thornton, J.D., Woodruff, A.: Sotto Voce: exploring the interplay of conversation and mobile audio spaces. In: Proceedings of the SIGCHI Conference on Human Factors in Computing Systems, pp. 431–438. ACM, New York (2002). doi:10.1145/503376.503454

3. Bellotti, V., Back, M., Edwards, W.K., Grinter, R.E., Henderson, A., Lopes, C.: Making sense of sensing systems: five questions for designers and researchers. In: Proceedings of SIGCHI Conference on Human Factors in Computing Systems (CHI), pp. 415–422. ACM, New York (2002). doi:10.1145/503376.503450

4. Benford, S., Crabtree, A., Reeves, S., Flintham, M., Drozd, A., Sheridan, J.G., Dix, A.: The frame of the game: blurring the boundary between fiction and reality in mobile experiences. In: Proceedings of SIGCHI Conference on Human Factors in Computing Systems (CHI), April, pp. 427–436. ACM, New York (2006). doi:10.1145/1124772.1124836

5. Benford, S., Giannachi, G.: Performing Mixed Reality. MIT Press, Cambridge (2011, in press)

6. Benford, S., Schnädelbach, H., Koleva, B., Anastasi, R., Greenhalgh, C., Rodden, T., Green, J., Ghali, A., Pridmore, T., Gaver, B., Boucher, A., Walker, B., Pennington, S., Schmidt, A., Gellersen, H., Steed, A.: Expected, sensed, and desired: a framework for designing sensing-based interaction. ACM Trans. Comput.-Hum. Interact. 12(1), 3–30 (2005). doi:10.1145/1057237.1057239

7. Bowers, J.: TONETABLE: A multi-user, mixed media, interactive installation. In: Proceedings of COST G-6 Conference on Digital Audio Effects (DAFX-01) (2001)

8. Bowers, J.: Improvising machines: Ethnographically informed design for improvised electro-acoustic music. ARiADATexts (4) (2002). URL http://www.ariada.uea.ac.uk/ariadatexts/ariada4/index4.html

9. Brignull, H., Rogers, Y.: Enticing people to interact with large public displays in public spaces. In: Proceedings of the IFIP International Conference on Human-Computer Interaction (INTERACT 2003), pp. 17–24 (2003)

10. Capra, M., Benford, S., Giannaci, G., Flintham, M., Greenhalgh, C., Crabtree, A., Tandavanitj, N., Adams, M., Farr, J.R.: Deliverable D12.7: Evaluation of Day of the Figurines II, final report from touring Day of the Figurines. Technical report, University of Nottingham (2007)

11. Carpenter, L.: Cinematrix, video imaging method and apparatus for audience participation. US Patent, Nos. 5210604 (1993), 5365266 (1994)

12. Clark, C., Pinch, T.: The Hard Sell. Harper Collins, New York (1995)

13. Crabtree, A., Rodden, T.: Hybrid ecologies: understanding cooperative interaction in emerging physical-digital environments. Pers. Ubiquitous Comput. 12(7), 481–493 (2008). doi:10.1007/s00779-007-0142-7

14. Dalsgaard, P., Hansen, L.K.: Performing perception—staging aesthetics of interaction. ACM Trans. Comput.-Hum. Interact. 15(3), 1–33 (2008). doi:10.1145/1453152.1453156

15. Dix, A., Sheridan, J.G., Reeves, S., Benford, S., O'Malley, C.: Formalising performative interactions. In: Proceedings of 12th International Workshop on Design, Specification and Verification of Interactive Systems (DSVIS), pp. 15–25 (2005). doi:10.1007/11752707_2

16. Dourish, P.: Where the Action Is: The Foundations of Embodied Interaction. MIT Press, Cambridge (2001)

17. Dow, S., Lee, J., Oezbek, C., MacIntyre, B., Bolter, J.D., Gandy, M.: Wizard of Oz interfaces for mixed reality applications. In: Extended Abstracts on Human Factors in Computing Systems (CHI), pp. 1339–1342. ACM, New York (2005). doi:10.1145/1056808.1056911

18. Gaver, W., Beaver, J., Benford, S.: Ambiguity as a resource for design. In: Proceedings of Conference on Human Factors in Computing Systems (CHI), pp. 233–240. ACM, New York (2003). doi:10.1145/642611.642653

19. Geser, H.: Towards a sociological theory of the mobile phone. Unpublished report (2001)

20. Goffman, E.: The Presentation of the Self in Everyday Life. Doubleday, New York (1959)

21. Goffman, E.: Frame Analysis: An Essay on the Organization of Experience. Harper & Row, New York (1974)

22. Grudin, J.: Interface. In: Proceedings of the 1990 ACM Conference on Computer Supported Cooperative Work (CSCW), pp. 269–278. ACM, New York (1990). doi:10.1145/99332.99360

23. Harrison, S., Dourish, P.: Re-place-ing space: the roles of place and space in collaborative systems. In: CSCW'96: Proceedings of the 1996 ACM Conference on Computer Supported Cooperative Work, pp. 67–76. ACM, New York (1996). doi:10.1145/240080.240193

24. Heath, C., Luff, P., vom Lehn, D., Cleverly, J.: Crafting participation: designing ecologies, configuring experience. Vis. Commun. 1, 9–34 (2002)

25. Huhtamo, E.: On the origins of the virtual museum. In: Nobel Symposium (NS120) on Virtual Museums and Public Understanding of Science and Culture (2002)

26. Huizinga, J.: Homo Ludens: A Study of the Play-Element in Culture. International Library of Sociology and Social Reconstruction. Routledge & Kegan Paul, London (1944)

27. Lamont, P., Wiseman, R.: Magic in Theory: An Introduction to the Theoretical and Psychological Elements of Conjuring. University of Hertfordshire Press, Hatfield (1999)

28. Lasen, A.: A comparative study of mobile phone use in London, Madrid and Paris (2002). http://www.surrey.ac.uk/dwrc/papers/CompStudy.pdf. Unpublished report

29. vom Lehn, D., Heath, C., Hindmarsh, J.: Exhibiting interaction: conduct and collaboration in museums and galleries. Symb. Interact. 24(2), 189–216 (2001)

30. vom Lehn, D., Hindmarsh, J., Luff, P., Heath, C.: Engaging constable: revealing art with new technology. In: CHI'07: Proceedings of the SIGCHI Conference on Human Factors in Computing Systems, pp. 1485–1494. ACM, New York (2007). doi:10.1145/1240624.1240848

31. Marshall, J., Benford, S., Pridmore, T.: Deception and magic in collaborative interaction. In: CHI'10: Proceedings of the 28th International Conference on Human Factors in Computing Systems. ACM, New York (2010). doi:10.1145/1753326.1753397

32. Marx, G.T.: Murky conceptual waters: The public and the private. Ethics Inf. Technol. 3(3), 157–169 (2001)

33. Niemi, J., Sawano, S., Waern, A.: Involving non-players in pervasive games. In: CC'05: Proceedings of the 4th Decennial Conference on Critical Computing, pp. 137–140. ACM, New York (2005). http://doi.acm.org/10.1145/1094562.1094583

34. Paradiso, J.: The Brain Opera technology: New instruments and gestural sensors for musical interaction and performance. J. New Music Res. 28(2), 130–149 (1999)

35. Preece, J., Rogers, Y., Sharp, H.: Interaction Design. Wiley, New York (2002)

36. Reeves, S., Benford, S., O'Malley, C., Fraser, M.: Designing the spectator experience. In: Proceedings of SIGCHI Conference on Human Factors in Computing Systems (CHI), pp. 741–750 (2005). doi:10.1145/1054972.1055074

37. Rosen, C.: Piano Notes: The Hidden World of the Pianist. Penguin, Baltimore (2002)

38. Salen, K., Zimmerman, E.: Rules of Play: Game Design Fundamentals. MIT Press, Cambridge (2003)

39. Sanneblad, J., Holmquist, L.E.: "Why is everyone inside me?!" Using shared displays in mobile computer games. In: Proceedings of International Conference on Entertainment Computing (ICEC) (2004)

40. Schnädelbach, H., Koleva, B., Flintham, M., Fraser, M., Izadi, S., Chandler, P., Foster, M., Benford, S., Greenhalgh, C., Rodden, T.: The Augurscope: A mixed reality interface for outdoors. In: Proceedings of SIGCHI Conference on Human Factors in Computing Systems (CHI), pp. 9–16. ACM, New York (2002). doi:10.1145/503376.503379

41. Sheridan, J., Dix, A., Lock, S., Bayliss, A.: Understanding interaction in ubiquitous guerrilla performances in playful arenas. In: Proceedings of British HCI Conference (2004)

42. Smith, J.: Digital dance hall: the fan culture of dance simulation arcade games. In: O'Hara, K., Brown, B. (eds.) Consuming Music Together. Computer Supported Cooperative Work, vol. 35, pp. 193–209 (2006). doi:10.1007/1-4020-4097-0_10

43. Stewart, J., Bederson, B.B., Druin, A.: Single display groupware: a model for co-present collaboration. In: CHI'99: Proceedings of the SIGCHI Conference on Human Factors in Computing Systems, pp. 286–293. ACM, New York (1999). doi:10.1145/302979.303064

44. Sudnow, D.: Ways of the Hand: The Organization of Improvised Conduct. Routledge & Kegan Paul, London (1978)

45. Terrenghi, L., Quigley, A., Dix, A.: A taxonomy for and analysis of multi-person-display ecosystems. Pers. Ubiquitous Comput. 13(8), 583–598 (2009). doi:10.1007/s00779-009-0244-5

46. Vogel, D., Balakrishnan, R.: Interactive public ambient displays: transitioning from implicit to explicit, public to personal, interaction with multiple users. In: UIST'04: Proceedings of the 17th Annual ACM Symposium on User Interface Software and Technology, pp. 137–146. ACM, New York (2004). doi:10.1145/1029632.1029656
47. Watson, R.: Ethnomethodology, consciousness and the self. J. Conscious. Stud. 5(2), 202–223 (1998)
48. Wilson, S.: Information Arts: Intersections of Art, Science and Technology. MIT Press, Cambridge (2002)
49. Z, P.: Audible image/visible sound: Donald Swearingen's Living Off The List. 21st Century Music 8(1) (2000)

Chapter 9
Conclusion

It has hopefully become clear, underlined by the growing body of literature concerned with technology-based interactions in public settings referred to within this book, that designing spectator and performer interfaces is an increasingly important aspect of mainstream HCI. This relevance also comes at a time when computers continue to migrate from the workplace into the domains of art, performance and entertainment, diversifying in their application and featuring ever more in the public settings that form the backdrops to our everyday experiences. Situations such as these present significant new challenges for interface design, and will require better understandings and strategies within HCI for directing the design of interfaces situated in all manner of public settings.

The overarching aim of this book has been to provide a step forward in this area, firstly articulating in empirical and concrete instances the challenges posed, and secondly in providing detailed ways in which to address those challenges in interface design. In summarising how this has been done within this book, in this chapter we return to the initial questions and key aims posed at the start, and begin to reflect upon them in light of the studies and framework that have been presented. Also in closing we will discuss some practical matters regarding the use of this book, look at recent developments of related work, and finally briefly cover some directions for where we go next in understanding interaction with technology in public settings.

9.1 Revisiting Opening Questions and Aims

- How might interfaces support users in performing their interactions within a wide range of expression, and fit well with such activities?

A performer's expressive interactions have been considered in terms of revealed or amplified manipulations and effects, as introduced first in Chap. 4. Expressive actions have also been placed within a taxonomy that provides guidance not only on the ways in which expression might be designed into an interactive system, but also how this design can be thought of as one class of a wider range of systems,

S. Reeves, *Designing Interfaces in Public Settings*, Human-Computer Interaction Series, 177
DOI 10.1007/978-0-85729-265-0_9, © Springer-Verlag London Limited 2011

as suggested in complementary 'magical', 'secretive' and 'intriguing' strategies. In addition to this, the skilled work of professional performers and how their activities may come to 'fit' within an interactive design has been addressed through understanding the spatial nature of manipulation and the potential for interference, as detailed in Chap. 5's study. Thus, designing for interference becomes an important consideration when supporting activities which frequently take place in some form of 'sensor range'.

Expressivity and its particular combination of manipulations and effects, along with other strategies, have also been placed within the context of a performer-spectator dynamic. This leads to the next question of third parties.

- What are the ways in which a third party might experience a user's interaction with an interface?

From the initial examination of how third parties have begun to come under scrutiny within the literature on the workplace, museums and galleries, to Chap. 4's study of the ways in which visitors became audience to the 'intriguing' strategy of the Telescope's design, understanding the third party's experience has permeated the treatment of interaction presented in this book. Through repeatedly addressing this topic, we have seen how the notion of the third party may be broken down into a variety of framework components.

Some key topics for designers to consider when addressing the 'how' of the spectator experience have been manipulations and effects, as well as the ways in which these may be combined to produce different characters of interactional experience for the spectator, such as the 'magical' or 'expressive' strategies.

The basic distinction between performers and spectators has also been expanded upon to consider a variety of different roles, such as non-professional audience or participant 'spectators' and professional actor and orchestrator 'performers'. In addition to this, the third party experience has been considered in an even wider context with the introduction of the frame, fracturing 'spectator' type roles further in order to address how designers might cater for special kinds of third parties, such as the unwitting bystander.

- How are participants made aware that a performance is occurring and understand the boundaries and limits of the performance, especially in public settings where performance may be interleaved with other activities?

A key feature presented within the framework was the adaptation of Goffman's concept of framings. The kinds of designs made possible by a designer's awareness of the frame and the challenges it presents was conceptualised in a number of ways, such as through thinking of actors and orchestrators as constructing the frame which is then interpreted by participants, audience and bystanders. Chapter 7's study of Uncle Roy All Around You provided an example of a game design that purposefully made the frame ambiguous via setting the game on city streets and providing suggestive clues for the player. The framework provides designers with ways to address the frame through the identification of two strategies, either extending the frame to include objects and people that are not strictly part of it, or shrinking the apparent frame of the experience and deploying a number of props and actors 'outside' of that frame (Uncle Roy All Around You employed both of these). In addition to this, the framework sensitises designers to the subdivisions of the frame that may be present, such as front-of-house, centre-stage and behind-the-scenes, as well as the ways in which particular roles are configured by their place or 'position' within the frame, and how the limitations of the constructed frame often create bystanders unwitting of its intended interpretation.

- How does transition between users occur (for example when a current user hands an interface over to a new user in a setting such as a crowded public gallery), and how might we reflect this in design?

A further feature provided to designers concerned with managing a participant's understanding of performance boundaries and limits has been the concept of the transition. The discussions of transition described how the framed settings of behind-the-scenes, centre-stage and front-of-house, and the roles that operate within them, may be used to configure and set up transitions. Uncle Roy All Around You's intervening orchestrators and their support by other orchestrators who were feeding them information on participants was made seamless by the nature of the behind-the-scenes setting (i.e., on city streets, see below) and their theatrical orientation to that intervention. We have also identified how the physical design of an interface may enable transitions to occur spontaneously as a result of non-professional coordination around the interface, as in Chap. 4's Telescope device. Further to this, we have also seen how moving members of a particular subdivision of the frame to another setting with the support of actors or orchestrators can be a method of creating transition. The transitions in Chap. 6's Fairground: Thrill Laboratory between audience member and participant rider were achieved via a movement of the audience firstly to a behind-the-scenes setting for the donning of equipment with the help of orchestrators, and then a centre-stage position via a live transmission, the data from which subsequently was woven into the ongoing performance by actors. Other techniques may be used, such as the performative routines and briefings found in Desert Rain. These investigations, then, have provided salient issues for the designer to keep in mind when attempting to construct interfaces whether they merely permit or actively encourage transition.

- How do orchestrators conduct their work and the ongoing shaping of a performance, typically from 'behind-the-scenes'?

Some key practices and common features of orchestrators have been described, particularly within Chap. 6. More specifically, these have been: the working knowledge developed as part of orchestration, the physical distribution of orchestrators and the need for mutual awareness between them and actors in weaving together a coherent performance, intervention and its associated overheads, and the orchestrator's role in enabling transition. Providing technologies that support such practices should be a key concern for designers, as well as an awareness of the part each setting plays in configuring the framing of environments for successful orchestration; delimiting any centre-stage setting by necessity often will configure a corresponding behind-the-scenes area. This awareness should also be coupled with a more general understanding of the common occurrence of behind-the-scenes spaces within a diverse series of settings, rather than just the more obviously performative, theatrical ones (e.g., within museums and galleries, the work conducted behind-the-scenes being significant in the production of exhibits that will form the 'centre-stage' [21]). In the case of Uncle Roy All Around You, for instance, in Chap. 8, we saw how the anonymity of city streets was used as an *orchestration tool* that provided a setting behind-the-scenes for orchestrators, as well as assisting a host of practices like intervention and monitoring of players.

Moving on from these questions, we can now also review the key aims of the book, and answer the question of the ways in which these aims have been addressed.

1. The framework provides a set of sensitising concepts.

Rather than being seen as providing a proscriptive set of rules and regulations, the framework's recommendations should instead be seen as sensitising concepts. This is a familiar idea within HCI literature, drawing inspiration from Blumer's discussions of the analytic sensibilities of symbolic interactionism. He states that, "[w]hereas definitive concepts provide prescriptions of what to see, sensitizing concepts merely suggest directions along which to look" [6, p. 148]. Issues like the design of the frame, the way that manipulations and effects may be experienced by audience and bystanders, and even the breaking down of interaction with interfaces in public into basic roles offer to designers new, perhaps not previously considered set of "directions along which to look" in understanding how their interaction design may be applied to the setting of interest.

2. The framework provides a shared language.

The framework provides a series of concepts and components that are applicable across a wide variety of settings. As Chap. 2 demonstrated, there are common concerns between a range of communities such as artists, technologists, designers, curators and computer scientists. For instance, the engagement of the spectator in participating with an exhibit is frequently a topic to address for museum curators, and artists have increasingly attempted to shift the position of the 'passive' audience member to active participant.

The sensitising concepts of the framework are described in language which mainly draws on a theatrical metaphor, inspired by Goffman's dramaturgy. In being communicated through metaphor, this language becomes mutable and ready for wider appropriation. 'Participants' may be 'players', 'actors' may be 'members of staff', 'audience' may be 'fans', 'orchestrators' may be 'sound and light technicians', 'centre-stage' may be 'city streets', and so on.

Returning to the introduction's suggestion of the framework as a boundary object, the above examples provide some of the ways in which the framework may be "plastic enough to be adaptable across multiple viewpoints" and at the same time "maintain continuity of identity", being what Star might more specifically term an "ideal type" form of boundary object [32]. Thus, although the framework may be "weakly structured in common use", by virtue of its mutable language and general concepts drawn from a wide-ranging series of settings, it becomes "strongly structured in individual site-use" [32].

3. The framework offers a collection of constraints and strategies.

Spreading technology creates a rich set of challenges for new kinds of spectator interfaces, and therefore opens up a complex design space of possibilities. The framework provides implicitly, through both its construction and through what topics it does and does not speak to, a number of limitations and boundaries to managing that design space. Although this inevitably results in a narrowing of potential forms of design, a perspective informed by framework concepts enables designers to approach public settings in two ways. Firstly the implicit constraints of the framework, in talking about certain topics and having a particular perspective on interaction, may actually open up previously unconsidered aspects of design, such as importance of the bystander, the (typically implicit) construction of the frame and how it is experienced by its members, or how spectators may experience manipulations and effects. Secondly the model or pattern of interaction communicated through the framework's sensitising concepts offers a palette or 'toolbox' of strategies that provide structures with which to design within.

This toolbox consists of the following:

- The identification of basic non-professional spectator and professional performer roles, such as audience, participant, orchestrator and actor.
- Dividing interaction into manipulations and effects as conducted by performer roles and experienced by spectator roles.
- Providing strategies of 'magical', 'secretive', 'intriguing' and 'expressive' combinations of those manipulations and effects.
- Circumscription of the frame as a boundary the designer may construct around those roles.
- Strategies of expanding or shrinking the frame according to the way in which the status of objects and people is to be interpreted.
- Techniques to design transition by the division of the frame into various settings.

In addition to this there are a number of orchestration strategies that the framework draws in from the literature, such as the construction of monitoring and intervention tools in managing distributed and mobile settings. Building upon this, the framework also highlights the use of orchestrators in managing transitions.

4. The framework constructs a new perspective on interaction in HCI.

As detailed above, the framework helps constrain this complex design space, but also provides strategies and sensitising concepts in order to navigate it successfully. In doing so it presents a novel offering to HCI, and, whilst not necessarily resolving all questions, contributes to a conversation over third parties to interaction and performance that has begun to emerge in recent years.

However, in promoting this new perspective, it is worth considering how, contrastingly, there is also a 'stronger' interpretation of the framework that is possible. This stronger claim proposes that the flexible language of the framework and its sensitising concepts apply *beyond* the segment of HCI literature it is situated within, and that the findings have implications for understanding how interaction with interfaces takes place in a *wide variety* of social settings in which computation is deployed, whether they are distributed virtual environments, online desktop machine-based games, tangible interfaces in workplaces or technology at a performance event. More generally, it has potential application in developing understandings of interaction with technology in workplace and other collaborative settings (particularly since many of its observations are developed from this literature). A further, even more 'strong' perspective could also see the framework being applied to non-computational settings.

This latter point should also include a note of caution, however. In particular it brings to the foreground the relationship between computational technology and framework concepts, and what role the nature of computation has had in shaping these concepts. Certain framework topics have elements in which technology plays a strong part in either making certain activities possible, or enhancing pre-existing practices. Within orchestration, for example, the possibilities for managing orchestrator and actor distribution over a large space, as well as monitoring participants and audience, are opened up by the introduction of computational tools. On the other hand, some framework topics are derived from non-computational settings and then applied to computational ones. For instance, the possibility of bystanders can occur within many everyday interactions, however the point of drawing on such observations is to begin to consider how these phenomena impact HCI and in turn sensitise design sensibilities towards dealing with them. (In some sense, there is a parallel here with Laurel's consideration of bringing theatrical metaphors to desktop computing [19].)

9.2 Using This Book in Practice

In the introduction it was suggested that this book has potential applications for a wide variety of researchers, practitioners, designers and artists working with technology in public settings.

At a fundamental level, the framework in this book is primarily an *analytic* framework, which has reflected upon a wide range of explicit and implicit performance practices and scenarios, in order to build a tool that provides structure for designers in addressing the often complex and difficult design spaces of public and semi-public environments. In a broad sense, then, this book hopefully provides a guiding *theoretical* orientation for researchers of technology-mediated interactions, in order to understand one way (there will be others, of course) that interactions in public settings may be conceptualised.

However, this book in general may be practically employed in quite different ways depending upon the reader. For artists working with technology, perhaps rather than providing inspiration for their design (since many of the concepts will be intuitively familiar already), this book and its framework can provide a common reference when collaborating with others, such as technologists (and vice versa). In other situations, say, for computer scientists or technologists perhaps with limited knowledge of how interaction takes place in public and who are not collaborating with others who have this experience, this book can be read as a series of explicit design guidelines and recommendations for any interfaces which may be deployed in museums, galleries, city streets, exploratoria, and so on. Thus, reflecting upon this book, it does not necessarily offer an explicit 'instruction manual' for how to go about designing interaction for public settings, but rather provides a resource with which to communicate design concerns in varying levels of detail.

This book also has a range of styles in which it may be practically used. On the one end of the scale, concepts in the book may offer a way of systematically approaching the myriad possibilities opened up by situating technology in public, sensitising its user and highlighting issues not previously considered. As a result of this, for instance, perhaps individual conceptual issues become a consideration, such as the role of the bystander (perhaps unobvious for some), the importance of the transition and moment of handover, or even that monitoring and intervention tools for orchestration should be developed. Alternatively, in offering a systematic and structured way to begin tackling the design space, users of the framework may start by considering the 'big issues', broadly conceptualising their interaction design from the outset in terms of a series of roles, stages, framings and transitions between these. Or instead, the framework might provide a less distinct but still useful background perspective with which to address technology design in public, and, rather than providing a checklist or series of tools to draw on as a resource, features as a document that co-designers can commonly be aware of and use as a point of shared reflection.

Finally, a (possibly obvious) caveat is in order, for those working with the concepts presented in this book. Any framework or model of interaction will necessarily contain some characterisations of the real, ongoing and moment-by-moment nature of social conduct. As such there is always a trade-off between developing useful, applicable-in-practice concepts and rendering an ironic version of interaction, which, by its very nature simplifies or 'misses' the detailed and nuanced nature of interaction. It is possible, for example, to become too prescriptive with such a framework, perhaps quite rigidly imposing concepts derived from it to interactional settings. Such a tendency must be guarded against.

9.3 Conversations Within HCI and Other Fields

As mentioned earlier in this book, initial versions of the framework for interaction with technology in public settings (including [2, 26], and studies [11, 25, 27, 31]) have been engaged with by others within a broad range of technology-based research.

Most particularly, the issue of the spectator experience of interaction with technology has been a pertinent concern in a wide variety of contexts within HCI. For instance, it has featured in discussions on interactions in nightclubs [14], massively-multiplayer online games [12], mobile interaction with large public displays [30], rally spectating [16], mobile pervasive contexts [1], and digitally-enhanced live-action role playing [17].

In addition to featuring in recent discourse on the role of the spectator in human-computer interaction, we must also examine here the ways in which others have critiqued or built upon initial fragments of the framework that have been published, and this section will briefly reflect upon the ways in which they impact this book. (Where relevant, some of these 'conversations' with the work presented in this book have been touched on in previous chapters. For instance, we have seen already in the previous chapter how vom Lehn et al. emphasised the dynamism in roles, transitions and the observability of manipulations and effects [20].)

The notion of framing has been extended by others. In particular, Montola and Waern [24] further subdivide the framing (with reference to [2]) into various distinct "stages of awareness" such as "unaware", "ambiguous" and "conscious", suggesting Uncle Roy All Around You employs a "socially expanded game" design which crosses social boundaries, "inviting non-players to participate in a way or another". They also provide distinctions between different "invitations" the game's design may offer to the player, such as "invitation to play" where the design explicitly offers participation, "invitation to participate" where participation is offered but does not require such a major role. Finally, there is "invitation to spectatorship" where the design offers a spectator-only role and "invitation to refuse" which provides the player an opportunity to reject participation. Further refinements could use this to develop the levels of awareness between the bystander and audience roles, however it is important to consider that part of generating frameworks involves a necessary simplification of the findings derived from studies, and thus distinctions may at times be necessarily limited.

A related branch of work on trajectories in the interactional experience, which we have briefly covered in Chaps. 5 and 7, is also relevant to the development of concepts in this book. Their discussions are particularly instructive in enriching notions of transition with the framework. In two related papers [3, 5], the structured design of various "temporal trajectories" that participants may experience in interactive scenarios is presented. Trajectories express a "mapping or path between fictional time in an underlying story universe [. . .] and the actual time [that] is experienced by participants". Two such trajectories that feature in the design of systems they explore (and which we have encountered already in this book) are "canonical trajectories"—trajectories that represent the designed, intended, and authoritative temporal path through an interactive experience—and "participant trajectories"—trajectories which participants actually experience, and may well diverge from the intended canonical trajectory.

Benford et al.'s discussion of trajectories is then expanded to consider more generally the structure of interactive experiences, in terms of space, roles and interfaces as well as time. Critical moments in the design of transitions are when users cross between spaces, change roles, engage with new interfaces, and so on. Concepts we have met over the course of this book, such as handover, may play an important role in these transitions, along with orchestrator work in maintaining alignments between, say, canonical and participant trajectories or role transitions. As a result we can think more broadly and expansively about the importance of transition as a key design concept in the structure of technology-based interactions in public settings, featuring not only transitions between roles and handing over interfaces (as we have seen in this book), but also transitions between canonical trajectories and participant trajectories.

Building upon this, Benford and Giannachi have recently developed this work on trajectories into a larger discussion of mixed reality performance [4]. In their book they broadly synthesise a wide number of ongoing conversations within HCI, including their own work on trajectories [3, 5], and the work of others, specifically including discussions of ecologies [9], seamful design [7], concepts of space and place [15], and the use of 'record and replay' techniques both in performance and data analysis [8]. In addition to this, Benford and Giannachi also integrate several topics that this book has covered in detail, such as notions of orchestration, dramaturgical perspectives on interaction in public, framings, the roles assumed in performance-like situations, transitions between those roles, and concepts of distinct, constructed performative settings (such as front-of-house). In this way, it provides a useful companion to for the concepts presented in focussed detail within this book, as these are set in the context of a wider-ranging framework that provides design understandings for developing mixed reality performances.

Parts of the framework have also been used and built upon in the analysis of computer-based stage magic. Marshall, Benford and Pridmore studied a series of magic tricks in which interaction was (to varying degrees) mediated or intervened in using video tracking systems controlled by computer [22]. During the course of these tricks, the computer was sometimes hidden from the spectator, sometimes revealed to them, and at other times was used to misdirect the spectator. In their study, they examined how interactive technology can play a role in various features of magical performance, such as in misdirecting spectator attention or setting up false expectations for the spectator. They identify hiding and revealing strategies of manipulations and effects as fundamental in these interactions, as well as the importance of splitting spectator attention between interface components (such as using physical separation, or magician's 'patter'), thus creating indirection in causal mappings between manipulations and effects (see [11]). Developing this, however, Marshall et al. extend the taxonomy of manipulations and effects, describing how a performer "often reveals only *some aspects* of manipulations while hiding others, simultaneously occupying several areas of [the taxonomy]" (emphasis added). This can lead to a modification of thetaxonomy (i.e., Figs. 8.2 and 8.4, which considers the spectator's perspective only) in which competing spectator and performer perspectives are mapped onto the taxonomic space, highlighting the differences and convergences between the two. In order create this design practically, Marshall et al. increased the number of 'channels' of interaction, including further physical artefacts in addition to the computer interface itself. This strategy then affords the potential for this splitting of the taxonomic space.

Interestingly, Marshall et al. also relates this to Benford et al.'s work on trajectories and transitions as outlined above. In this case, performers (magicians) and spectators follow different temporal trajectories with alternative narratives associated with them; for example, Marshall et al.'s spectators experience the performer's

narrative "patter [. . .] making clear the external story of the trick, and hiding the se-
cret [story]". This is particularly relevant when understanding not only how users in
different roles experience potentially very different perspectives on the taxonomic
space, but also how that space has a temporal progression.

A final concept that Marshall et al. suggest in extension to some of the concepts
that have been presented in this book is the notion of "deceptive feedthrough" where
certain manipulations result in two forms of effects: those that the manipulator is
aware of, and hidden, additional effects that they are unwittingly performing. This
can provide a strategy for setting up "false expectations" for a spectator, a further
key component of many magical performances.

9.4 Directions for Designing Technology in Public

It is relatively safe to assume that deployments of interactive technologies in our
public places will continue in the immediate future, and, correspondingly diversifying notions of 'work' within CSCW and HCI [10]. Presumably this trend will
continue for as long as interactive technologies are seen as beneficial and useful
ways to (for example) engage the public with exhibits in museums, to offer new expressive possibilities for artists and performers, or offer augmented ways to provide
information in busy public spaces such as train stations or airports. This section explores both some of the limitations with this book and proposes a number of routes
that may offer interesting developments of its contents.

This book has pulled together a number of different settings, developing inspiration from workplace studies, and following on to look at experiences involving
museums, galleries, performance art, music performances, and mobile technology
in public, for example. However, the domain competence or craft knowledge in
such areas as these has only been addressed to a limited degree, with much being
drawn from what is frequently an anecdotal literature (such as documentation of
performance art events). In many ways the study of such settings could be conducted in a much deeper fashion, with a more systematic and complete collection of
craft knowledge from practitioners providing further confirmation, contradiction or
development of framework concepts. Future work should build this collection by involving further investigation of the domain competence of groups such as performers, exhibition designers, and other design, art or educational communities. With
wider and more probing surveys of such areas (perhaps uncovered with sustained
engagement via ethnography), basic framework concepts such as roles, transitions
and frame ambiguity may be enriched. Indeed, as with [4] and the corresponding
continuing discussion on spectatorship in HCI mentioned earlier, we are perhaps
seeing the beginning of such work developing already.

Whilst the approach ventured in this book has steered away from Goffman's em-
brace of all social interaction as performance, another direction for developing the
strand of work presented here is to reconsider the framework's relevance beyond
just the explicit and less markedly explicit framings of performance that it has examined, and return to Goffman's original conception of everyday performance, and

everyday framings. In some senses this would be a test of the 'strong claim' posed earlier in this chapter, addressing the question of whether some more typical settings in which technology is used (such as returning to classical workplace CSCW studies) may be thought of in terms of roles such as orchestrator, audience, bystander, and transitions, spatial settings (e.g., behind-the-scenes) and so on.

Exploring such everyday 'performance' could help in determining whether the employment of theatrical and other metaphors within the framework necessarily bind its observations and design issues to more deliberate performance settings. In some sense, everyday social interaction continually features practical skills such as looking, watching, determining context (or 'framings') and so on, as well as the assuming of 'roles'. It is unclear, however, if such metaphors derived from the various delineations and boundaries set up by explicit performance are still tractable as design guidelines within the less constrained and freely flowing nature of everyday 'performance'.

The framework also opens up and exposes the possibility of the investigation of unusual framework configurations. Examples of this would be revealed (public) orchestration (i.e., moving orchestration that occurs behind-the-scenes to a centre-stage setting), or uncommon transitions such as bystander to orchestrator, or participant to bystander (e.g., in some 'nested' framing of a performance). To some extent, public (or at least semi-public) orchestration was a feature of Chap. 6's Fairground: Thrill Laboratory through aspects such as the positioning of the control area at the back of the room just behind the audience, and it being implicated within the performance through being pointed out by the host.

Unusual configurations could even extend to finding ways in which such configurations provide counter examples that challenge or 'break' how the framework's concepts and organisation has been defined. One particularly interesting example would involve technology itself pushing into framework components, such as developing an interface that acts as actor or orchestrator. Artists often break or challenge the status quo, and it is apparent that within some performance and art pieces this repositioning of interface as orchestrator or actor has already occurred (e.g., [18] and [13]). For instance, in an installation by the artist Ken Rinaldo called The Flock [29], a number of computer-controlled robotic arms were endowed with the ability to react to each other and visitor movement and sound, embodying forms of emergent behaviour. Rinaldo's later work, Autopoiesis, pushed this concept further by providing the robotic sculptures with a 'memory' that created modified behaviours over time. These robotic actors, therefore, incorporate relationships they have shared with participants previously into their current 'performance'. Finally, at the more extreme end of replacing the (professional) actor role with the interface itself are systems such as AARON [23], a drawing program by Harold Cohen that is able to draw scenes described to it. This software has gone through a long maturing process, initially from basic childlike doodles to something approaching what might be expected of a competent artist. Similar examples can be found for musical performance in which the interface assumes the actor role (e.g., Aglaopheme [33, p. 431]). Challenging new configurations of performance offer the potential for intriguing developments of the concepts presented in this book.

Finally, this book has for the most part been focussed upon relatively modest numbers of audience, participants, actors and orchestrators. Scaling these observations up to large crowd spectatorship (e.g., festivals, stadia) should provide new opportunities for understanding whether certain framework concepts are no longer relevant, need modification, or come to gain greater prominence in design for those circumstances. This is coupled with the growing prevalence of large screen displays, sophisticated mobile devices and infrastructures (e.g., wifi networks) being deployed across festivals and stadia. Initial work examining crowd-scale groups of people has begun to develop frameworks such as that presented within this book, calling for a consideration of crowds themselves as a distinct interactional unit [28]. Further work will need to investigate inter- as well as intra-crowd interactions in greater depth, responding to the subtleties of events in which diverse, distinct groups of people congregate into large-scale formations.

References

1. Ballagas, R.A., Kratz, S.G., Borchers, J., Yu, E., Walz, S.P., Fuhr, C.O., Hovestadt, L., Tann, M.: REXplorer: a mobile, pervasive spell-casting game for tourists. In: CHI'07: CHI'07 Extended Abstracts on Human factors in Computing Systems, pp. 1929–1934. ACM, New York (2007). http://doi.acm.org/10.1145/1240866.1240927
2. Benford, S., Crabtree, A., Reeves, S., Flintham, M., Drozd, A., Sheridan, J.G., Dix, A.: The frame of the game: Blurring the boundary between fiction and reality in mobile experiences. In: Proceedings of SIGCHI Conference on Human Factors in Computing Systems (CHI), April, pp. 427–436. ACM, New York (2006). doi:10.1145/1124772.1124836
3. Benford, S., Giannachi, G.: Temporal trajectories in shared interactive narratives. In: CHI'08: Proceeding of the Twenty-Sixth Annual SIGCHI Conference on Human Factors in Computing Systems, pp. 73–82. ACM, New York (2008). doi:10.1145/1357054.1357067
4. Benford, S., Giannachi, G.: Performing Mixed Reality. MIT Press, Cambridge (2011, in press)
5. Benford, S., Giannachi, G., Koleva, B., Rodden, T.: From interaction to trajectories: designing coherent journeys through user experiences. In: CHI'09: Proceedings of the 27th International Conference on Human Factors in Computing Systems, pp. 709–718. ACM, New York (2009). doi:10.1145/1518701.1518812
6. Blumer, H.: Symbolic Interactionism: Perspective and Method. University of California Press, Berkley (1986)
7. Chalmers, M., Galani, A.: Seamful interweaving: Heterogeneity in the theory and design of interactive systems. In: DIS'04: Proceedings of the 2004 Conference on Designing Interactive Systems, pp. 243–252. ACM Press, New York (2004). doi:10.1145/1013115.1013149
8. Crabtree, A., Benford, S., Greenhalgh, C., Tennent, P., Chalmers, M., Brown, B.: Supporting ethnographic studies of ubiquitous computing in the wild. In: Proceedings of Conference on Designing Interactive Systems (DIS) (2006)
9. Crabtree, A., Rodden, T.: Hybrid ecologies: understanding cooperative interaction in emerging physical-digital environments. Pers. Ubiquitous Comput. **12**(7), 481–493 (2008). doi:10.1007/s00779-007-0142-7
10. Crabtree, A., Rodden, T., Benford, S.: Moving with the times: IT research and the boundaries of CSCW. Comput. Support. Coop. Work **14**(3), 217–251 (2005). doi:10.1007/s10606-005-3642-x
11. Dix, A., Sheridan, J.G., Reeves, S., Benford, S., O'Malley, C.: Formalising performative interactions. In: Proceedings of 12th International Workshop on Design, Specification and Verification of Interactive Systems (DSVIS), pp. 15–25 (2005). doi:10.1007/11752707_2

12. Ducheneaut, N., Yee, N., Nickell, E., Moore, R.J.: "Alone together?": Exploring the social dynamics of massively multiplayer online games. In: CHI'06: Proceedings of the SIGCHI Conference on Human Factors in Computing Systems, pp. 407–416. ACM, New York (2006). doi:10.1145/1124772.1124834

13. Edmonds, E., Turner, G., Candy, L.: Approaches to interactive art systems. In: GRAPHITE'04: Proceedings of the 2nd International Conference on Computer Graphics and Interactive Techniques in Australasia and South East Asia, pp. 113–117. ACM, New York (2004). doi:10.1145/988834.988854

14. Gates, C., Subramanian, S., Gutwin, C.: DJs' perspectives on interaction and awareness in nightclubs. In: DIS'06: Proceedings of the 6th Conference on Designing Interactive Systems, pp. 70–79. ACM, New York (2006). doi:10.1145/1142405.1142418

15. Harrison, S., Dourish, P.: Re-place-ing space: the roles of place and space in collaborative systems. In: CSCW'96: Proceedings of the 1996 ACM Conference on Computer Supported Cooperative Work, pp. 67–76. ACM, New York (1996). doi:10.1145/240080.240193

16. Jacucci, G., Oulasvirta, A., Salovaara, A., Sarvas, R.: Supporting the shared experience of spectators through mobile group media. In: GROUP'05: Proceedings of the 2005 International ACM SIGGROUP Conference on Supporting Group Work, pp. 207–216. ACM, New York (2005). http://doi.acm.org/10.1145/1099203.1099241

17. Jonsson, S., Montola, M., Waern, A., Ericsson, M.: Prosopopeia: experiences from a pervasive LARP. In: Proceedings of the 2006 ACM SIGCHI International Conference on Advances in Computer Entertainment Technology, p. 23. ACM, New York (2006). http://doi.acm.org/10.1145/1178823.1178850

18. Kac, E.: Ornitorrinco and Rara Avis: telepresence art on the internet. Leonardo 29(5), 389–400 (1996)

19. Laurel, B.: Computers as Theatre. Addison-Wesley, Longman, Reading, Harlow (1993)

20. vom Lehn, D., Hindmarsh, J., Luff, P., Heath, C.: Engaging constable: revealing art with new technology. In: CHI'07: Proceedings of the SIGCHI Conference on Human Factors in Computing Systems, pp. 1485–1494. ACM, New York (2007). doi:10.1145/1240624.1240848

21. MacDonald, S.: Behind the Scenes at the Science Museum. Berg, Oxford (2002)

22. Marshall, J., Benford, S., Pridmore, T.: Deception and magic in collaborative interaction. In: CHI'10: Proceedings of the 28th International Conference on Human Factors in Computing Systems. ACM, New York (2010). doi:10.1145/1753326.1753397

23. McCorduck, P.: Aaron's Code. New York, Freeman (1990)

24. Montola, M., Waern, A.: Participant roles in socially expanded games. In: Strang, T., Cahill, V., Quigley, A. (eds.) Pervasive 2006: Workshop Proceedings, pp. 165–173 (2006)

25. Reeves, S., Benford, S., Crabtree, A., Green, J., O'Malley, C., Pridmore, T.: The spatial character of sensor technology. In: Proceedings of ACM Conference on Designing Interactive Systems, pp. 31–40 (2006). doi:10.1145/1142405.1142413

26. Reeves, S., Benford, S., O'Malley, C., Fraser, M.: Designing the spectator experience. In: Proceedings of SIGCHI Conference on Human Factors in Computing Systems (CHI), pp. 741–750 (2005). doi:10.1145/1054972.1055074

27. Reeves, S., Fraser, M., Schnädelbach, H., O'Malley, C., Benford, S.: Engaging augmented reality in public places. In: Adjunct Proceedings of SIGCHI Conference on Human Factors in Computing Systems (CHI) (2005)

28. Reeves, S., Sherwood, S., Brown, B.: Designing for crowds. In: NordiCHI'10: Proceedings of the 6th Nordic Conference on Human-computer Interaction. ACM, New York (2010)

29. Rinaldo, K.E., Grossman, M.S.: The Flock. In: Proceedings of IEEE Computer Graphics Visual (SIGGRAPH). ACM, New York (1993)

30. Scheible, J., Ojala, T.: Mobilenin combining a multi-track music video, personal mobile phones and a public display into multi-user interactive entertainment. In: MULTIMEDIA'05: Proceedings of the 13th Annual ACM International Conference on Multimedia, pp. 199–208. ACM, New York (2005). http://doi.acm.org/10.1145/1101149.1101178

31. Schnädelbach, H., Egglestone, S.R., Reeves, S., Benford, S., Walker, B.: Performing thrill: designing telemetry systems and spectator interfaces for amusement rides. In: Proceedings of

SIGCHI Conference on Human Factors in Computing Systems (CHI), pp. 1167–1176. ACM, New York (2008). doi:10.1145/1357054.1357238

32. Star, S.L.: The structure of ill-structured solutions: boundary objects and heterogeneous distributed problem solving. In: Gasser, L., Huhns, M.N. (eds.) Distributed Artificial Intelligence, vol. 2, pp. 37–54. Morgan Kaufmann, San Mateo (1989)

33. Wilson, S.: Information Arts: Intersections of Art, Science and Technology. MIT Press, Cambridge (2002)

Index

A

AARON, 187
Accidental input, 145
Actor, 166
Affordances, 10
Ambient Wood, 16, 59
Ambiguity in design, 16, 126–131, 164
AR Quake, 19
Audience, 160
Augmented reality
  registration issues, 47
Augurscope, 15, 153
Autopoiesis, 187
Avatar Farm, 120

B

Body of knowledge, 83, 104
  application of, 104
Boundary objects, 180, 181
Brain Opera, 18, 144
Breaching experiments, 33, 35, 127
Bystanders, 160
  in museums, 15

C

Can You See Me Now?, 16, 86, 88, 120, 136,
  163
CAVEs, 152
Collaboration
  as a gloss, 12
  'flatness' of, 13
  'non-flat', 62
Computer-mediated communication, 12
Craft knowledge, 20
Crowd interaction, 18, 187, 188

D

Dance Dance Revolution, 152
DanceSpace, 88
Data
  chronology, 35
  collection 'in the wild', 35
  emergent concepts, 40
  forms of data, 33
  replay, 97
  role of the author, 36–38
  simulations, 33, 48
  transcription, 34
  use of video recordings, *see* video
Desert Rain, 17, 119, 120, 166, 167
Destabilising performance, 127
Deus Oculi, 165
Division of labour, 61, 112, 113
Dramaturgical perspective, 19, 29, 32, 144

E

Effects, 148
Ethnomethodology, 29–32
Expressive interfaces, 150, 153, 155
Expressive latitude, 17, 145

F

Feedback in performance, 147, 160
Formal interaction models, 10
Frame, 4, 20, 21, 135–138, 158–160
  actual and perceived, 162, 163
  boundaries of, 130, 131, 161, 162
  conceptual extensions by others, 184
  constructors and interpreters, 160
  extending of, 162, 163
  extensions by others, 184
  feedback in, *see* feedback in performance
  induction into, 127, 128